MEMORY

THE KEY TO CONSCIOUSNESS

MEMORY

THE KEY TO CONSCIOUSNESS

Richard F. Thompson
Stephen A. Madigan

Joseph Henry Press
Washington, D.C.

Joseph Henry Press • 500 Fifth Street, NW • Washington, DC 20001

The Joseph Henry Press, an imprint of the National Academies Press, was created with the goal of making books on science, technology, and health more widely available to professionals and the public. Joseph Henry was one of the founders of the National Academy of Sciences and a leader in early American science.

Any opinions, findings, conclusions, or recommendations expressed in this volume are those of the author and do not necessarily reflect the views of the National Academy of Sciences or its affiliated institutions.

Library of Congress Cataloging-in-Publication Data

Thompson, Richard F.
  Memory : the key to consciousness / Richard F. Thompson, Stephen A. Madigan.
      p. cm.
  Includes bibliographical references and index.
  ISBN 0-309-09311-2 (hardcover)—ISBN 0-309-54949-3 (pdf) 1. Memory. 2. Learning, Psychology of. 3. Memory—Physiological aspects. 4. Learning—Physiological aspects. I. Madigan, Stephen A. II. Title.
  BF371.T484 2005
  153.1'2—dc22

                          2005007404

Printed in the United States of America.

Preface

Memory is the most amazing phenomenon in nature. The fact that we can remember literally billions of bits of information—facts, language, our own experiences, athletic skills, musical knowledge—is truly astonishing. Without memory we could not be conscious of the world; we would, in fact, have no minds.

Our intention in writing this book is to provide a popular account of current scientific understanding of memory and learning. Over the past several decades, memory research has accelerated greatly and has expanded its techniques, ramifications, and applications, and we want to convey the excitement and importance of this research to general readers. It is not difficult to find many striking, surprising, and interesting facts about memory in this rich research literature.

Do people have photographic memories? Can we remember better while hypnotized? How do we learn language? Can we have false memories? Can emotions influence memories? How can we improve our memory? Where are memories stored in the brain?

Can we someday read memories by measuring the activity of the brain? Can our brains someday be "plugged" into computers?

Psychological science has already produced a wide-ranging and successful applied science of memory, including new, improved procedures for eliciting valid recollections in legal settings, for diagnosing and treating memory deficits, for devising systems for the efficient assimilation and retention of information, and many others.

Much of the new information from this explosion of new knowledge is very relevant to understanding how the brain acquires and stores memories. We touch on this literature lightly where it is most relevant but only in a nontechnical manner.

We hope readers will enjoy this tour through the fascinating and many-chambered structures of memory.

Richard F. Thompson
Stephen A. Madigan

Contents

1

What Is Memory?

Memory is the most extraordinary phenomenon in the natural world. Our brains are modified and reorganized by our experiences. Our interactions with the physical world—our sensory experiences, our perceptions, our actions—change us continuously and determine what we are later able to perceive, remember, understand, and become.

Every person has perhaps billions of bytes of information stored in long-term memory. This "memory store" is the vast store of information you possess as a result of learning and are not aware of unless you call it up. It includes all vocabulary and knowledge of language, all the facts that have been learned, the personal experiences of a lifetime, and much more—all the skills learned, from walking and talking to musical and athletic performance, many of the emotions felt and in fact ongoing experience, and the continuous sensations, feelings, and understandings of the world we term *consciousness*. Indeed, without memory there can be no mind.

Most animal species display some behaviors, such as reflexes and instincts, that do not greatly depend on learning from experience. They are instead part of a species' evolved biological makeup and appear in individuals as a result of genetics and fetal development. You might think of this as being like your computer's read-only memory that has built-in instructions and data. In some species this kind of "hard-wired" behavior seems to constitute most of the species' repertoire of behaviors. But many other species have another kind of memory that has functions similar to the random access memory of your computer—a kind of memory that allows the recording, maintenance, and utilization of new information. The evolution of this kind of memory and capacity for learning was a major step in the development of complex forms of life. Why this capacity evolved isn't hard to understand: An animal with a such a memory system can process information that is no longer directly available in the environment, as, for example, when a squirrel is able to remember in the winter where it stored nuts the previous fall.

Memory: Four Portraits

This book examines some of the basics of current scientific understanding of memory, starting with descriptions of the memories of four individuals to illustrate some of the remarkable properties of the human memory system.

A Life Without Memory

The most famous case history of a memory disorder is that of HM (initials are used to protect the patient's privacy). HM was a young man with severe epilepsy that could not be controlled with drugs. As a result of neurosurgery to treat the epilepsy, HM lost the ability to form new long-term memories, a condition called anterograde amnesia. His memory is only moment to moment. He can no longer remember his own experiences for more than a few minutes. As he once expressed it:

Right now, I'm wondering, have I done or said anything amiss? You see, at this moment everything looks clear to me, but what happened just before? That's what worries me. It's like waking from a dream. I just don't remember.

If you were introduced to HM and talked with him for a while, you would get the impression of a normal man with an above-average IQ. If you left and then returned a few minutes later, he would have no memory of having met and talked with you earlier. His immediate "working memory," however, is intact. If you ask him to remember a phone number you've just read to him, he can repeat it to you, but he cannot easily memorize it so as to recall it later. He has learned to use trick associations to remember things, but this works only as long as he can keep repeating the association to himself. Distract him and the memory is completely gone. Readers may recall the popular film *Memento*, whose hero suffered from the same disorder as HM.

Although HM cannot store his own experiences in long-term memory, he can learn and store motor skills relatively normally. Suppose you were his tennis instructor. As you teach him various skills over a series of lessons he improves as well as anyone else would. But each time he is brought to the lesson he has to be introduced to you again and you have to remind him that he is learning tennis.

HM provides a dramatic illustration of the distinction between short-term and long-term memories and the fact that they involve different brain systems, as do motor skill memories. His long-term memories of things learned and experienced before his surgery, incidentally, are relatively intact. (We will have much more to say later about HM and other examples of amnesia.)

A Mnemonist

Rajan Mahadevan was the son of a prominent surgeon in Mangalore, India. Rajan liked to astound his school friends by reciting the complete railway timetable for the Calcutta railway system. Later he contacted Guinness World Records Limited in

London for suggestions on how to establish a memory record. He was told to focus on π, the Greek letter pronounced "pie." π is the number 3.14. . . (the ratio of the diameter and circumference of a circle), and it is an endless and apparently irregular sequence of digits with no patterns or predictability (3.14159265. . .). Rajan set to work. On July 14, 1981, he stood before a packed meeting hall in Mangalore and started reciting π from memory. He recited numbers for 3 hours and 49 minutes, reaching 31,811 digits of π without a single error, winning him a place in the Guinness book. He later became a graduate student in psychology at Kansas State University, where he studied and was studied. His extraordinary memory was for numbers, not words, and he used strategies to help him remember (more about this later). Later, in 1987, a Japanese "memorist," Hideaki Tomoyoni, recited the first 40,000 digits of π and replaced Rajan in the Guinness book.

Life with Too Much Memory

The most famous case history of a person with what is often referred to as "photographic" memory was recorded by the distinguished Russian psychologist Alexander Luria, who named his subject "S."

> I gave S. a series of words, then numbers, then letters, reading to him slowly or presenting them in written form. He read or listened attentively and then repeated the material exactly as it had been presented. I increased the number of elements in each series, giving him as many as thirty, fifty or even seventy words or numbers, but this, too, presented no problem for him. He did not need to commit any of the material to memory; if I gave him a series of words or numbers, which I read slowly and distinctly, he would listen attentively, sometimes ask me to stop and enunciate a word more clearly, or, if in doubt whether he heard a word correctly, would ask me to repeat it. Usually during an experiment he would close his eyes or stare into space, fixing his gaze on one point; when the experiment was over, he would ask that we pause while he went over the material in his mind to see if he had retained it. Thereupon, without another moment's pause, he would reproduce the material that had been read to him.

It was of no consequence to him whether the series I gave him contained meaningful words or nonsense syllables, numbers or sounds; whether they were presented orally or in writing. All he required was that there be a 3–4 second pause between each element in the series, and he had no trouble reproducing whatever I gave him.

As the experimenter, I soon found myself in a state verging on utter confusion. An increase in the length of a series led to no noticeable increase in difficulty for S., and I simply had to admit that the capacity of his memory *had no distinct limits*; that I had been unable to perform what one would think was the simplest task a psychologist can do: measure the capacity of an individual's memory. I arranged a second and third session with S.; these were followed by a series of sessions, some of them days and weeks apart, others separated by a period of several years.

But these later sessions only further complicated my position as experimenter, for it appeared that there was no limit either to the *capacity* of S.'s memory or to the *durability of the traces he retained*. Experiments indicated that he had no difficulty reproducing any lengthy series of words whatever, even though these had originally been presented to him a week, a month, a year or even many years earlier.

Such feats of memory seem to be beyond most of us. Indeed such individuals are extremely rare; only a handful have been identified in the past 100 years or so. At the same time, actors routinely memorize entire plays, musicians memorize long musical scores, and adherents of some religions commit vast amounts of sacred text to memory. With appropriate strategies and training, we can all do much better at memorizing, as we will see later.

Musical memory can be quite extraordinary, and very little is known about it. A classic example concerns the eminent conductor Arturo Toscanini. At one point he wished to conduct his NBC orchestra in a rather obscure piece, the slow movement of Joachim Raff's Quartet no. 5. The libraries and music stores in New York were searched for the score, but none could be found. Toscanini, who had not seen the music for decades, wrote down all the orchestral parts for the entire movement. Much later, a copy of the score was discovered and compared to Toscanini's manuscript.

He had made exactly one error! But is Toscanini like the rest of us?

False Memories

The preceding case histories and our own common experiences have led many of us to assume that memory is much like a tape recorder or video recorder, holding a perfectly accurate record of what has been experienced. Nothing could be further from the truth. Memory is extraordinary, but it is far from perfect. A classic case in point is John Dean's testimony to a congressional committee about his conversations with President Richard Nixon and others concerning the Watergate cover-up. The first meeting he held with the president was on September 15, 1972. Dean described this and other meetings in astonishing detail in written testimony prepared later for a congressional committee. There was no way to check the accuracy of Dean's memory at the time. But in 1974 the president released transcripts of the tape recordings he had made of these meetings.

Ulrich Neisser, a leading authority on human memory, compared Dean's testimony of the September 15 meeting with the tape transcript of the meeting:

> Comparison with the transcript shows that hardly a word of Dean's account is true. Nixon did not say *any* of the things attributed to him here: He didn't ask Dean to sit down, he didn't say Halderman had kept him posted, he didn't say Dean had done a good job (at least not in that part of the conversation), he didn't say anything about Liddy or the indictments. Nor had Dean himself said the things he later describes himself as saying: that he couldn't take credit, that the matter might unravel some day, etc. (Indeed, he said just the opposite later on: "Nothing is going to come crashing down.") His account is plausible, but entirely incorrect. In this early part of the conversation Nixon did not offer him any praise at all, unless "You had quite a day, didn't you?" was intended as a compliment. (It is hard to tell from a written transcript.) Dean cannot be said to have reported the "gist" of the opening remarks; no count of idea units or comparison of structure would produce a score much above zero.

But despite all the inaccuracies, the basic message of Dean's testimony, that President Nixon knew about the break-in and the cover-up, was true. So his memories did at least reflect reality.

A more serious issue is whether people can be made to remember things that did not really happen. Can false memories actually be implanted? Elizabeth Loftus, a leader in the study of human memory and its foibles, has explored this issue in depth, as we will see later. Here we give one rather charming example that occurred recently. This involved Alan Alda, who is known best as Hawkeye Pierce from the TV show *M*A*S*H*. What people may not know is that Alda is a lifelong science buff and host of *Scientific American Frontiers*, a television program dedicated to communicating scientific theories to the public.

Alan Alda visited Loftus at the University of California, Irvine, to work on a show about memory. A week before Alda arrived, Loftus sent him some questionnaires, ostensibly designed to learn about his personality, in particular food preferences. When Alda met Loftus, she explained to him that she and her colleagues had analyzed the data he sent back and discovered that Alda had once gotten very sick after eating too many hard-boiled eggs as a child. (So far as Loftus knew, this had actually never happened.) Later, Loftus and her researchers had a picnic lunch with Alda. There was a smorgasbord of delicious food, most importantly some hard-boiled and deviled eggs. When offered some of these eggs, Alda refused to eat them. Was this because Loftus had induced in him a false memory about his childhood and eggs? In any event, Alda's avoidance of eggs on that occasion was filmed and is a part of the *Scientific American Frontiers* program on memory.

The Many Varieties of Memory

One of the major achievements of modern memory research is the discovery that there are several different kinds of memory systems with different properties and different brain mechanisms. A convenient classification of these forms of memory is shown in

Figure 1-1. The rest of this chapter describes the main features and properties of these different memory systems and uses them to introduce the major phenomena of memory that this book will discuss.

Explicit Declarative Memory: Episodic and Semantic

Larry Squire, of the University of California, San Diego, has argued eloquently for the basic distinction between declarative and nondeclarative forms of memory (Figure 1-1). Declarative or explicit memory is what most people mean by memory. The words "explicit" and "declarative" here signify the ability of individuals to consciously and deliberately access and describe the contents of their memory. Even here there are two different aspects to explicit memory. The first is autobiographical or *episodic* memory, the memories of your own experiences. The second is *semantic* memory, the sum total of knowledge you have—your vocabulary, understanding of mathematics, and all the facts you know. The distinction between these two is easy enough to see in Table 1-1.

Endel Tulving, of the University of Toronto, has made the difference between semantic memory and episodic memory into something more than a matter of definition. His conception of episodic memory puts it at the center of the highest human mental capacities: It is the ability to consciously and deliberately perform "mental time travel." This ability can be seen in any example of ordinary, everyday recollection. One day we asked a colleague to write a narrative description of everything he could remember about his trip from home to campus that morning. What he produced appears in Box 1-1. In one sense this act of recollection is not extraordinary because any mentally normal person is capable of it. In another sense it is extraordinary: A very large amount of information was stored and maintained in memory, without any intent on the part of the subject to memorize or retain it. Note also that what he remembered did not consist of striking, unusual, emotional, or important events. Most of it really has to be called mundane. Yet there it is in memory. Try

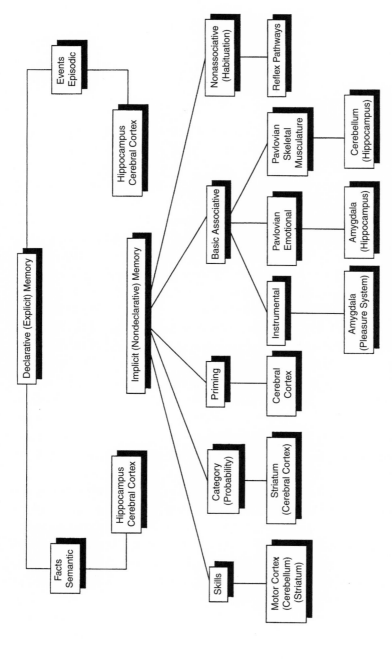

FIGURE 1-1 A schematic of the different types or forms of memory and the brain structures involved.

TABLE 1-1 Two Kinds of Declarative Memory

Semantic Memory	Episodic Memory
Where is the Eiffel Tower?	What did you have for breakfast?
What does "adumbrate" mean?	What was the last movie you saw?
Name the Seven Dwarfs	How much did you pay for that CD?

this kind of recollection yourself and you will find that you also have the strong subjective sense that what you are recalling is accurate. Try this kind of recollection for *yesterday* morning's events, and you will quickly discover another characteristic of the ordinary workings of episodic memory: swift forgetting!

Do you think our memories of our own experiences are really different from our memories of facts? Some authorities think that the only real difference is how well things have been learned. Each of us can remember dramatic experiences in our own lives and when they occurred. Memories of our own experiences are often learned in one "trial," although we may rehearse memories important to us. On the other hand, memories for specific items like words in a foreign language may take many trials to learn. When was the first time you learned the meaning of the word "tomato"? You have heard "tomato" so many times you can't possibly remember when you first heard it. Actually you were probably so young when you learned the word that it is buried in "infantile amnesia." People can't remember anything that happened to them before about age 3 or 4. Chapter 3 treats the developmental aspects of memory.

We are consciously aware of both these aspects of explicit memory. The hippocampus and surrounding cerebral cortex of the medial temporal lobe (see Figure 1-2) are the brain structures critical for declarative memory. On the other hand, there is some evidence that the brain systems in the cerebral cortex that store autobiographical or episodic memory and fact or semantic memories may differ.

There is another important kind of explicit memory not mentioned in Figure 1-1: short-term memory. Short-term memory

BOX 1-1 Ordinary Recollection and Episodic Memory

I backed the car out and turned around to get on the street, but I had to wait as three cars passed by. I was talking to Nancy about how she was going to get home as I had the car for Monday. This caused me to miss the turn on to Olympic and continue on to Overland as we normally do; this morning I was supposed to drop Nancy off at a co-worker of hers, so I turned on Pico instead. I was just barely able make the green light to turn across the traffic and head east on Pico; a red 280ZX turned with me from the opposite direction on to Pico. The traffic was intermediately heavy on Pico; the road surface was rough. Nancy was telling me as we drove by Rancho Park where she jogged the other day that she did not recommend running along Pico because of the traffic. There were a few joggers warming up in the parking lot next to the golf course. As I drove by the 20th Century Fox studios I saw a sign for the movie *The Verdict*, saying it was nominated for five Oscars, but I thought it actually didn't win any last night. Several Honda Accords seemed to hover around me at this point. I was driving in the left-most lane, looking for Cardiff. I had to ask Nancy for the street name and where exactly it was. She said it was just past the bagel shop with a green and yellow sign, in the same block as the synagogue we visited a couple of weeks ago. I thought briefly about the circumcision we witnessed and veered into a sort of turning lane. A car screeched and I realized the cross-traffic had stopped to let a pedestrian cross. I tried to cross over, but I was in third gear so I didn't move. A red and white Cadillac came past me real close to get in its left-turning lane and turned right behind me. I watched it briefly in the mirror. The traffic cleared and we crossed over. Cars were parked on both sides, making it tight. I looked at the left side for a white house where Cheryl lives but had to ask Nancy to make sure; I interrupted her as I did so. I found an opening and stopped to let her out. We agreed she'd come at 5 p.m. by bus; she said she'd leave at 4:30. I said that I would get her to USC (University of Southern California) at 5:15, but she disagreed. We kissed goodbye. I looked in the mirror and saw a new silver BMW and thought it was Erin, who was going to meet with them—it was. He pulled up alongside as I released the trunk with the switch on the floor. He leaned over in his car; I pulled down the window and said, "So you all are going to work this morning." He said something back. The sun roof was open in his car. He backed away as we said goodbye so I could pull out. A car was coming from the other direction as I pulled out. There was a woman in it. (I have written 25 minutes now and can go on, but I have to go to a meeting. This is only about one-fifth of the drive in, however.)

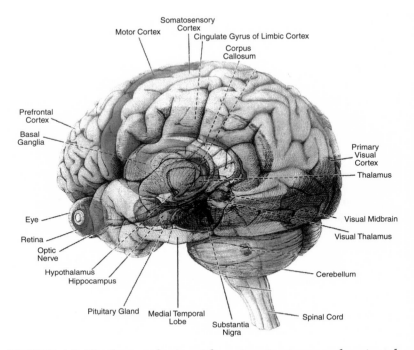

FIGURE 1-2 The human brain with major structures and regions labeled. The entire surface of the brain is covered by a several millimeter thick layer of neurons that forms the cerebral cortex. Key structures for memory include the cerebral cortex, the hippocampus, the basal ganglia and the cerebellum.

generally refers to retention and retrieval of very recently presented information, such as a new telephone number you just looked up. It may last no more than a few seconds. Research on short-term memory has led to the idea of "working memory," which includes retaining new information but also involves transformation and use of that information, retrieval of knowledge from long-term memory to integrate with the new information, and awareness of your surroundings. The concept of working memory is closely related to what is commonly referred to as consciousness or awareness. As you will see in Chapter 2, working memory also seems to be closely related to general intelligence.

Implicit-Procedural Memory

As Figure 1-1 indicates, there is a major distinction between explicit episodic memory and another form of memory called implicit procedural. To a first approximation, explicit episodic memory deals with *knowing that*; implicit-procedural memory deals with *knowing how*. We've already seen an example of the implicit-procedural memory system in the form of patient HM's ability to learn new motor skills. One of the main reasons that memory theorists originally postulated the existence of these two different systems was the fact that certain kinds of brain damage seemed to impair explicit-declarative memory but not implicit-procedural memory. In general, implicit memory does not necessarily involve being aware of the memory.

Can people learn while they are under general anesthesia for surgery? Seem unlikely? There is actually some evidence for this extreme example of implicit memory! In one study patients were played a tape of the story of Robinson Crusoe during cardiac surgery. When they had recovered from the anesthesia, they were asked if they remembered anything that happened during surgery and they all stated that they remembered nothing. They were then asked to free associate to the word "Friday," and five of the 10 responded with "Robinson Crusoe." A group of 15 control patients were not played the tape, and when asked to free associate to "Friday," none of them responded with "Robinson Crusoe"!

Much of this little book on memory is about declarative memory. The other major category—implicit memory—is something of a grab bag. It is defined more or less as memory without awareness and involves several different kinds of memories. But even if we are not aware of these types of memories they are still very important, as they are involved in learning to walk and talk. These aspects of implicit memory will be treated briefly here and expanded on in later chapters. The various brain systems involved are indicated in the drawing of the human brain in Figure 1-2. Don't be concerned if this looks complicated now; the key forms of memory and their brain systems will be made clearer in later chapters.

Habituation

> If a drop of water falls on the surface of the sea just over the
> flower-like disc of a sea anemone, the whole animal contracts
> vigorously. If, then, a second drop falls within a few minutes of
> the first, there is less contraction, and finally, on the third or
> fourth drop, the response disappears altogether. Here in this ma-
> rine polyp with the primitive nerve net is clearly exhibited one
> of the most pervasive phenomena of the animal kingdom—dec-
> rement of response with repeated stimulation (habituation). Al-
> most every species studied, from amoeba to man, exhibits some
> form of habituation when the stimulus is frequently repeated or
> constantly applied. The ubiquity of the phenomenon plus its
> obvious survival value suggests that this kind of plasticity must
> be one of the most fundamental properties of animal behavior.

You can verify this the next time you are at the seashore.
Touch a sea anemone repeatedly and it will cease to contract. If
you encounter a caterpillar, touch it lightly and it will curl up.
Touch it repeatedly and it will cease curling up.

There are many examples of habituation in humans. City
dwellers become habituated to the many noises of the city environment. A city dweller camping out in the forest will find the
silence "deafening." We are constantly exposed to many different
kinds of stimuli, sights, sounds, touches. If we were to respond to
each stimulus we wouldn't have time to do anything else. We
constantly habituate to most stimuli, particularly if they have no
consequences for us.

Habituation has been widely used to study the learning ability and mental capabilities of human infants. It is easy to record
the heart rate of a newborn infant or even a fetus. If a loud sound
is presented the infant's heart rate will increase briefly. If the
sound is repeated several times, the heart rate will cease increasing to the sound; it habituates. We can use measures like this to
ask the infant what she knows long before she can talk.

The occurrence of habituation has a number of characteristics or properties. For example, the more rapidly a stimulus is
presented the more rapid is habituation, weaker stimuli lead to
more rapid habituation, and so on. These same properties occur

in all animals that have been studied, from simple creatures like the sea anemone to humans. This led scientists to think that the basic neuronal mechanism of habituation is common to all these creatures, which in turn suggests that the mechanism must be very simple. Indeed, the "memory trace" (the actual neural process underlying habituation) is rather well understood.

Basic Associative Learning

Basic associative learning includes the kind of learning first discovered by Ivan Pavlov, the great Russian physiologist. Pavlov received a Nobel Prize in 1904 for his pioneering research on digestion. He discovered the conditioned response later. Incidentally, Pavlov was a frugal man. He deposited his Nobel Prize money in a bank in St. Petersburg. After the Russian revolution in 1917, he went to withdraw his money, only to be told that the communist government had confiscated it. Pavlov was completely nonpolitical and simply worked at his research. However, his discoveries were so important that the Soviet government supported him amply, building a major institute for him in Leningrad (formerly and now again St. Petersburg).

Pavlovian conditioning has had some bad press over the years, in part because communist theory embraced it to show that everything is learned—hence they could teach everyone to be good communists. Actually, Pavlov believed that there are marked individual differences among people that are not due to learning. He based this belief on his studies of the different temperaments of different individual dogs that he studied.

Pavlov's earlier work on digestion led him naturally to his work with the conditioned salivary response. A dog was presented with the ringing of a bell followed by the placement of meat powder in its mouth. Initially, the bell produced no effect, but the meat powder of course elicited copious salivation. After a few pairings of bell and meat powder, the bell came to elicit salivation without meat powder. Surprisingly, we still have not identified the critical brain systems for salivary conditioning. In part because of the difficulties in accurately measuring salivation, particularly in people, other forms of Pavlovian conditioning have been more widely used.

Eye-Blink Conditioning

One of the most widely studied forms of Pavlovian conditioning is very simple: conditioning of the eye-blink response. A tone or light serves as the conditioned stimulus. It is followed in less than a second by a puff of air to the eye, which elicits a blink. After a number of pairings of tone and air puff, the tone alone elicits closure of the eyelid. This conditioned response is very precisely timed so that the eye blink is maximally closed at the exact moment in time when the air puff is delivered. If the interval between tone onset and air puff is a quarter of a second, the lid will be maximally closed at a quarter of a second after the tone onset; if the interval is a half second, the lid will be maximally closed at a half second; and so on. In animal studies the same is true for the learning of any discrete movement (e.g., the limb flexing of a response to an electrical shock to an animal's paw). Most studies of this form of learning in people have used the eye-blink response.

Eye-blink conditioning is an elementary example of a skilled movement. Work by one of the present authors (RFT) and his associates has shown that the memory traces for this form of learning are formed and stored in localized regions of the cerebellum (see Figure 1-2), but the hippocampus is also involved in this kind of learning. The term *memory trace* refers to the physical storage of the memory in the brain. In this case it appears to be in a very localized place in the brain where the neurons have actually undergone physical changes that code and store memory. It may also be the case that memory traces for complex skilled movements are stored in the cerebellum (Figure 1-2). We will have more to say about memory storage in the cerebellum.

When you are learning a new motor skill, such as a golf swing, you concentrate your efforts on the precise movements. This effort engages the highest area of the brain, the cerebral cortex, particularly the motor areas of the cortex. However, once the swing is thoroughly mastered and highly skilled, the best thing to do is not think about it at all and just let it happen. Evidence suggests that the memories for such complex skills are stored in the cerebellum. We are consciously aware of engagement of the cerebral cortex, as in learning the swing, but are not aware of engagement of the cerebellum. We think it stores the memories for the automatic performance of skilled movements. This type of learning, from eye blink to a golf swing, requires many trials, that is, many repetitions of the behavior before it becomes "natural."

Emotional Learning

Another widely studied form of Pavlovian conditioning is *conditioned fear*. In brief, a neutral stimulus like a tone is followed by a strong electric shock to the paws of a rat. Even one experience is enough to train the rat to fear the tone. The next time the rat hears that tone, it will experience fear, typically expressed by changes in its heart rate, freezing (becoming motionless), or other behaviors. Fear can also easily be conditioned in humans by pairing a neutral stimulus or situation with an unpleasant event, for example, a very loud sound. Learned fear can develop in one trial. Part of Chapter 7 is devoted to this very important form of Pavlovian conditioning. It accounts for most of our fears, even our likes and dislikes, and phobias. Some people have developed intense "irrational" fears, perhaps for crowds, or snakes, or even running water. The critical brain region for learned fear is the amygdala, but the hippocampus is also involved.

Instrumental Learning

A third category of basic associative learning is called *instrumental or operant conditioning*, where the person or animal is able to control the outcome of a situation. In Pavlovian conditioning the person is unable to control the situation. She is given the stimulus, perhaps a picture of a snake followed by a very loud sound, regardless of what she does. But in instrumental learning she could press a lever when she sees the snake to prevent the loud sound from occurring. In some common examples in animal studies, a rat is trained to press a lever to obtain a food reward or avoid a paw shock, or a pigeon is trained to peck a key for food. B. F. Skinner, a pioneering scientist in the study of learning, termed this type of situation operant conditioning. The animal or person learns to operate on the situation to obtain the desired outcome.

Much of the elementary learning people do is of this sort, although after early childhood the rewards and punishments are more complex. Approval of others, especially peers, is a powerful reward, just as disapproval is a powerful punishment, particularly in the teenage years but also throughout our lives. Instrumental learning may occur in one trial or may require many trials.

The amygdala is a major brain structure involved in learning to avoid an unpleasant or dangerous event, although other brain structures also are involved. On the other hand, learning to obtain rewards involves yet another brain system, the brain "pleasure system," which is also critical for drug addiction. The striatum also seems to be involved in some aspects of reward learning, as in well-learned habits.

Priming

Priming is the kind of memory shown by the surgical patients mentioned earlier who had been anesthetized. They had no awareness or explicit memory of having heard the story of Robinson Crusoe during surgery. But half of them free-associated the name Robinson Crusoe to the word "Friday." Free association is the common method for measuring priming memory.

In a standard priming test, people first read a list of common words (*office, trouble, hillside*, . . .) and have to rate the pleasantness of each word. This rating of pleasantness, incidentally, is irrelevant. It is simply a way to get the person to pay attention to the words. What you are doing here is "priming" or activating the words in the person's long-term memory (their "mental dictionary"). Then at some later time they are given a test such as completing word fragments (for example, $t \_ o \_ b \_ e$). The test does not ask them to explicitly remember anything (nor were they asked to learn or memorize anything originally). Nevertheless, it is easy to show that they will complete the word fragment as $t r o u b l e$ much more often than someone who saw a list that did not have this word in it. Once again, it has been studies of brain-damaged subjects that have led memory theorists to conclude that the kind of memory measured by these implicit procedures is basically different than the memory assessed by explicit memory tests. Many investigators have reported that amnestics such as HM can perform at normal or near-normal levels in implicit tests—even though their memory for the word list is nonexistent when they are asked to use their explicit memory ("Try to recall as many of the words in the list as you can").

In a brain imaging experiment performed by Larry Squire, Marcus Raichle, and other colleagues, normal people studied a list of words. (See Box 1-2 for a description of brain imaging procedures.) Some subjects had to remember and state the words they had studied (explicit memory). In this case a brain structure critical for explicit memory, the hippocampus, became more active. Other subjects were given the priming test, where they said the first words that came to mind upon seeing the first two letters of each word. In this case a region of the right visual areas of the cerebral cortex became active. Indeed, damage to this region of the cortex in a patient markedly impaired priming memory, but the patient *was* able to remember the actual words in an explicit memory test as well as normal people. Explicit memory involves awareness, but priming memory does not, and the two forms of memory seem to involve different areas of the brain.

The existence of priming memory has interesting implications. It would seem that we have some kind of memory storage for experiences we are not very aware of. Some fragments of these memories are there in the brain but cannot be consciously retrieved. This kind of learning had also been described as incidental learning. We learn bits and pieces of experiences, particularly

---

BOX 1-2 Human Brain Imaging—A Window on the Mind

Brain imaging has provided a quantum leap in our ability to study the workings of the human brain. For the first time we can actually watch increases and decreases in the activity of brain regions as they occur without having to do surgery or insert electrodes. In this way brain structures and areas that are critically involved in various forms and aspects of learning and memory can be identified. These methods were, of course, first developed for medicine and have revolutionized medical diagnosis.

Current methods most widely employed for behavioral brain imaging make use of the remarkable fact that increases in the activity of any local group of neurons in the brain result in a rapid increase in blood flow to that particular area. By measuring these local increases in blood flow we can determine which brain areas are most active in a particular learning situation.

One commonly used brain imaging procedure is positron emission tomography (PET). In essence, radioactive biological probes are administered to the subject, usually injected into the bloodstream, and the radiation emitted from the brain (or other target tissue) measured with an array of radiation detectors. This method uses positrons, elementary particles with the mass of an electron but a positive charge. Isotopes of several common elements—for example, carbon or oxygen—emit high levels of positrons. When a positron encounters an electron, the two annihilate each other and are converted to two gamma rays, which can easily be detected and localized in the brain. These "radio-labeled" substances have to be injected into a person, which does not seem like a very good idea. Luckily, they have very short half-lives, decaying quickly (in about 2 minutes for oxygen 15), so there is no harm to the person.

---

unimportant experiences, without being particularly aware of doing so. Incidentally, the importance of implicit memory and priming was identified over 100 years ago by Hermann Ebbinghaus, a German philosopher, educator, and pioneer in the study of memory who spoke of how the accumulated experiences of a lifetime "remain concealed from consciousness and yet produce an effect which authenticates their previous existence."

The radioactive isotopes must be made in a cyclotron, and because of the short half-lives, the cyclotron must be located at the imaging facility site. Since carbon is common to all organic compounds and nitrogen to many, the PET method can be used to study a wide variety of biological functions, including protein synthesis and neurotransmitter-receptor actions.

A more recently developed imaging method is magnetic resonance imaging (MRI), which involves placing the patient or research subject in a very strong magnetic field. Changes in a property of hydrogen protons known as "spin" are then produced when the MRI machine sends in a radio signal at a frequency that causes some proportion of protons to enter an "excited" state. This in turn generates a signal that MRI detectors pick up and later convert to an image of the tissue in the scanned brain areas.

In brain studies the primary research method is called functional MRI (fMRI) and makes use of the same general biological phenomenon as PET—namely regional changes in blood flow. If the amount of oxygen carried by the hemoglobin changes, the degree to which hemoglobin disturbs a magnetic field also changes. Thus, fMRI measures changes in blood oxygenation due to changes in local regional blood flow, which in turn occur when neural activity in a given region of the brain changes.

The fMRI method has a number of advantages over the PET procedure. One is that it is noninvasive, does not require an injection, and does not involve any radioactive substance. fMRI also has much better spatial resolution than PET (it can localize neural activity in relatively small regions) and also better temporal resolution (it can detect changes in neural activity in a much smaller time frame than that required by PET).

Probability and Category Learning

If you were a gambler, imagine what you would do in the following situation. You are presented with two levers (as in a two-armed "one-armed bandit") and must pull one of them every five seconds. Some of the time you win a reward from each lever. Although you are not aware of it, the "house" (i.e., the experimenter) has rigged the situation so that the right lever pays off 57 percent of the time and the left lever 43 percent of the time. If you play for a long time, what do you think you will end up doing? Believe it or not you will reach a steady state where you pull the right lever 57 percent of the time and the left lever 43 percent of the time. Your behavior will come to match the exact probabilities of pay-off, even though you are unaware of this and even though you would have done better by pulling the right lever all the time.

This surprising result was found in a series of studies by the brilliant Harvard psychologist Richard Herrnstein, who characterized this behavior as the "matching law." Even more remarkable, exactly the same result occurs if a rat has to press levers or a pigeon peck keys, with differing probabilities of reward. Mammals, including humans, and birds respond in exact proportion to the probability that reward will occur. In general, people are unaware of the fact that they are matching reward probabilities. Probability learning requires *many* trials.

Mark Gluck, of Rutgers University, developed an important elaboration of this type of probability or category learning in a game he termed *weather forecasting*. Four different cards are used, and one, two, or three of the cards are presented on each trial. The person playing the game has to guess from each presentation whether it will rain or be sunny. Sounds simple, right? But Mark rigged the situation so that the probability that a given card or combination of cards might mean rain was less than one. For example, one card predicted sunshine 57 percent of the time and rain 43 percent of the time. The player is not told this, only "right" or "wrong" on each trial. The player can't simply memorize the relations between cards and weather because the relationships are considerably less than perfect.

At the beginning of the game, people more or less guess rain or shine at random on each trial. With much practice they actually improve substantially in their predictions of the weather. But they are unaware of why they are improving; that is, they cannot state what is governing their successful behavior.

In a series of studies, Larry Squire, Barbara Knowlton, Mark Gluck, and associates, working at the University of California, San Diego (Barbara is now at the University of California, Los

Angeles), tested amnestics, like HM, with damage to the hippocampus and medial temporal lobe. They actually showed improvement with practice, just as normal people do, but they could not
remember the game afterward. On the other hand, patients with
Parkinson's disease, with damage to the striatum, were unable to
improve with practice, even though they could remember the
game afterward. The striatum appears to play a key role in this
type of unconscious category or probability learning.

Skills

Parkinson's patients also have difficulty starting or initiating vol-
untary movements, clearly indicating that the striatum is involved in motor control and presumably in motor skill learning
as well. We noted earlier that the well-learned memories for motor skills appear to be stored in the cerebellum. But we also noted
the important role of the motor areas of the cerebral cortex in the
initial learning of motor skills. The striatum is also somehow
involved in motor skill learning, although little more is known.

Overview

This book focuses on those aspects of memory we think are most
important to you, the reader. The ability to store new information and experience into long-term or permanent memory is the
hallmark of memory. But people also forget. How accurate are our
memories? Believe it or not, it is relatively easy to establish false
memories, to convince people they have certain memories that in
fact they do not have.

Normal aging is accompanied by minor impairments in long-
term memory ability, what has been termed "benign" forgetting.
This is completely different from Alzheimer's disease, in which
most memories, new and old, eventually disappear.

Amnesia is typically an inability to form long-term memories
that can result from brain injury, but here the memories for some
period prior to injury may still be present.

Emotional memories, fear and anxiety, are compelling. Intense anxiety when remembering and reliving traumatic events can exert disruptive effects on people for years. The problem is not so much being able to remember such traumas but instead being able to forget them.

Perhaps the most important learning people do is the acquisition of their native language. Indeed, language sets us apart from all other species. It allows us to describe anything, even things that do not exist. Nothing defines humanity so much as our ability to communicate abstract thoughts to others.

These are all aspects of long-term memory. We also distinguish between short-term or "working" memory and long-term memory. Short-term memory, often termed immediate memory, is how long you can remember a new telephone number you just looked up—a few seconds. Working memory includes new information but also retrieval of knowledge from long-term memory and awareness of one's surroundings, what is commonly referred to as consciousness or awareness. Long-term memory is the vast store of information you possess and are not aware of unless you call it up. How the three pounds of tissue that are the brain accomplish these extraordinary functions of memory is one of the greatest mysteries and one of the most exciting fields of science today.

2

Memories of the Here and Now

We begin our exploration of the human memory system by considering *primary memory*, a term used by the psychologist-philosopher William James in 1890 to refer to the contents of our immediate, ongoing awareness. Since James's time, it has been variously called *immediate memory*, *short-term memory*, and *working memory*. The modern version of James's concept of primary memory originated in research by the British psychologist Donald Broadbent and the American psychologist George Miller, who analyzed the problems of attending to and processing events that occurred simultaneously or in quick succession. Intense experimental study of these problems has produced detailed understanding of consciousness, attention, perception, and memory. More recently, work has started on understanding of the brain systems responsible for these basic human capacities.

The Two-Store Model of Memory

A decade of memory research led to the diagram shown in Figure 2-1. Based on the work of Richard Atkinson and Richard Shiffrin, it is a schematic of how information flows through the various aspects of our declarative memory system, and it is usually referred to as the *two-store model of memory* (even though it actually consists of three memory stores).

Sensory Memories

Imagine that you are a subject in a psychology experiment in which you are shown an array of letters such as the following:

H T D R
B F Q G
L N S K

You see the array for only 50 milliseconds (one-twentieth of a second), and you have to recall as much of the display as you can.

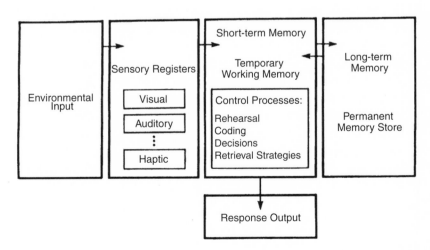

FIGURE 2-1 Atkinson and Shiffrin's model of the short-term and long-term memory systems.

Some people appear to possess a rare ability to take in and retain large amounts of visual information. You, however, are much more likely to be able to recall only four or five letters and their locations. Interestingly, you would perform at about the same level if the experimenter showed you an array of common objects rather than random letters of the alphabet. This apparent limit on perception and memory was originally known as the *span of apprehension* ("apprehension" in the sense of grasping something). Actually, all of us possess a high-capacity, high-resolution visual memory, one that holds a lot more information than the span of apprehension seems to indicate. This is the good news. The bad news is that for most of us, our visual short-term memory lasts only about a fifth of a second.

How this was first determined is an interesting detective story. In 1960 George Sperling, now at the University of California at Irvine, took a closer look at the span of apprehension and the belief that it is only four or five stimulus objects. He succeeded in showing that immediate visual sensory memory has a capacity much greater than this. Sperling argued that the image of the array might be fading during the few seconds it took the person to report what they had seen (our first example of how the act of remembering can actually cause forgetting). He tested this hypothesis in a simple and elegant series of experiments in which he used a device that projected the array of letters very briefly and then presented a cue to the subject to report only one row of the array (for example, a high-pitched tone to signal recall of the first row, a medium-pitched tone for the second row, and a low-pitched tone for the third row). The cue occurred at various time delays after the image had been presented, ranging from 0.02 second to 1 second. He repeated this over and over with the cue in different random and unpredictable locations in different arrays. The key finding was that if the cue was presented less than 0.1 second after the array had vanished, people could typically report most of the letters in any given row but could not do so if the cue was delayed for 0 .5 second or more. Sperling reasoned that this must mean the memory image of the array contained information about *all* of the letters and that the capacity of this form of memory was therefore actually much greater than four or five elements.

Sperling's experiments are also important because they provide an example of what appears to be a simple decay of information from memory. Visual information enters a sensory register or "iconic" memory where it is held in detail for a brief period. Some of this information is transferred to a short-term memory store if it is attended to, and some may even get transferred to a more permanent long-term memory; but much information from sensory memory is not attended to, is not stored, and is simply lost. (The process of attention and its importance in memory creation are discussed in more detail later in this chapter.)

Visual sensory memory can also be easily interfered with and essentially erased. Suppose you see a row of digits such as *5 3 8 4* flashed on a computer monitor for 30 milliseconds, followed by a blank screen. You will be able to remember all four digits in order almost all of the time. But suppose the row of digits is followed immediately not by a blank screen, but by a row of symbols such as # # # # that occupies the same location on the screen as the digits. Under these conditions, you won't be able to recite the digits easily. In fact, you might find yourself telling the experimenter that you didn't even *see* any digits! This is a simple demonstration of what's called *backward masking*, an effect that seems to occur because the symbols overwrite the digit information in the iconic memory store before it can be transferred to the next stage of processing. If you think about it, this seems to say that in ordinary, moment-to-moment vision, information is continuously being erased from iconic memory as new information enters the visual system.

As Figure 2-1 suggests, there are short-term sensory memory stores for other senses as well: hearing (the acoustic store), touch (the haptic store), and smell (the olfactory sensory store). They all seem to have the same general function and properties as Sperling's iconic memory: They preserve sensory information for very brief periods but are highly susceptible to loss of information from decay and interference.

Are there people with "photographic memories" who can perceive and remember a 3 by 4 array of random letters after a single 50 millisecond exposure? There have been a few reports of such individuals, but they have not withstood scientific scrutiny very well. At the same time, there definitely are individual differences in the capacity of visual short-term memory, and recent research has begun to identify the brain regions where these differences may reside. Working independently, Jay Todd and Rene Marois at Vanderbilt University and Edward Vogel and Maro Machizawa at the University of Oregon tested undergraduate subjects whose average performance ranged from an average of one or two correct to five or more correct in tests of memory for briefly presented arrays of colored dots and squares. Both research teams found that low- and high-capacity subjects differed in levels of brain activity in the parietal cortex, a region of the brain known to be involved in the processing of visual and spatial information.

The Short-Term Store

The concept of *memory span* was known to psychologists long before the two-store model of memory was developed. It refers to the longest randomly ordered sequence of stimuli—digits, letters, words—that a person can recall in order after one brief presentation. Test someone with the digits sequences shown here, reading them at a rate of two per second. A list

2, 7, 5, 1
2, 7, 5, 1, 4, 8, 9
2, 7, 5, 1, 4, 8, 9, 3, 6, 1, 7

of four digits is easy recalled; a list of seven digits is noticeably harder; and a list of 11 digits is next to impossible to recall perfectly. Young adults have a memory span of seven or eight for randomly ordered digits.

This basic limit on our ability to recall very recent events is represented in Figure 2-1 by the short-term memory or working memory store, which is thought of as a temporary storage system that has a relatively small capacity. The concept of a short-term memory store was also inspired by the observation that the last few events of a sequence tend to be relatively easy to recall. This is called the *recency effect*. If you present subjects with lists of 15 common words at a rate of one word per second and have them recall the words as soon as the list ends, in any order they can recall them, then you will get results like those shown in Figure 2-2. Recall of the first few words in the list is relatively good but drops off toward the middle of the list; then recall rises steeply toward the end of the list. This whole pattern is called the *serial position effect in immediate recall*. According to the two-store model, the recency effect occurs because the last five or six words in the list are still available in the short-term store at the time of the test.

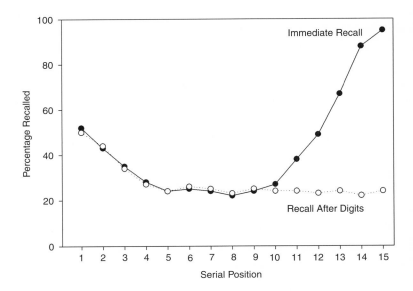

FIGURE 2-2 *The serial position effect in recall of a sequence of 15 words. The prominent recency effect can be eliminated by a brief distraction such as reciting a list of digits.*

An interesting fact about the recency effect in this kind of experiment is that it is very fragile. Suppose we change the experiment so that the subject has to recite just three digits that appear after the fifteenth word and then recall the words. As shown in Figure 2-2, the recency effect disappears almost completely! In this regard, the short-term store is just like the sensory store because its contents can be readily displaced by new incoming information that requires attention and competes for "space" in short-term memory.

This fact has an important practical implication: Being able to recall the contents of short-term store after a short, distraction-free interval does not mean that you will also be able to recall them as easily after a longer interval filled with other events, as many witnesses to crimes or traffic accidents have discovered.

Long-Term Store

We'll complete our exploration of the two-store model by looking at some of the most important properties of long-term storage or long-term memory. According to the model shown in Figure 2-1, information moves from short-term store to a larger and more permanent storage system. Whether or not this happens depends largely on the process of *encoding* that is applied to information while it is still in short-term store. For example, suppose in trying to remember a telephone number you've just looked up, you repeat it to yourself (an act called "maintenance rehearsal"). This typically succeeds in keeping the information active and accessible in the short-term store, but is a poor strategy for creating a new memory record that will last over time and in the face of distractions. Something more is needed.

George Miller, a pioneer in the study of cognitive psychology and memory, suggested that this "something more" often consists of the process of *chunking*. Miller described the capacity of short-term memory as "the magical number 7, plus or minus 2." By this he meant we can hold about seven chunks of information in short-term memory. The word "chunk" here means something like "psychological unit" or "perceptual unit." Look back at the example of the letter array used in Sperling's experiments. It represents 12 chunks of information because the letters, being randomly chosen and arranged, each represent one psychological or perceptual unit. But suppose you were tested in the Sperling experiment with arrays like this:

$$H \quad O \quad L \quad D$$
$$B \quad A \quad R \quad K$$
$$L \quad I \quad N \quad E$$

The number of letters you could recall would now be much greater because, while there are still 12 letters, they represent a much smaller number of chunks (just three familiar words). The same principle applies to memory span. The letter sequence *O U T S T A N D I N G* consists of 11 letters but only one chunk, and is easily accommodated by short-term memory and easily transferred into long-term memory. This also explains why memory span for meaningful sentences is far greater that for randomly ordered digits or words. You would not have much trouble remembering a 14-word sentence such as *the wicked old witch led the two trusting children into the deep dark forest* even when it is shown to you word by word at the very fast rate of 10 words per second.

Chunking also seems to be the basis of some kinds of learning. For example, if you are shown a list of 30 unrelated words, one at a time for one second each, you may be able to recall only about six to eight of them if you're tested right away. But if you are shown the same words a second time, the amount you can recall increases, and will continue to increase every time you are given an additional learning trial until you get to the point where you can easily recall all 30 words. One important reason you've been able to overcome the "7 plus or minus 2" limit is that in the course of learning you have formed information-rich chunks, each of which may contain several words. See Box 2-1 for an example of how the chunking principle can be applied to create a memory span of over 70, and for a discussion of memory improvement in general.

BOX 2-1 Chunking, Recoding, Remembering

Can we learn to improve our short-term memory? The answer is *yes*, with some qualifications. In one experiment the subject was a young man who was an enthusiastic amateur runner. At the beginning of the project he had a normal memory span for digits, about seven. He was given massive amounts of practice in which he applied a special encoding or chunking procedure to the digits sequences. He would try to *recode* a set of digits into something that was familiar and meaningful: times in foot races of different distances. For example, *3 5 4 5 1* might be encoded as "near world record for a one-mile race," and this seemed to reduce the five digits to one chunk. With a great deal of practice and effort, he was also able to "chunk chunks" until he got to the point where he could recall up to 70 digits after hearing the sequence just once.

What do you suppose happened when he was then given some tests with randomly ordered letters of the alphabet? His memory span was right back to where it had started—around seven letters! This is a good illustration of what strategies for memory improvement most often consist of. Rather than increasing the actual capacity of a memory store, *they work by improving the way a person encodes information into long-term memory*. This basically means using what you already know—what's already in your long-term memory—to assimilate new information. Many kinds of mnemonic devices are based on this principle, such as the sentence codes you learned as a child to represent the notes of the treble clef or the rhymes that represent spelling rules. And if it's ever important for you to learn and never forget which kind of camel has two humps and which has one hump, just remember what you see when the B in *Bactrian* and the D in *Dromedary* are rotated 90º to the left.

In general, how well new information is stored in long-term memory depends very much on *depth of processing*, an important concept developed by Fergus Craik and Robert Lockhart of the University of Toronto. A semantic level of processing, which is directed at the meaning aspect of events, produces substantially better memory for events than a structural or surface level of processing. For example, if you respond to each word in a list that an experimenter wants you to remember by thinking about the pleasantness of each word, your memory for the word list will be much better than if you had instead paid attention to the number of letters in each word or to some aspect of their perceptual appearance. Interestingly, the same result occurs if you want to remember faces. As you look at a face, judge the person's trustworthiness or temperament. Your later recognition of the face will be considerably better than it would be if you had instead focused on facial features only.

Forming Long-Term Memories

Even with minimal exposure to an event, some information about that event seems to register in long-term memory. An example of this is called the Hebb-Melton effect, in which subjects are given a sequence of memory span tests for random nine-digit sequences such as the following:

$$4\ 8\ 5\ 2\ 6\ 3\ 7\ 1\ 9$$
$$5\ 7\ 2\ 9\ 3\ 6\ 2\ 8\ 1$$
$$8\ 1\ 5\ 7\ 3\ 4\ 2\ 6\ 9$$
$$4\ 8\ 5\ 2\ 6\ 3\ 7\ 1\ 9$$

The subjects are not told that a given digit list may be repeated (for example, the first and fourth sequences in this example). What is found is that recall of the second occurrence of a given list is better than recall of the first occurrence. In simple terms, some learning or transfer of information into a more permanent form must have occurred when the repeated sequence was first presented and tested, even though the memory task involved would require only transitory short-term memory.

It sometimes seems that all that is required to produce a durable long-term memory is perception of a meaningful stimulus event. This was demonstrated in dramatic experiments by Ralph Haber at the University of Rochester and Lionel Standing at Bishop's University. In these experiments, undergraduate students were shown a large number of slides of color magazine photos that depicted a wide variety of scenes, people, and objects. Each slide was shown for four or five seconds. A few days later subjects were shown a series of pairs of pictures in which one picture was "old" (seen previously in the experiment) and one was "new" (not previously seen) and they were asked to pick out the old pictures. After viewing 1,000 pictures, they scored an amazing 90 percent correct in this recognition test. They did pretty well even when the "new" test pictures were mirror-image versions of the original pictures!

The memory system of the human brain seems to have an astonishing capacity for this kind of material. In one of Standing's experiments, subjects were shown 10,000 slides over a two-day period, with each slide exposed for five seconds. The performance of subjects on the recognition memory test indicated that they had retained information for at least 6,600 of the pictures. This doesn't mean that the subjects were storing highly detailed representations of each picture in memory, but it does suggest that some information of the visual scene in each slide had been stored directly in visual long-term memory.

There is an interesting connection between what is known about the capacity of visual long-term memory and the use of mental imagery in learning and memorizing. Many schemes for rapidly assimilating and retaining information are based on the use of visual mental imagery (see Box 2-2).

A third example of how readily long-term memory can be formed from brief experiences can be found in studies of what are called *priming effects*. In one experiment, Carolyn Cave had subjects name pictures of common objects as fast as they could. One year later the subjects were retested with some of the pictures they had seen and named a year before, along with some new pictures. She found that subjects were faster at naming the previously seen and named pictures than the new pictures—even when they couldn't remember having seen the pictures originally. This is astonishing: A brief experience in a memory experiment created memory traces that lasted at least a year.

Attention, Consciousness, and Memory

Psychologists think of attention in terms of how we allocate our perceptual and mental resources to some aspects of a complex environment. If you are reading a book and someone speaks to you, your behavior can range from not hearing the person at all and being aware of (and remembering) what you are reading to being fully aware (and remembering) what was said to you and not remembering what you are reading. Two key assumptions of

BOX 2-2 Memory and the Mind's Eye

Some of the most effective methods for memorizing material quickly and effectively are based on use of "the mind's eye"—our ability to visualize objects and places and to form mental images from them. Some of these methods (mnemonic devices) have been known since antiquity. One is the *method of loci* (locations). Suppose you want to memorize a list of things you must do or a set of words in a fixed order. The best way to proceed is to form a mental image of each of the things to be remembered as occupying a place along a travel route you already know well. Then, when you have to retrieve the information, just take a stroll (a mental one) along the route. You will find that the things you have to remember come to mind quite easily.

Another simple mnemonic system is the *rhyming peg word method*. Suppose you have to memorize a list of 10 words (*cash, doll, band, farm, hill, gang, knee, lime, mail, nose*) in a way that preserves information about the order of the words as well as the words themselves. This is not easy to do if you use a learning strategy such as repeating the word list over and over, but it's a breeze if you use the rhyming peg word system. All you need to do is first learn the "peg words" for the numbers 1 through 10:

1 is a gun	6 is sticks
2 is a shoe	7 is heaven
3 is a tree	8 is a gate
4 is a door	9 is a pine
5 is a hive	10 is a hen

The next step is to form a mental image of the words you have to memorize, associating each word with successive peg words. For "one" imagine a *gun* lying on a pile of *cash*; for "two" think of a *shoe* with a *doll* stuffed in it; and so forth. This system is amazingly effective. It is also easy to learn to use, unlike some mnemonic systems that require a great deal of initial memorization and practice.

The use of mental images in mnemonic devices is just one example of the important functions of visual mental imagery in human memory and cognition. The modern study of mental imagery was started in the 1960s by Allan Paivio of the University of Western Ontario in a wide-ranging program of research that led to Dual Code Theory, which argues convincingly for the existence of separate verbal and visual systems for representing information in memory.

all theories of attention are that there are limits to our attentional resources as well as limits on how well we can divide attention. Think of a flashlight beam that can illuminate only so much space at any one time.

The scientific study of selective attention is another intriguing detective story. How can you determine if someone is attending to something? Typically you see if they remember what they were attending to or supposed to be attending to. Suppose you played two different stories through two earphones of a headset. If you ask people to pay attention to the right ear, they will remember that story but be unaware of the story in the left ear, and vice versa. This led to the notion of a selective filter. The unattended message was "filtered out" before it reached awareness.

This filter model was appealing. But Anne Treisman, a leading authority on human cognition, added a twist. At a certain point in the unattended message spoken to the left ear, the listener's own name was spoken. The person immediately became aware of the unattended message. Somehow, the unattended message was being evaluated someplace in the brain and was determined to be important or unimportant. This has been called the "cocktail party effect." You are talking to someone at a crowded and noisy party. You are unaware of the contents of the conversation going on behind you until your name is spoken. Suddenly you attend to that conversation and ignore the person speaking directly to you.

Notice the implication here that the sensory and perceptual systems of the brain can detect, analyze, and filter out information about events in the external environment before you become consciously aware of them. Exactly how this preconscious processing happens is currently a major issue in cognitive neuroscience and brain science, but it is clear from the results of many different kinds of experiments that the processing of sensory information by the brain does not always lead to conscious awareness of an event; it depends, among other things, on how your attentional resources have been deployed.

In one such experiment, subjects saw a rapidly presented

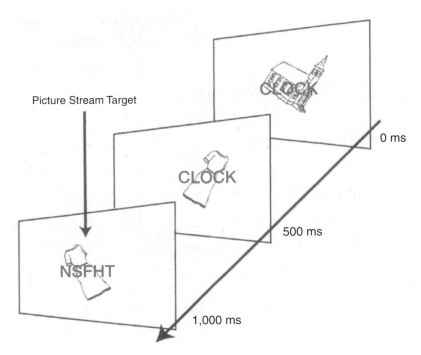

FIGURE 2-3 A rapidly presented stream of pictures, words, and random letter strings.

stream of either meaningless strings of letters or familiar words superimposed on pictures (see Figure 2-3) while undergoing a brain scan by MRI. Their task was to detect repetitions of pictures and ignore the verbal material, or vice versa. Normally, the brain activations produced by a random string of letters and by a real word are usually quite different. However, when subjects in this experiment were instructed to attend and respond to the pictures only, the brain activations for the superimposed nonsense words and real words were about the same, even though the subjects were looking directly at the words. (Try looking at one of the pictures without perceiving the word; it seems impossible.) At the end of the experimental session, subjects could remember many of the words if they had been directed to pay attention to them, but had *no memory at all* for the unattended words. It seems that focusing of attention on one kind of event (the pictures) precluded processing of the other kind of event (the words)—even though the perceptual and memory systems of the brain would be able under normal conditions to detect and identify the words and to bring them into conscious awareness in a few fractions of a second.

Another striking demonstration of this "inattentional blindness" was conducted by Daniel Simons and Christopher Chabris at Harvard University. Using an experimental procedure first devised by Ulrich Neisser, they had undergraduate subjects look at a video depicting a group of students moving about and passing a basketball around. The subjects were instructed either to keep track of the number of times the ball was passed (the easy task) or to keep separate tallies of the number of air passes and bounce passes (the difficult task). They were not told that something unusual would happen in the middle of the video: A person wearing a gorilla suit entered the scene, paused in the middle of the group of basketball passers, beat on its chest, and then exited (Figure 2-4). What Simons and Chabris found was that at least 35 percent of the subjects did not report seeing the gorilla in the easy task, and more than 50 percent failed to see the gorilla when the counting task was difficult! It is important to understand that in this experiment the person in the gorilla costume was easily visible for several seconds and would always be seen by someone asked to simply look at the video but not required to do any counting. Simons also found that subjects counting basketball passes by students in black shirts were more likely to report seeing the gorilla than subjects who had to count passes by students in white shirts. This is what you would expect if the student observers had "set their attentional filters" to select one kind of stimulus event and filter out others.

Consciousness

Most discussions of attention lead to the issue of consciousness and awareness.

FIGURE 2-4 You can fail to see the person in the gorilla costume if your attention is focused on the students passing the basketball around.

Some theorists believe that the primary brain system responsible for consciousness is the cerebral cortex. A compelling case for this view was made by the neuroscientist Larry Weiskrantz at Oxford University in elegant studies of a person with "blindsight." This individual had extensive damage to the primary visual areas in the cerebral cortex. As far as the patient was concerned, he was totally blind in a large part of his visual field. When presented with a spot of light somewhere in his visual field and asked to point to it, he would say, "what spot of light? I don't see anything." If you persist and tell the patient just to point anywhere he will humor you and point at random—except that he doesn't point at random; he always points accurately to the spot of light. But he doesn't see it at all; he is not aware of the spot of light and has no working memory of it. But other visual systems in his brain are able to direct his pointing. Such patients also avoid objects. In walking through a room they walk around chairs and other objects all while insisting that they can't see any of the objects.

As mentioned in Chapter 1, some perception and memory formation can occur without consciousness, at least judging from experiments performed on patients under deep surgical anesthesia. If a list of words is read to them while they are anesthetized, they will later, when awake, have no episodic memory at all of the words or, for that matter, any aspect of the surgery. But if you give them an *implicit* test for the words, they will show evidence of having "registered" more of the words than control subjects who were not read the words. This priming memory seems to involve auditory-visual association areas of the cerebral cortex. Perhaps awareness or consciousness is what we can describe verbally at a given moment in time—the contents of our working memory.

Where does this leave animals? Evolution works in very small steps to change the structures and functions of animals. If humans have awareness or consciousness, it seems reasonable to suppose that nonhuman animals have a similar capacity. It must have evolved gradually from small beginnings in simpler animals because it has adaptive value. But how can it be assessed in animals, who cannot speak? We can teach them how to tell us. In ingenious experiments, monkeys with damage to the visual cortex showed blindsight. They can be trained to tell us that they cannot see a light, yet they can point to it. These monkeys, like humans, have lost awareness of the visual stimulus.

There is other good evidence that some species have a form of conscious episodic memory much like that of humans. Anthony Wright has studied "list memory" in monkeys using procedures not so different from those used with human subjects. This research has produced evidence for common processes in nonverbal monkeys and verbal humans. For example, monkeys show recency effects and serial position effects (see Figure 2-2) that resemble those of humans in important ways.

When a questionnaire was sent to many neuroscientists asking them to rank animals in terms of degree of consciousness, the results were just what might have been expected. Primates and possibly sea animals ranked highest, then carnivores, then rodents, and so on. The neuroscientists expressed serious doubt about the consciousness of flies and worms. The result of the questionnaire is of course merely opinion, but here opinion corresponds rather closely with the evolution of the forebrain and cerebral cortex.

Working Memory and Its Brain Systems

As is true for most really important ideas in science, the two-store model of memory has been criticized in virtually every conceivable way, but basics of the model of it have stood the test of time. When Atkinson and Shiffrin first proposed the two-store model of memory some 30 years ago, they described short-term store as a temporary "working memory" that could be used in flexible ways to adjust to the demands of processing information. Over time this idea has become a central one in studies of memory, mind, and brain. For many contemporary theorists, working memory is much more than a small, passive memory store; instead, it is an essential part of conscious awareness, with important connections to attention and mental ability.

Alan Baddeley of Cambridge, England, a leading authority on working memory, characterizes it as the temporary storage of information in connection with performing other, more complex tasks. He proposes a multicomponent system, comprising an attentional system, the *central executive*, aided by "slave" systems responsible for temporary storage of either visual or verbal material. He coined the very apt terms *visuospatial sketchpad* for visual temporary storage and *phonological loop* for temporary storage of verbal speech material. As we shall see, his view appears to correlate well with findings on the brain mechanism of working memory.

The involvement of the prefrontal cortex in working memory in monkeys was first reported by C. F. Jacobsen at an international congress in 1935. Frontal-lobe lesions in the brains of monkeys produced a marked taming effect on the animals. A neurosurgeon, Egon Muniz, was in the audience. He immediately saw the relevance of this effect for humans, and at his clinic in

Portugal he began removing the frontal lobes in humans to treat psychiatric problems. Unfortunately, Jacobsen had also described a severe deficit in working memory following the lesion in monkeys. Thousands of human operations later it was realized that this damaging procedure was of little help in the treatment of mental illness. A most unfortunate chapter in the history of psychiatry, the procedure is no longer used today.

A standard task now used to test short-term memory in monkeys (and human infants) is the delayed response. A monkey is shown two food wells; one is baited with a preferred food, and both are covered with identical objects. An opaque screen is placed between the animal and the objects for a short period of time. The screen is lifted and the animal must reach out and displace the object over the food to obtain it (see Figure 2-5). Note that this is not a visual discrimination as such but rather memory of a location, a kind of spatial short-term memory. Normal animals can learn to perform correctly with delays of many seconds. Destruc-

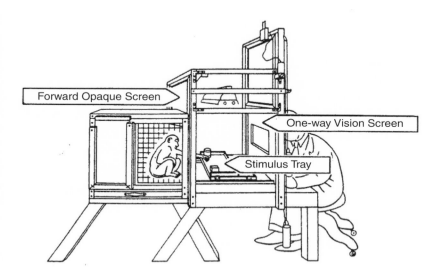

FIGURE 2-5 Testing a monkey's short-term memory.

tion of a localized region of frontal cortex severely disrupts the animal's ability to perform this task, even at relatively short delays.

In a visual discrimination task, the animal must learn to choose one of two different objects to obtain a reward, that is, to learn to recognize particular objects. Again, normal animals can learn to do this well even with delays of many seconds. Lesions of a different region of prefrontal cortex impair this task, even with relatively short delays.

Much of our current information about the monkey prefrontal cortex has come from two scientists, the late Patricia Goldman-Rakic at Yale University and Joachim Fuster at the University of California at Los Angeles. In addition to lesion studies, they have analyzed the activity of single neurons in a monkey's prefrontal cortex while the animal is performing delay tasks. They found neurons that increase their firing rates during delay periods, as though they are holding the needed information in working memory.

Important studies by Brenda Milner at McGill University showed that patients with prefrontal damage are greatly impaired in remembering the temporal sequence of events, although memories for the events themselves are not impaired. Thus, Milner would show a patient a series of pictures of paintings, one at a time, and at some point show the patient two paintings and ask which was seen first. Patients with prefrontal damage are much impaired on this task (which is typically easy for nonimpaired people), although they remembered perfectly well having seen the paintings earlier.

If any one term summarizes these rather diverse aspects of prefrontal damage it is *executive function*, a process that makes use of specific short-term memory stores from the posterior visual and verbal areas to store and search for long-term memories. It is not the memories that are impaired but rather the ability to manipulate and process them: exactly what Baddeley termed the "central executive."

There is evidence from the human clinical literature that damage to a fairly localized area in the left parietal cortex massively impairs short-term memory of verbal material. A classic example is the case of KF, who was studied by Elizabeth Warrington and Timothy Shallice in England. KF appeared to have relatively normal visual short-term memory but had virtually no verbal digit span. He could repeat back two digits at most. This is strikingly reminiscent of Baddeley's phonological loop. Other patients with damage to right-hemisphere visual association areas have a dramatic and selective loss of visual short-term memory ability—Baddeley's visuospatial sketch pad.

But what do the phenomena of short-term visual memory and short-term verbal memory have to do with the prefrontal cortex? Lesions of the human prefrontal cortex do not impair short-term memory processes or, for that matter, many aspects of longer-term memory. Extensive studies by Arthur Shimamura at the University California at Berkeley and by other groups showed that frontal lobe damage seems to impair more the processes than the facts of memory. Thus, such patients are much impaired in the *retrieval* of information. They have a particular problem with "source" memory, meaning they can remember facts they recently learned, but not where and when they learned them. We saw earlier that this type of memory is termed *episodic* and refers to events you have experienced, and that this kind of memory is contrasted with semantic memory—for example, your vocabulary—that is not tagged to your own life experiences.

A case can be made that Baddeley's central executive function is performed by the prefrontal cortex, that the visuospatial sketchpad operates in the posterior visual association cortex, and that the phonological loop may use the short-term verbal memory area in the posterior cortex. In humans (as in monkeys) there are extensive interconnections of these short-term visual and verbal memory areas with regions of prefrontal cortex.

Extensive imaging studies in humans have demonstrated the role of the prefrontal cortex in memory retrieval, a key aspect of working memory. There is an intriguing asymmetry in the retrieval function of the prefrontal cortex. The left prefrontal cortex seems particularly involved in retrieving semantic information, whereas the right prefrontal cortex is more involved in retrieving episodic information, perhaps consistent with the fact that in most people language functions are located in their left hemispheres.

The frontal lobes have expanded enormously from monkeys and apes to humans. It has been known for many years that people with large lesions of the frontal lobes in both hemispheres have great difficulty inhibiting inappropriate behaviors. The classic case is Phineas Gage, who had a metal rod blown through his skull that obliterated his frontal lobes. He changed from a modest, reliable, hard-working individual to a very erratic and emotional person given to irrational rages (see Box 2-3).

BOX 2-3 Frontal Lobes and Personality:
The Story of Phineas Gage

One of the most obvious and striking effects of frontal lobe damage in humans is a marked change in social behavior and personality. Perhaps the most publicized example of personality change following frontal lobe lesion is that of Phineas Gage, first reported in 1868. Incidentally, Fred Gage, a recent president of the Society for Neuroscience and a pioneer in the study of new neurons being formed in the adult brain, is a descendant of Phineas. Gage was a dynamite worker and survived an explosion that blasted an iron-tamping bar (3 feet 7 inches long and 1.25 inches wide) through the front of his head. After the accident his behavior changed completely. He had been of average intelligence and was "energetic and persistent in executing all his plans of operation." After the injury his personality was described as follows:

> This equilibrium or balance, so to speak, between his intellectual faculties, and animal propensities seems to have been destroyed. He is fitful, indulging at times in the grossest profanity, manifesting but little deference for his fellows, impatient of restraint or advice when it conflicts with his desires, at times pertinaciously obstinate, yet capricious and vacillating, devising many plans of operation, which are no sooner arranged than they are abandoned in turn for others appearing more feasible. A child in his intellectual capacity and manifestations has the animal passions of a strong man.

But the frontal lobes do not function simply to inhibit bad behavior. We know they play a critical role in overseeing memory; that is, they perform the executive function in memory. When you try to remember something that doesn't immediately come to mind, the frontal lobes show a marked increase in activity. The memory you are searching for, perhaps something you earlier saw or heard, is not stored in the frontal lobe. Rather, such memories are thought to be stored in cortical areas more toward the back of the brain. But the frontal lobes seem to be the system that is searching through your memory banks. A frustrating aspect of this kind of memory search is called "tip of the tongue." You know that you know the word or name, but you just can't remember it at the moment. Sometimes, if you stop trying to remember it and think about something else, the memory suddenly pops into your head, as if during this period the frontal lobes have been busily searching through your vast memory stores until they find the memory you want. As we will see later, such memory searches are not random but rather are guided by associations among the items in memory. This executive function of the frontal lobes in memory is critically important in short-term or working memory. Brain imaging work with normal humans suggests that a major executive function of the frontal lobes in working memory is to inhibit irrelevant or outdated memories. Think of the memory demands on the referee in an ice hockey game. In order to assign credit to players for goals and assists, he must continually keep track of the last two or three players to have control of the puck. Given the nature of hockey, this changes quickly, and the information in the referee's working memory has to be updated equally quickly.

There is growing evidence that this prefrontal cortex is critically involved in the mental disorder known as schizophrenia. Such patients characteristically have thought disorders, including marked impairment in working memory. Recent evidence, much of it from the work of Patricia Goldman-Rakic, shows that patients with schizophrenia have a significantly reduced metabolic rate in the prefrontal cortex and in fact have a reduced amount of neural tissue in the prefrontal cortex.

Recent studies by Adrian Raine and his associates at the University of Southern California have implicated the prefrontal cortex in violent behavior. These researchers did imaging studies of the brains of normal subjects and convicted murderers. Most of those who had been convicted of murder apparently killed in violent rage, usually one victim and often a relative or friend. But some were mass murderers who killed many times before being caught. Their killings were carefully plotted and not impulsive. Raine and his associates found that impulsive-rage killers had much reduced prefrontal activity compared to normal subjects when performing a task that engages the prefrontal cortex. Interestingly, the mass killers had normal prefrontal activation. It is tempting to conclude that the rage killers had reduced frontal control of impulsive behavior, whereas the mass killers had normal prefrontal function (though clearly they had other abnormalities as well).

Working Memory and Intelligence

Exploring the concept of working memory and its brain substrates has taken us into unexpected territory such as personality, schizophrenia, and criminality. It also takes us directly into one more important area: intelligence. Working memory tasks usually require a person to transform information, to keep track of changes and update memory, to retrieve information, to divide attention, and to make comparisons. If this sounds to you like a description of intelligent behavior, you're right. Many studies of working memory have shown a close connection between working memory efficiency and general cognitive ability. Correlations of working memory scores and cognitive ability (or IQ) are large and positive, meaning that people with good working memories tend to have above-average cognitive ability as measured by standardized tests (the SAT and GRE, for example). Even performance with the humble memory span test with digit lists is correlated with other cognitive abilities, such as SAT verbal scores. The correlation is not large, but it can be made much larger by a simple change in the classic digit-span test that requires the subject to repeat the digit list *backward.* This is a much harder test than the usual digit span test, and the reason seems to be that the backward digit span test requires more working memory resources. You have to mentally manipulate, scan, and reorganize the digit list; you can't simply hold in it short-term memory and then "dump" it.

Working memory appears to be a special function of the frontal lobes. Is it possible that people who differ in their working memory abilities also differ in the structure or capacity or functioning of their frontal lobes? There are good reasons for thinking this is so. First, there is significant natural variation among people in brain structure, including variation in gray matter volume, which is related to the number of cortical neurons. A large proportion of this variation appears to be heritable and is therefore genetic in origin. In one study of 10 pairs of identical twins, it was found that the correlation of gray matter volume was an astounding +.95, meaning that the two members of each twin pair had essentially identical gray matter volumes. One of the four main dimensions of the Wechsler Adult Intelligence Scale is in fact called Working Memory, and scores on this dimension also have relatively high heritability.

It has not yet been shown that the size of the frontal lobes in different individuals is correlated with working memory performance. Also, at this time, it is not clear that the extent of brain activations is correlated in any simple way with working memory performance. One MRI study found positive correlations between reasoning task scores and frontal lobe activations during problem solving, but some PET studies have found *decreased* levels of activation in people with high IQs, as if those individuals found the tests easier than subjects with lower IQs. Stay tuned.

3

The Early Development of Memory

The development of memory by the human brain from conception to adulthood is an extraordinary story. The physical differences among the infants shown in Figure 3-1, who are arranged in order of increasing age from 2 to 18 months, are easy enough to see. Harder to see—but suggested by the differences in the sizes of their heads—are their brains, which have been growing, processing information, and creating memories, starting several months before birth.

The human brain has upward of a trillion nerve cells. A number like this is much too large for most of us to grasp (nevertheless, politicians seem to have no difficulty tossing such numbers around when they talk about federal budgets and deficits). A better idea of how large this number is comes from looking at how fast new neurons multiply over the nine months of the brain's development. From conception to birth the growing human brain adds new neurons at the astonishing rate of 250,000 every minute!

Actually, a newborn baby's brain has more neurons than at

FIGURE 3-1 Babies from 2 to 18 months of age.

later ages. Some neurons die as the brain is shaped and sculpted by experience. We used to think that the total number of neurons present in the brain at birth was it. Some would die, but no new neurons would form. We now know that this is not the case. The brain forms neurons throughout life. We will look more closely at these surprising facts and how they relate to learning and memory later.

Have you ever encountered a young baby you didn't know? Perhaps a chance encounter in an elevator with an infant lying in her carriage. She looks at you, at your face, with an intense blank stare. One has the impression that behind that stare is an incredibly powerful computer clicking away at high speed. Beginning well before birth, experience shapes the brain.

At what point in the development of the brain does learning first occur? The growing brain of the fetus shows a simple form of learning a month or more before birth. If a loud sound is presented close to the mother, her fetus will show changes in heart rate and also make kicking movements. If the sound is given repeatedly, these responses will gradually cease or habituate. If the nature of the sound is markedly changed, the fetus will again respond. This must mean that the fetus has learned something about the properties of the initial sound.

Habituation is the most basic form of learning. It is simply a decrease in response to a repeated stimulus and occurs in a wide range of animals, in addition to humans. Habituation of such responses as looking at an object is widely used to study learning in newborns and young babies. You might be interested to learn that the rate of habituation of responses in very young infants is correlated with later measures of IQ in the growing child—faster habituation is associated with higher IQ. We know a good deal about how habituation occurs in the nervous system too, as we will see later.

Learning in Utero

What kinds of stimuli does the developing fetus experience? In heroic studies in which mothers have swallowed microphones, it is clear that sounds from the outside penetrate the womb. Not just loud sounds, but even conversations close to the mother can be detected. The voice that comes through loud and clear is the mother's own voice. At birth an infant can hear more or less like a partially deaf adult, with thresholds considerably higher than those of normal adults (20 to 40 decibels higher), but by about six months of age an infant's hearing is virtually normal.

Although the eyes develop early, as the fetus grows there is little light in the womb. A newborn baby has visual acuity resembling that of a rather nearsighted adult, somewhere between 20/200 and 20/600, but the direction of gaze can be somewhat controlled by the newborn. The newborn appears to be largely color-blind, but by two to three months color vision is normal. The reasons for the poor vision of the newborn lie not in the eyes but in the brain. The development of the visual part of the brain, and the role of experience in this development, is an extraordinary chapter in neuroscience (see Box 3-1).

It used to be thought that the mind of the newborn is a blank slate and that the world is a vast and meaningless sea of sensations. Part of the reason for this is that a newborn has little ability to control her movements. A young baby cannot lift her head, roll over, or even point at objects with her arms. How do you ask such a helpless little creature what she sees or knows? As it happens,

BOX 3-1 The Visual System

The *lens* of the eye works much like the lens of a camera. It focuses a rather clear image of the visual world on the *retina*, the sheet of photoreceptors and neurons lining the back of the eye (see Figure). As in a camera, the image on the retina is reversed. Objects to the right of center project images to the left part of the retina and vice versa, and objects above the center project to the lower part and vice versa. The shape of the lens is altered by the muscles of the *iris* so that near or far objects can be brought into focus on the retina. The amount by which the lens must be altered also provides cues about the distance of nearby objects.

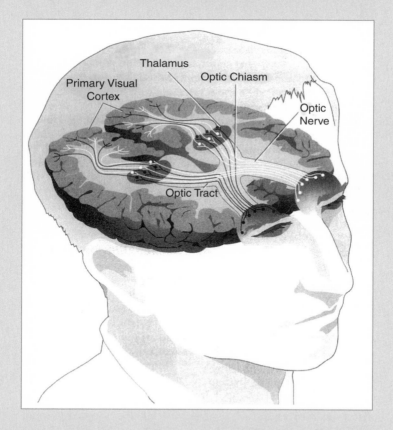

The visual system.

BOX 3-1 Continued

All visual systems begin with photoreceptors, which are cells that respond to light energy. Photoreceptor cells all contain one or more pigments that respond chemically to light, and much is known about the biochemistry of these pigments. Structurally, the visual chemical that responds to light is called *retinal*, a variation on the vitamin A molecule (which explains why one should eat foods containing vitamin A for good eyesight) and is associated with proteins called *opsins*.

There are two types of photoreceptors in the vertebrate eye—rods and cones. In general, the *rods*, which mediate sensations of light versus dark and shades of gray, are much more sensitive to light than the cones: They have much lower thresholds and can detect much smaller amounts of light. *Cones* mediate acute detail vision and color vision. In the human eye there are three types of cones: one type that is the most sensitive to red light, one that is the most sensitive to green, and one that is the most sensitive to blue.

Some animals, particularly nocturnal animals like rodents, have mostly or entirely rods, and others have mostly or entirely cones. Humans, apes, and monkeys have both rods and cones. Indeed, the retina of the macaque and other old world monkeys appears to be identical to the human one: Both macaques and humans have rods and three types of cones. It is now thought that the genes for the rod and cone pigments evolved from a common ancestral gene. Analysis of the amino acid sequences in the different opsins suggests that the first color pigment molecule was sensitive to blue. It then gave rise to another pigment that in turn diverged to form red and green pigments. Unlike old world monkeys, new world monkeys have only two cone pigments, a blue pigment and a longer-wavelength pigment thought to be ancestral to the red and green pigments of humans and other old world primates. The evolution of the red and green pigments must have occurred after the new world and old world continents separated, about 130 million years ago. The new world monkey retina, with only two color pigments, provides a perfect model for human red-green color blindness. Genetic analysis of the various forms of human color blindness suggests that some humans may someday, millions of years from now, have four cone pigments rather than three and see the world in very different colors than we do now.

The ultimate job of the eye is to transmit information about the visual world to the brain. It does this through the fibers of the *optic nerves*. The cell bodies of the optic nerves, the *ganglion cells*, are neurons situated at the back of the eye in the retina and send their axon fibers to the brain. When a small spot of light enters a vertebrate eye, the lens focuses it on a particular place on the retina. As the spot of light is moved about, its image moves about on the retina. Suppose you are recording the electrical activity from a single ganglion cell, perhaps by placing a small wire near it. In darkness it will have some characteristic rate of discharge—say, it fires one response every second. When the light strikes the retina, it activates some rod and cone receptors. If these receptors are in the vicinity of the ganglion cell that is being monitored and are connected to it through the neural circuits in the retina, the light will have some influence on the rate of firing of the ganglion cell. Depending on the neural circuits, the ganglion cell will be excited (fire more often than the spontaneous rate) or inhibited (fire less often).

In mammals the anatomical relations of projection from the visual field to the retina to the brain are a bit complicated. In lower vertebrates such as the frog there is complete crossing of input: all input to the right eye (the right visual field) goes to the left side of the brain, and vice versa. Such animals have no *binocular vision*. Primates, including humans, have virtually total binocular vision; the left half of each retina (right visual field) projects to the left visual cortex, and the right half of each retina (left visual field) projects to the right visual cortex. The optic nerves actually project to the thalamus, and the thalamus in turn projects to the visual cortex. This means, of course, that the right cortex receives all of its input from the left visual field, and the left visual cortex receives all of its input from the right visual field. Removal of the left visual cortex eliminates all visual input from the entire right half of the visual field of both eyes.

Although a single eye can use various cues to obtain some information about depth, or the distance of objects, much better cues are provided by binocular vision, in which input from the two eyes can be compared by cells in the visual cortex. Among mammals, predators such as cats and wolves have good binocular vision; hence, they can judge the distance to prey very accurately. Many animals that are prey, such as rabbits and deer, have much less binocular vision. Instead, their eyes are far to the sides of their heads so that they can see movements behind them. The excellent binocular vision of primates is probably due to the fact that they live in trees, or at least their ancestors did. If one mistakes the distance to a branch that one is leaping for, one's genes will not be propagated!

The projections from the visual thalamus to the visual cortex are such that a given neuron in layer IV of the visual cortex receives input *from one eye or the other but not from both*. In fact, the cells of layer IV of the visual cortex are organized in columns in such a way that one column will respond to the left eye, an adjacent column will respond to the right eye, and so on.

babies do one thing extremely well: they suck. They can also move their eyes and head from side to side to look at objects, and they can kick. We can use these simple behaviors and their habituation to ask the infant what she sees, hears, and can learn.

Newborn babies will learn to suck on an artificial nipple to turn on certain types of sounds. They particularly like the sound of their mother's voice, much more than the speech of another mother. They have learned enough about their mother's voice in utero to recognize it after birth. An infant can also display one response to its mother's voice and another response to a stranger's voice prior to birth. This was shown in a study of near-full-term fetuses in which each fetus was exposed to the recorded sound of its mother's voice or the voice of a stranger. Fetal heart rate increased in response to the mother's voice and decreased in response to the stranger's voice. Newborn babies also prefer their native language to foreign languages.

> Zak, my three-year-old, liked to rest his head on my enlarged abdomen and talk to his little sister-to-be. A few hours after Marie was born, I was breastfeeding her and she lay there with her eyes nearly closed. Zak came up and began talking to her. Immediately her eyes flew open and she stared at him. She clearly recognized his voice from her earlier experience in utero. She did not respond like this to the voices of strangers.

Similar results have been obtained for more complex speech, as shown by the remarkable study dubbed the "cat in the hat" experiment. Pregnant women read aloud twice a day during the last six weeks of pregnancy. Each mother was assigned one of three children's books, one of which was Dr. Seuss's *The Cat in the Hat*. The mothers-to-be who were assigned this story read it aloud faithfully twice a day for the entire six-week period. Recordings were made of the readings of all three stories. Three days after birth the infants were tested using the sucking response on a pacifier on all three stories. Infants that had, for example, been read *The Cat in the Hat* in utero sucked so as to produce this story over the other two, even if the story was read by another mother. (Never underestimate the power of Dr. Seuss!) Exactly how the babies learned to recognize this particular story from experience in utero is a mystery, but learn it they did.

Learning in Newborns

What do newborns see? Or, more specifically, what do they like to look at? Faces are very potent stimuli for humans and other primates. If shown her mother's face versus other women's faces, a baby just a few hours after birth will look more at her mother's face. What exactly tells the infant it is her mother? If the women wore scarves over their hair and part of their heads, the babies no longer showed any preference for their mothers. They apparently had learned a kind of global perception of the mother's head rather than attending to smaller details of the face.

Shown drawings of faces versus drawings of mixed-up faces, newborns prefer to look at faces. Newborns show an extraordinary ability to learn about individual faces. When shown pictures of different individual women's faces and then shown composite faces made up from individual faces that they had either seen or not seen before, babies show a clear preference for composites made up from faces they had seen before. This learning occurs in less than a minute in human infants as young as eight hours old!

Equally remarkable is the sophistication of the kind of learning that human infants are capable of, even very early in postnatal development. Cross-modality matching refers to a process by which information experienced exclusively in one sensory modality (such as tactile stimulation) can "transfer" for use in connection with stimuli or events in another modality (such as vision). This was shown in a study in which infants first experienced a pacifier of a given shape (such as example A in Figure 3-2) solely by sucking on it—the infants never saw it. When the infant sucked hard enough on the pacifier, a computer monitor would present a visual display to the infant. The display showed a picture of the pacifier being sucked on or a picture of a differently shaped pacifier (such as example B) in a random order. Infants as young as 12 hours old spent more time looking at the picture of

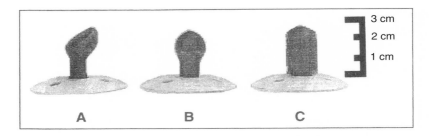

FIGURE 3-2 Infants can visually recognize the shape of the pacifier simply by sucking it.

the pacifier they had in their mouth during the testing. (As testing progressed, there was a shift to spend more time looking at the new pacifier; this is the novelty preference effect again.) It is not known how the infant brain is able to accomplish this kind of "going beyond what's given"—that is, of abstracting information. It has become clear in recent years that many psychologists—including the renowned child cognitive psychologist Jean Piaget—have severely underestimated the learning and cognitive abilities of human infants.

Faces

Adults recognize individual human faces far more accurately than individual monkey faces, and the opposite is true for monkeys (see Figure 3-3). These differential abilities seem to be due to early learning. Using the looking-preference procedure, studies have shown that six-month old infants are equally good at discriminating between individual human and individual monkey faces they have or have not seen before, but by nine months the infants are like adults: They readily distinguish between old (previously seen) and new human faces, but they no longer discriminate between old and new individual monkey faces.

There is a face "area" in the human brain, a localized region of cerebral cortex termed the *fusiform gyrus*. Patients with damage to this area can still identify faces as faces, but they can no

FIGURE 3-3 Human and monkey faces.

longer recognize individual faces (a condition called *proso-pagnosia*). They cannot recognize their own relatives or even spouses by face, only by voice. Indeed, they cannot even recognize themselves in the mirror—if they happen to bump into a mirror, they might apologize to the face in the mirror. If recording electrodes are placed in this brain area, nerve cells show face-selective responses.

There is a similar area in the monkey brain. This discovery, made by Charles Gross then at Harvard, is a dramatic case of serendipity. Gross and his associates were studying the responses of single neurons with a recording electrode in a region of the monkey cerebral cortex thought to be a higher visual area. The monkeys were anesthetized and then presented with various simple visual stimuli—spots of light, edges, and bars—the standard elementary visual stimuli used in such studies. The neurons in this area responded a little to those simple stimuli but not to sounds or touches, so it seemed to be a visual area. But the neurons were not very interested in their stimuli. After studying one neuron for a long time with few results, they decided to move on to another. As a gesture, the experimenter said farewell to the cell by raising his hand in front of the monkey's eye and waving goodbye. The cell responded wildly to this gesture. Needless to say, the experimenters stayed with the cell. This particular cell liked the upright shape of a monkey's hand best. Other neurons in this region responded best to monkey faces. This region of cerebral cortex in the monkey corresponds more or less to the face area in the human cerebral cortex.

Is the face area formed by experience and learning or is it built into the brain? The answer seems to be both. A newborn infant prefers to look at faces rather than nonfaces but must learn to identify its mother's face or other faces. This learning can be very rapid, so there must be a "face area" in the brain that is formed by the organization of the neuronal circuits in this region of the cerebral cortex. It is innate. But individual faces must be learned. Further, it seems that the memories for individual faces may be stored in this localized face area, given the devastating loss of ability to recognize individual faces when the area is damaged.

Studies of infant memories for faces have been performed using tests that do not require verbal responses or complex motor movements. One such procedure is based on the measurement of "looking" preferences. In the response-to-novelty task, an infant first looks at a picture of a face; then at varying intervals the infant is shown two pictures—the previously seen one and a new one—and the experimenter records the amount of time the infant spends looking at each (see Figure 3-4). The typical finding is that the infant spends more time looking at the new picture, which implies that the infant has retained information about the original picture.

As Learning Develops

An ingenious method of studying memory in young infants was introduced by Carolyn Rovee-Collier at Rutgers University. She

FIGURE 3-4 A toddler looking at two pictures.

hung a mobile over an infant's crib and attached a ribbon to the infant's foot. When the infant saw an object she had seen before, she kicked more, showing that she remembered having seen it. This kind of task is termed *operant training* or *conditioning*. The infant is in control of her behavior. This procedure was initially developed by B. F. Skinner many years ago to probe the learning abilities of animals.

Two- or three-month-old infants were trained in the task and showed excellent retention at 24 hours. When tested with a different item, they did not respond at all. They showed both memory and discrimination at 24 hours. In a series of studies the duration of memory was determined to be a function of the infant's age and to be virtually a straight-line function, reaching many weeks at 18 months. So memory improves dramatically with age.

Even longer-lasting memories have been found for babies using imitation. Babies love to imitate. If you stick out your tongue at a young infant, she will do the same to you (see Figure 3-5). Imitation is one of the most powerful learning tools available to

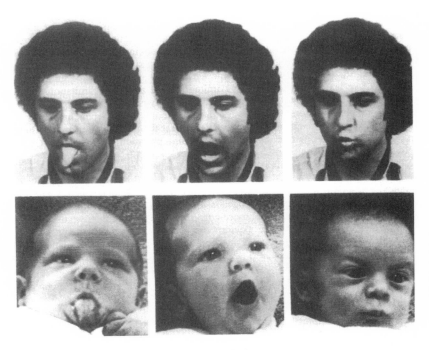

FIGURE 3-5 An infant imitating an adult.

infants and young children. Using imitation children learn to mouth their first words and to master the nonverbal body language of facial expressions and posture. Infants are also capable of deferred or delayed imitation. When shown a sequence of actions modeled by an adult, such as removing a mitten from a puppet's hand, infants repeat the behavior. At six months of age infants are capable of imitating the action 24 hours after seeing it. At nine months, babies can remember for a month, but by the age of 20 months most toddlers remember this task for a year! This kind of memory is called *recall memory*. The baby has to remember how to remove the mitten. Simply recognizing the puppet is not enough. In general, recall memory is more difficult than recognition memory for adults as well as children and is especially difficult when it involves information about the order of events or actions.

Infantile Amnesia

Babies clearly develop long-term memories for past experiences beginning at the age of about six months or even earlier. By the end of the first year of life they are beginning to learn and remember words. Obviously, adults retain skills and information acquired during infancy and early childhood, yet adults seem unable to consciously remember and describe anything of their own experiences before about age 3. This is called *infantile amnesia*.

Sigmund Freud first described infantile amnesia. Freud thought the period extended back to age 6, but more recent studies indicate that it may extend to age 3 or 4. Freud initially thought this might be due to repression of existing memories but apparently later abandoned this idea.

As we have seen, infants learn and remember very well indeed, beginning at birth and continually improving with age. Why adults cannot remember much if anything about their own experience before age 3 or 4 is a mystery. We are referring here to what is called *autobiographical memory*. Such memories are described in words (that is, declarative memory, deliberate conscious recollection). Such memories are usually time tagged; we remember more or less when and where important events occurred in our lives. This is particularly true for very emotional experiences. Some researchers argue for autobiographical memory going back to as young as age 2, but the claim is controversial and the relevant research is hard to do. For example, in some studies researchers report having found memories in young adults of independently verified events such as injuries and hospitalizations that occurred around age 2, but a major and obvious problem here is the difficulty of ruling out the argument that such "recollection" may be based on later family discussions and reminders of the events.

Infantile amnesia has important relevance in real-world situations. Someone who claims to remember having been sexually molested at the age of six months is likely to have a *false memory*. Recent work suggests that infantile amnesia has much to do with language. It appears that we cannot describe in words events that occurred in our lives before we knew the words to describe them. Sound confusing? Enter the "magic shrinking machine." Investigators at the University of Otaga in New Zealand exposed children to a unique event at an age when they could just barely talk. They visited the homes of toddlers two to three years of age, bringing with them the magic shrinking machine. The child would place a teddy bear in the machine, close the door, and pull on levers. The machine would make odd sounds. The child would then open the door and—behold—the teddy bear was now much smaller. The toddlers greatly enjoyed this. Their language skills were also evaluated at that time.

A year later the investigators returned with the machine. The children, now a year older and with much improved language skills, recognized the machine. However, when asked to remember what it did, they used only the few words they knew a year earlier when they first saw the machine. People cannot reach back in time to non–verbally coded memories and describe them with words. These observations may provide at least part of an explanation of infantile amnesia. A complementary explanation concerns the fact that certain regions of the cerebral cortex, where we think language is learned and stored, require several years after birth to mature fully.

You may find it surprising that with all of the available evidence, there is still a great deal of controversy about the nature of infant memory. The debate centers on the vexing concept of consciousness. Recall that one of the defining features of episodic memory is that it consists of conscious recollection of events from one's personal past. Some theorists claim that human infants lack this form of memory. We think the issue is irrelevant. As Carolyn Rovee-Collier points out, many of the basic processes of learning, retention, and forgetting can be found in infants in much the same way as in adults. What is different is language. Infants cannot store memories verbally because they haven't yet learned to speak. As with the magic shrinking machine, preverbal memories cannot be expressed verbally, and words are the only tool we have to study consciousness, as when people describe their experiences.

What Things Are and Do

Looking at objects in a room, we see chairs, tables, and so on. For a long time it was believed that young infants did not actually see objects as separate entities. Again, the problem is that young infants are incapable of interacting with objects. Elizabeth Spelke and her associates at the Massachusetts Institute of Technology completed an ingenious series of studies which indicated that by three months of age infants do perceive objects as distinct from backgrounds. They do not have to manipulate objects to know this, as earlier thought. Visual experience of objects and the way that experience shapes the brain are enough.

Infants also seem to grasp the basic notion of cause and effect. In one study a film showed a red brick moving across a screen until it encountered a green brick at which point the red brick stopped and the green brick moved off. If the two bricks collided and there was a pause before the green brick moved, the infant responded as though surprised. Using variations on this scenario, infants as young as six months of age showed some appreciation of cause and effect.

Some scientists have argued that Pavlovian conditioning may be the basis for the understanding of causality. Due to experiences with the world, the brain has come to be so wired over the course of evolution. Remember Pavlov's basic experiment: A bell rings and a few seconds later meat powder is put in a dog's mouth, which causes the dog to salivate. After a few such experiences, the bell alone elicits salivation. It doesn't work the other way around: Put meat powder in the dog's mouth and then sound the bell. That bell would be of no help in predicting food. Since Pavlovian conditioning occurs in a wide range of animals, from relatively simple invertebrates to humans, we argue that cause and effect is "understood" by virtually all animals possessing brains. It forms the basis of adaptive behavior, behavior based on the ability to predict consequences.

When Things Go Missing

Young infants seem to think that if an object is suddenly hidden and they can no longer see it, it has ceased to exist. Dangle an enticing object such as a toy insect in front of an infant and he will happily reach for it. Before he reaches it, cover it with a towel. The infant suddenly looks blank and shows no interest in the towel. Instead, cover the toy with transparent plastic and he will pull the plastic off to grab the toy. It appears that when the object is covered such that it cannot be seen, the infant does not remember it is there.

Between about 7 months and 12 months of age, there is dramatic growth in an infant's ability to remember that hidden objects still exist. The same is true for young monkeys. The task used to study the development of this memory ability is called *delayed response*, and it is very simple. The infant, human or monkey, is shown a board with two wells in it. A desired object, a small toy or raisin, is placed in one well, and the two wells are covered with identical blocks. A screen is then interposed so that the tiny subject cannot see the board for a brief time. The screen is then raised, and the infant reaches the blocks and pushes one aside (he is allowed to push only one). With a delay of a second or less while the screen is down, a seven-month-old human infant quickly learns to go to the baited well. If the delay period while the screen is down is increased beyond a second or so, the task quickly becomes very difficult for the seven-month-old. However, there is a dramatic increase with age in the infant's ability to remember where the object is hidden. By the age of 12 months the infant can easily remember for 10 seconds or more where the object is.

Monkeys show exactly the same progression in memory for hidden objects. But monkeys are born a good deal less helpless than humans and mature much more rapidly. At 50 days of age the infant monkey can remember for about one second the location of an object, and by 100 days can easily remember delays of 10 seconds or more. These are examples of the early development of a raw memory ability.

This simple test was developed more than 50 years ago to chart the growth of memory ability in monkeys but has only more recently been used with human infants. Instead, a seemingly similar task was developed years ago for human infants by the pioneering Swiss child psychologist Jean Piaget. He called his "task A and not B." Actually, the task is the same as delayed response but is done a little differently. What is dramatically different is the performance of young infants.

Suppose only the left well is baited with a toy repeatedly, so it is always correct. The screen is lowered for only a second or so each time. The seven-month-old (human) learns this very well. Then, in full view of the infant, the other well is baited instead. The screen is lowered and raised after one to two seconds. The infant immediately goes to the wrong well, the one that had earlier been baited repeatedly, even though she saw the other well being baited. As the infant grows older, she can perform correctly at longer and longer delay intervals. In more recent work, infant monkeys showed exactly the same results as infant humans on A, not B, but over a shorter period of development.

It is somewhat bemusing that these two tasks existed separately and independently for many years—delayed response for monkeys and A, not B, for humans—perhaps because in earlier years the two disciplines of child psychology and animal behavior did not interact.

These two tasks, particularly the A, not B, seem to involve two kinds of processes. On the one hand, in both tasks the infant has to remember where the missing object is over a brief period of time. The real surprise comes when young infants always choose the incorrect well, even though they see the other well being baited. If they had simply forgotten which well was baited, they should choose each well equally. But in fact they do remember that one well was repeatedly baited in the past and are unable to prevent or inhibit their response to this well. Learning to inhibit responses or behaviors that are incorrect or inappropriate is a key aspect of memory.

As it happens, a good deal is known about the brain system that underlies our ability to remember where objects are and to inhibit the wrong responses. The critical region of the brain is in the cerebral cortex in the frontal lobe—that is, the prefrontal cortex. It was discovered many years ago that small lesions in this region on both hemispheres in adult monkeys completely abolished the animal's ability to perform the delayed response task at any delay. The lesion changed an adult monkey into an infant monkey, at least in this task. When adult monkeys with these small brain lesions were tested in the A, not B, task, they behaved just like young humans and monkeys. At delays of as little as two seconds, they chose the well that had previously been baited repeatedly, even though they saw the other well being baited. Growth in the ability of infant humans and monkeys to perform these tasks correspond closely to the maturation of this critical region of the frontal cortex. The number of synapses (neuronal connections) grows rapidly from birth to one year of age.

What about adult humans who have damage to this region of the frontal lobe? The delayed response and A, not B, tasks are much too simple for adult humans, even if they are much impaired in their behavior. They can use words to hold the memory of where the object is during the delay period, using what is called working memory. But if a more sophisticated, analogous task is used, they show dramatic impairment in this kind of memory. The key task, famous in neuropsychology, is the Wisconsin card-sorting task. A deck of cards with various symbols is shuffled, and the person being tested is given the cards and told to sort them into categories. The investigator does not tell the subject the rules but only says "right" or "wrong" each time a card is sorted. Once the subject has mastered a category, the investigator, unbeknownst to the subject, changes the category. Normal people catch on quickly to the change in category, even though they are only told "right" or "wrong."

On the other hand, people with damage to the critical region of their frontal lobe find it almost impossible to correctly perform on the task. The problem comes when they have to change to another category. They can't. They might even say they need to change categories but can't do it. More precisely, they cannot inhibit responding to the earlier and now incorrect category. Shades of A, not B. They behave like human and monkey infants on this more complex A-B task. Incidentally, patients with the mental disorder schizophrenia also have great difficulty with the card-sorting task.

Counting

Rachel Gelman, now at Rutgers University, and her associates completed an interesting series of studies on the basic numerical abilities of children. It appears that the ability to count, at least a few items, is present as early as two years of age, well before language mastery. Indeed, infants as young as six months can distinguish one, two, or three objects. Toddlers do seem to understand the concept of counting, but their verbal behavior is not perfect. If there are two items, the child might count: "one," "two," but if three items, might count: "one," "two," "six." Yet the number of counts she states equals the number of objects.

In addition, human infants have a sense of "numerosity" similar to that of adults. This really means a number sense, a feeling about larger versus smaller numbers of items. In elegant studies, Elizabeth Spelke and her associates, then at the Massachusetts Institute of Technology, tested numerosity ability in six-month-old infants. They were able to discriminate groups of visual objects when one group was twice as large as the other but not when it was only one and a half times as large. The same thing happened when the infants were given auditory sequences. Charles Gallistel, now at Rutgers University, has summarized evidence indicating that animals also may possess a sense of numerosity.

Interestingly, there are neurons in the posterior association areas of the cerebral cortex in cats and monkeys that behave like counters. One of the present authors (RFT) conducted the study in cats (Figure 3-6). A given neuron would respond to each stimulus (sound or light) or every second stimulus, up to about seven stimuli. Similar results were obtained for the monkey. A frontal area becomes involved as well. Two closely analogous areas in the

Human

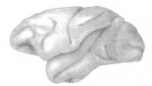

Monkey

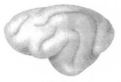

FIGURE 3-6 Regions in the cerebral cortex in cat and monkey where neurons respond to the number of objects and corresponding areas in the human brain.

Cat

human brain also are activated during numerical computations. A basic ability to count may be common among higher mammals and might be innate.

Theory of Mind

An experimenter shows a 5-year-old a candy box with pictures of candy on it and asks her what she thinks is in it. She of course replies, "candy," as would any adult (at least those not suspicious of psychological researchers). Then the child looks inside the box and discovers to her surprise that it actually contains not candy but crayons. The experimenter then asks her what another child who has not yet seen inside the box would think is inside it. The child says, "candy," amused at the deception. Things go a bit differently with a 3-year-old, however. His response to the initial question is the same—"candy"—but his response to the second question is surprising—an unamused "crayons." It may surprise you even more to know that in response to further questioning he also claims that he had initially thought there were crayons in the box and had even said that there were! This difference between 3- and 5-year-olds illustrates a critical difference in their conceptions of mind. That is, 3-year-olds do not yet realize that people have representations of the world that may be true or false and that people act on the basis of these mental representations rather than the way the world actually is. In contrast, 5-year-olds understand the nature of "false beliefs."

Although a sophisticated theory of mind does not develop until about age 5, even by age 1 babies have an amazing understanding of people. Suppose an adult is playing with a one-year-old and looks into two different boxes. When the adult looks into one box she has an expression of happiness, but when she looks in the other box she shows an expression of disgust. She then pushes the two boxes toward the one-year-old. What do you think happens? The baby happily reaches for the box that made the adult happy but won't touch the other box. The baby not only recognizes when a person is happy or disgusted but also understands that things can make someone feel happy or disgusted.

The development of a theory of mind in children is a striking example of social learning. Over the period from about three to five years of age, children learn by experience with others that people have ideas, thoughts, and emotions and that they act on the basis of these internal representations. They learn that the mind can represent objects and events accurately or inaccurately. As each child's theory of mind (actually theories about the minds of others) develops and becomes more sophisticated, the child is better able to predict the behavior of others, particularly as this behavior relates to the child.

The mind of a five- or six-year-old child is extraordinary. Not only does she have ideas about the minds of others, she is also aware that she has these ideas about ideas; she has self-awareness—so much so that by six to eight years of age children find it very hard not to think. It is easy to see how and why the child develops her theory of mind. The better her theories are about other individuals' minds and what their intentions are, the better she can respond to and even influence or control their behavior. The better her theory of mind, the better it is rewarded.

Some researchers believe that the beginnings of a theory of mind develop by way of imitation. As we saw earlier, children will imitate expressions. Partly as a result of imitation children learn that drooping shoulders in another person mean sadness. Facial expressions can mean happiness, sadness, anger, and so on. A primary aspect of the disorder autism is thought to be due to the lack of development of a theory of mind in autistic children.

Autism

Autism is one of the most common serious disorders of childhood. Earlier thought to be rare, it is now known to affect 1 in every 150 children age 10 and younger. If adults with autism are included, more than a million people in the United States have the disorder. It is much more common in boys than girls and the symptoms range from very mild to devastating. Individuals with severe cases can be profoundly retarded and unable to dress or even go to the bathroom without help. They often engage in meaningless repetitive behaviors, including self-injury, and may have temper tantrums and violent outbursts.

Children with the more severe forms of autism show a regular progression of symptoms that counter the normal development of learning in infants and children. At one year of age they still do not babble or point and by age 2 still cannot speak two-word phrases. A striking difference is that autistic infants and children do not imitate adults. If an adult pounds a pair of blocks on the floor, a normal 18-month-child will do the same, but young children with autism will not. Later, autistic children do not engage in pretend play, do not make friends, and do not make eye contact. They do make repetitive body movements and may have intense tantrums.

At the other extreme are people with Asperger's syndrome, discovered in 1944 by Hans Asperger, an Austrian pediatrician. It wasn't until 1994 that the American Psychiatric Association officially recognized Asperger's syndrome as a form of autism. Children with Asperger's syndrome are generally bright, sometimes gifted, and particularly adept at solitary repetitive activities like transformer toys or computer programming (see Box 3-2).

Asperger's syndrome is much more subtle and usually not diagnosed until about age 6 or older. Such children have difficulty making friends, cannot communicate with facial and body expressions, and have an obsessive focus on very narrow interests. All autistic children have one characteristic in common. They seem unable to recognize that other people have minds that differ from their own. They think that what is in their mind is in everyone else's mind and that how they feel is how everyone else feels. In short, they have never learned to develop a theory of mind.

Autism runs in families. If one identical twin has the disorder, the chances are 60 percent the other will too and a better than 75 percent chance that the twin without autism will exhibit one or more traits. It has been estimated that between 5 and 20 genes are involved in autism. One discovery of particular interest is the involvement of a gene on chromosome 7. A putative "language" gene maps to this same area. We will say more about this language gene in our treatment of language.

Several brain abnormalities have been associated with autism, but it is too early to draw firm conclusions. Some areas of the brain are smaller, particularly those involved in emotional behavior, and some areas are larger. There appear to be abnormalities associated with the cerebellum, an older brain structure earlier thought to be involved only with movement and motor control but now known to be involved in learning, memory, and cognitive processes as well. One particularly interesting finding from brain imaging work concerns the face area. Unlike normal people, this area does not become active at all in the brains of autistic individuals when they look at stranger's faces. However, when looking at the faces of loved ones, an autistic's face area and

BOX 3-2 The "Geek" Syndrome

At Michelle Winner's social-skills clinic in San Jose, California, business is booming. Every week dozens of youngsters with Asperger's syndrome file in and out of therapy sessions while their anxious mothers run errands or chat quietly in the waiting room. In one session, a rosy-cheeked 12-year-old struggles to describe the emotional reactions of a cartoon character in a video clip; in another, four little boys (like most forms of autism, Asperger's overwhelmingly affects boys) grapple with the elusive concept of teamwork while playing a game of 20 Questions. Unless prompted to do so, they seldom look at one another, directing their eyes to the wall or ceiling or simply staring off into space.

Yet outside the sessions the same children become chatty and animated, displaying an astonishing grasp of the most arcane subjects. Transformer toys, video games, airplane schedules, star charts, dinosaurs. It sounds charming, and indeed would be, except that their interest is all consuming. After about five minutes, children with Asperger's, a.k.a. the "little professor" or "geek" syndrome tend to sound like CDs on autoplay. "Did you ask her if she's interested in astrophysics?" a mother gently chides her son who has launched into an excruciatingly detailed description of what goes on when a star explodes into a supernova. Although Hans Asperger described the condition in 1944, it wasn't until 1994 that the American Psychiatric Association officially recognized Asperger's syndrome as a form of autism with its own diagnostic criteria. It is this recognition, expanding the definition of autism to include everything from the severely retarded to the mildest cases, that is partly responsible for the recent explosion in autism diagnoses.

There are differences between Asperger's and high-functioning autism. Among other things, Asperger's appears to be even more strongly genetic than classic autism, says Dr. Fred Volkmar, a child psychiatrist at Yale. About a third of the fathers or brothers of children with Asperger's show signs of the disorder. There appear to be maternal roots as well. The wife of one Silicon Valley software engineer believes that her Asperger's son represents the fourth generation in just such a lineage.

It was the Silicon Valley connection that led *Wired* magazine to run its geek-syndrome feature last December. The story was basically a bit of armchair theorizing about a social phenomenon known as assortive mating. In university towns and R.- and D. corridors, it is argued, smart but not particularly well-socialized men today are meeting and marrying women very like themselves, leading to an overload of genes that predispose their children to autism, Asperger's, and other related disorders.

Is there anything to this idea? Perhaps. There is no question that many successful people—not just scientists and engineers but writers and lawyers as well—possess a suite of traits that seem to be, for lack of a better word, Aspergery. The ability to focus intensely and screen out other distractions, for example, is a geeky trait that can be extremely useful to computer programmers. On the other hand, concentration that is too intense—focusing on cracks in the pavement while a taxi is bearing down on you—is clearly, in Darwinian terms, maladaptive.

But it may be a mistake to dwell exclusively on the genetics of Asperger's; there must be other factors involved. Experts suspect that such variables as prenatal positioning in the womb, trauma experienced at birth or random variation in the process of brain development may also play a role.

Even if you could identify the genes involved in Asperger's, it's not clear what you would do about them. It's not as if they are lethal genetic defects, like the ones that cause Huntington's disease or cystic fibrosis. "Let's say that a decade from now we know all the genes for autism," suggests Bryna Siegel, a psychologist at the University of California, San Francisco. "And let's say your unborn child has four of these genes. We may be able to tell you that 80% of the people with those four genes will be fully autistic but that the other 20% will perform in the gifted mathematical range."

Filtering the geeky genes out of high-tech breeding grounds like Silicon Valley, in other words, might remove the very DNA that made these places what they are today.

Time Magazine, May 6, 2002, pp. 50-51.

related brain areas become much more active than is true for normal people. Why autistic children do not develop a theory of mind and what brain abnormalities are responsible remain mysteries. The lack of imitative behavior in autistic children may prove to be a most important clue.

Some very basic psychological principles of learning have been applied with great success in the treatment of autism. For over 30 years, Ivor Lovaas has run a clinic at the University of California at Los Angeles that uses basic operant conditioning techniques to teach communication to autistic children. Many of these children lack even the rudiments of social speech, and the training process proceeds in small steps with the goal of developing normal social speech. For example, suppose the therapist's goal is to get an autistic child to respond appropriately to the question "What is your name?" The child does not respond, does not look at the therapist, and generally acts as if the therapist doesn't exist. The training proceeds by rewarding the child with snacks for paying attention, first, and then for making eye contact (which might have to first be "prompted" by the therapist). Then the therapist focuses on manually shaping the child's lips to prompt pronounciation of the first letter of his or her name and from there on rewards any of the child's behavior that represents a step (sometimes very small ones) toward the goal of getting the child to pronounce his or her first name when asked. This training can last for weeks before the goal behavior is achieved. The program then continues to more complex speech behavior, always building on what has been learned and always based on the principle of rewarding desired behavior, never unwanted behavior. It is quite amazing to see the results of the training: a formerly uncommunicative child who now uses normal, spontaneous social speech. Lovaas's success in treating autistic children lends further support to a statement made earlier: The limits of human abilities and their modifiability by learning are not yet known.

Critical Periods in Development

Perhaps the most dramatic example of a critical period in development is imprinting in birds. Birds like chickens, ducks, and geese that can walk and feed immediately after hatching, imprint on their mothers within the first day. The chick will stay close to its mother and follow her everywhere. The reader may have seen pictures of a mother duck leading her ducklings across a road, marching in single file.

If the mother is not present, the newborn chick will imprint on whatever object is present if it moves and makes noise. Imprinting works best for objects that look and sound like mother. In the laboratory, chicks have been imprinted on all kinds of objects, even little robots that move and make sounds. The classic example concerns the pioneering ethologist Konrad Lorenz, who imprinted a gaggle of goslings who were under the unfortunate impression he was their mother to follow him everywhere.

The critical period for imprinting is very brief. Once the chick has imprinted on the initial object, hopefully the mother, it will no longer imprint on other objects. Perhaps the closest example to imprinting immediately after birth in mammals occurs with olfactory learning. The human infant learns to identify and prefer the odor of his mother within the first day, especially if the mother is breast-feeding.

The now-classic example of a critical period in development for humans and other mammals is the visual system. Donald Hebb, a pioneer in the study of memory and the brain, has described clinical cases of people who were born and grew up with severe cataracts. They were essentially blind. Several had their cataracts removed as adults, after which their visual function, although improved, was still greatly impaired. They could see and quickly learned to identify colors, which are coded in the retina of the eye, but could not identify the shapes of objects. If presented with a wooden triangle, they could not identify it until they could touch and feel it. Object vision is coded in the brain, not the eye.

Being blind in one eye is almost as bad. The classic work on the critical period in vision development was done by two scientists then at Harvard, David Hubel and Torsten Wiesel, who worked initially with cats. If they kept one eye of a kitten closed from the time its eyes opened after birth until about two months of age, the kitten was permanently blind in that eye. If the same procedure was done on an adult cat, there was no vision impairment in the closed eye. This same massive impairment in vision occurs in monkeys and humans, the only difference is the duration of the critical period: For humans it extends to about five years of age. Children born with severe impairments in one eye (for example, a cataract or squint), if not treated, will become permanently blind in that eye. Indeed, even keeping one eye closed for a period of several weeks in a one-year-old child—for example, for a medical procedure—can cause damage. Better to keep both eyes closed. In all these cases the eyes themselves are fine; it is the visual area of the cerebral cortex that is damaged.

Hubel and Wiesel were able to determine the processes in neurons in the visual cortex that led to this devastating loss of vision after one eye had been closed. The basics of the normal human visual system are summarized in Box 3-1. As noted there, both eyes project to each side of the visual cortex. In adults the neurons in the visual cortex are the first to be activated when an object is seen (activity from the eye is relayed to the visual thalamus and on to the cortex). They receive this input from either the left eye or the right eye but not from both (see Figure). They in turn converge on other neurons in the cortex that are activated by input from both eyes, permitting binocular vision.

At birth the situation is quite different. These first-activated cortical neurons receive virtually identical input from both eyes. Over the critical period, if vision is normal in both eyes, a kind of competition occurs so that each neuron ultimately loses input from one eye or the other to yield the adult pattern. But if one eye is closed during the critical period, activation from the seeing eye gradually takes over all the connections in each of these neurons and the input from the shut eye dies away. We think a reason for this is that activation—the occurrence of neuron action potentials—is necessary to maintain synaptic connections in the critical period. Consequently, all input from the shut eye to the visual cortex vanishes.

This provides a particularly clear example of how genes and experience interact in human brain development. The basic connections, the neural circuits, are originally programmed by the genes and their interactions with the developing brain tissue. But the fine details of connections among neurons are guided by experience and learning. If one eye of a kitten is covered by an opaque goggle that transmits light but not detail, vision with that eye is still much impaired. Experience fine-tunes the organization of connections among neurons in the brain. These connections are termed *synapses*.

Synapses

If any one process is key to the organization of the brain and to the formation of memory it is the formation of synapses, the functional connections from one neuron to another. Each nerve cell has one fiber extending out to connect with another neuron, called the *axon* (Greek for "axis") and many other fibers extending out from the body of the cell that receive input from other neurons. These fibers are called dendrites (Greek for "tree," the dendrites on a neuron resemble the branches of a tree). Each dendrite is covered by small bumps or spines. Each spine is a synapse receiving an axon connection from another neuron (see Figure 3-7). Physically, synapses consist of a small synaptic terminal (presynaptic—before the synapse) in close opposition to a spine on the postsynaptic (after the synapse) neuron dendrite. There is a very small space between the two. When this presynaptic terminal is activated it releases a tiny amount of a chemical neurotransmitter that diffuses across to the postsynaptic membrane to activate the neuron. The number of synapses on a neuron is astonishing. A major type of neuron in the cerebral cortex may receive up to 10,000 synaptic connections from other neurons. The champions are a type of neuron in an older brain structure, the Purkinje neu-

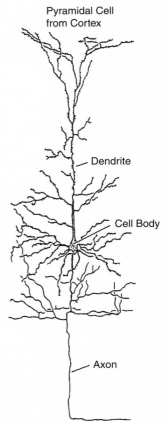

Pyramidal Cell
from Cortex

— Dendrite

— Cell Body

— Axon

*FIGURE 3-7 A typical neuron in the brain.
The dendrites are covered with little
bumps or spines. Each spine is a synapse, a
connection from another neuron.*

rons in the cerebellum, named for a famous anatomist. Each
Purkinje neuron (there are millions) receives upward of 200,000
synaptic connections from other neurons!

Synapses grow, form, and die from well before birth through
adulthood to death. The process of synaptic formation and growth
is called *synaptogenesis*. Thanks to the work of Peter
Huttchenlocker at the University of Chicago and many other scientists who have studied the brains of cadavers, we now have

solid data on the rates of synaptogenesis in various regions of the cerebral cortex in humans of all ages.

At birth the human brain is immature. New neurons are still forming and growing, synapses are multiplying, and myelin formation is far from complete (myelin is the insulating covering on nerve fibers that increases the speed of the electrical conduction of the neurons). The newborn brain is about one-fourth the size it will eventually reach, and most of its growth occurs in the first year of life. Most synapses connect to other neurons at terminals on dendrites. So the growth and elaboration of dendrites are closely associated with increased numbers of synapses.

At birth most of the connections, including dendritic growth and branching and synapse formation, are missing. Much of the growth occurs during the first year or so of life. At the end of this period the total number of synapses in the infant brain is twice that of an adult's. Following this early period of exuberant growth, there is a slow and prolonged period of elimination and pruning of excess synaptic contacts, which is not completed until late adolescence in many cortical areas. But new synapses, and indeed new neurons, form throughout life in some regions of the brain.

The growth of and decline in the numbers of synapses in various regions of the cerebral cortex are closely associated with critical periods in development. This is strikingly evident in the visual area of the human cortex. The total number of synapses is very low at birth, skyrockets to a peak at about 6 to 12 months of age, and then gradually declines until about age 10, after which it is relatively stable until old age. The period of maximum synaptogenesis closely corresponds with the period of maximum plasticity and maximum sensitivity to impairment in the visual system.

Hearing in infants is poor at birth but reaches virtual adult competence by about six months. This is closely paralleled by the growth of synapses in the human primary auditory cortex (Heschl's gyrus). By six months of age there has been a massive increase in the number of synapses, which approach adult levels by about three years of age and then gradually decline until about age 10.

Some musicians have perfect pitch; they can immediately identify the pitch of any note. The results of one study showed that all musicians who had perfect pitch began musical training before age 6. Those who began training after the age of 6 did not have perfect pitch, corresponding to the decline in synaptogenesis in the auditory cortex from age 3 to age 10. It is not known whether there are individuals with perfect pitch who did not begin musical training until after age 6 or so. But, of course, we must be careful about cause and effect in findings like this. Perhaps people with perfect pitch are so musically gifted that they naturally seek out musical training early.

The development of hearing is a clear example of a critical period. Many cases of early deafness can be helped by a device implanted in the inner ear, the cochlea. This device codes sounds into electrical impulses delivered to the cochlea to activate auditory nerve fibers. The development of cochlear implants has made it possible for some individuals who had been deaf from birth to learn to hear and understand speech. Interestingly, the implants are most effective if implanted before the age of 3. They decrease in effectiveness when implanted at older ages. Whether this is due to decreased plasticity in the auditory cortex or in the language areas of the cortex is not known. The growth of synapses in the language areas of the cortex also corresponds closely to the development of language functions.

As discussed earlier, infants show a dramatic increase in their ability to solve delayed response and A, not B, tasks from 7 to about 12 months of age and beyond. The prefrontal cortex, the region critical for these tasks, shows a rapid increase in the number of synapses from birth to one year of age and then remains high until at least age 5, declining in adolescence.

Enhancing Your Child's Mind

The Mozart Effect

Parents have always been interested in ways to improve their child's learning abilities and performance in school. A recent popular fad is the so-called Mozart effect. Stores now sell Mozart CDs for young children to "enhance" their intelligence. This fad derived from studies on college students in which it was reported that listening to a Mozart sonata enhanced their subsequent performance on spatial-temporal IQ-like tasks. What was also reported but widely overlooked in the popular press is that the Mozart effect lasted only about 10 minutes. There is, in fact, no evidence to support such an effect (see Box 3-3).

There is some evidence that musical training may enhance performance on some tests of mental abilities, but the effects are not great. To some extent, this is another chicken-and-egg problem. Does musical training enhance performance on the tests or do children who take musical training exhibit enhanced performance on the tests because of their particular interests and abilities? But early musical training perhaps increases the possibility the child will have perfect pitch, as we noted, presumably enhancing later musical capabilities. Actually, one recent and carefully done study found a greater increase in the IQ scores of children after taking music lessons than after taking drama or no lessons.

Enriched Environment

Raising animals in a rich environment can result in increased brain tissue and improved performance on memory tests. Much of this work has been done with rats. The "rich" rat environment involved raising rats in social groups in large cages with exercise wheels, toys, and climbing terrain. Control "poor" rats were raised individually in standard laboratory cages without the stimulating objects the rich rats had. Both the rich and the poor rats were kept clean and given sufficient food and water. Results of these studies were striking: Rich rats had a substantially thicker cerebral cortex, the highest region of the brain and the substrate of cognition, with many more synaptic connections, than the poor rats. They also learned to run mazes better.

The popular press made much of the enriched-environment

BOX 3-3 The Mozart Effect

Several years ago, great excitement arose over a report published in *Nature* which claimed that listening to the music of Mozart enhanced intellectual performance, increasing IQ by the equivalent of eight to nine points as measured by portions of the Stanford-Binet intelligence scale. Dubbed the "Mozart effect," this claim was widely disseminated by the popular media. Parents were encouraged to play classical music to their infants and children and even to listen to such music during pregnancy. Companies responded by selling Mozart effect kits, including tapes and players. (An aspect of the *Nature* account overlooked by the media is that the effect was reported to last only about 10 to 15 minutes.) The authors of the *Nature* report subsequently offered a "neurophysiological" rationale for their claim. This rationale essentially held that exposure to complex musical compositions excites cortical neuron firing patterns similar to those used in spatial-temporal reasoning, so that performance on spatial-temporal tasks is positively affected.

Several groups attempted to replicate the Mozart effect, with consistently negative results. One careful study precisely replicated the conditions described in the original study. Yet the results were entirely negative, even though the subjects were "significantly happier" listening to Mozart than they were listening to a control piece of postmodern music by Philip Glass. One recent report indicates a slight improvement in performance after listening to music by Mozart and Schubert as compared with silence. But listening to a pleasant story had the same effect, a finding that negates the brain model. Mood appeared to be the critical variable in this study.

Why did the Mozart effect receive so much attention, particularly if it lasts only minutes? Perhaps because the initial positive result was published in *Nature*, a scientific journal routinely viewed by the media as being very prestigious. Another factor, no doubt, is that exposing one's child to music appeared to be an easy way to make her or him smarter—much easier than reading to the child regularly. Moreover, the so-called neurophysiological rationale provided for the effect probably enhanced its scientific credibility in the eyes of the media. Actually, this rationale is not neurophysiological at all: There is no evidence to support the argument that music excites cortical firing patterns similar to those used in spatial-temporal tasks.

effect, and commercial devices were developed to "enrich" the environment of babies' cribs with bells, whistles, and moving objects. It turns out that the wrong conclusion was drawn from the animal literature. The data were clear; the rich rats had more developed brains than the poor rats. But when wild rats were examined, their brains were like those of the rich laboratory rats. Indeed, in one study a large area was fenced off outside the psychology building at the University of California at Berkeley, and rats were raised in this semiwild environment. They also developed rich rat brains. It seems that it was the poor rats whose brains developed abnormally, from being raised in isolation without the stimulation of normal rat life.

There are parallels in tragic cases where children have been raised in isolation. A California girl spent most of her first 14 years of life tied to a chair in a small room. She was never able to acquire normal language. There are also reports of impaired infant development in orphanages in Eastern Europe where the infants were left alone day and night except for feedings and changings.

What are the best things that concerned parents can do to enhance the cognitive development of their infants? The experts tell us to do what comes naturally. Talk to them, play with them, make funny faces, pay attention to them—spend time interacting with them. Mozart and noisy mobiles don't really help. It is people they want to interact with.

4

Ordinary Forgetting

Sherlock Holmes had very definite ideas about forgetting and its causes. In Arthur Conan Doyle's story *A Study in Scarlet*, Holmes gives Watson the following stern lecture:

> I consider a man's brain is like a little empty attic, and you have to stock it with such furniture as you choose. A fool takes in all the lumber of every sort that he comes across, so that the knowledge which might be useful to him gets crowded out, or at best jumbled up with a lot of other things so that he has difficulty in laying his hands upon it. . . . It is a mistake to think that that little room has elastic walls and can distend to any extent. Depend on it, *there comes a time when for every addition of knowledge you forget something you knew before.*

As we'll see, Holmes was invoking a fundamental principle of the Interference Theory of Forgetting, some 50 years before the theory was actually introduced. He was also suggesting an interpretation of what forgetting might consist of: difficulty in finding or locating information, rather than the actual loss of that information. This possibility was also raised by Hermann Ebbinghaus in 1885

in the opening paragraph of *On Memory*, the first systematic treatment of memory and forgetting:

> Mental states of every kind—sensations, feelings, images—
> which were at one time present in consciousness and then have
> disappeared from it—have not with their disappearance abso-
> lutely ceased to exist. Although the inwardly turned mind may
> no longer be able to find them, nevertheless they have not been
> destroyed and annulled, *but in a certain manner they continue
> to exist, stored up, so to speak, in the memory.*

This is a provocative statement, appearing to suggest that most or
all of what we consciously experience is stored and maintained in
memory, even though we may not have conscious access to those
memory records. Oddly, Ebbinghaus did not pursue this idea in
On Memory, nor is there any evidence that Sherlock Holmes actually tested his hypotheses about memory. But these two quotes
identify some of the basic problems that memory researchers
grappled with over the next 100 years.

The Forgetting Curve

The time course of memory was first described in detail by
Ebbinghaus over 100 years ago. He started with these general
observations:

> Left to itself every mental content gradually loses its capacity
> for being revived, or at least suffers loss in this regard under the
> influence of time. Facts crammed at examination time soon van-
> ish, if they were not sufficiently grounded by other study and
> later subjected to a sufficient review. But even a thing so early
> and deeply founded as one's mother tongue is noticeably im-
> paired if not used for several years.

Ebbinghaus then went on to study the details of this process. How
quickly are memories lost? Is there a steady loss until all of what
has been learned has been lost? What does the curve of forgetting
over time look like?

The general answer to this last question appears in Figure 4-1.
These data come from an experiment in which subjects had to
learn and remember a long list of words. Half of the subjects heard

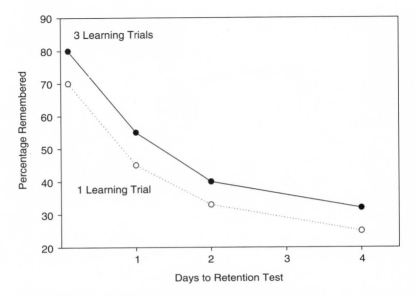

FIGURE 4-1 Forgetting of memorized materials over time.

the list just once and the other half heard the list three times. The subjects were then tested for retention of what they'd learned, either right away or at intervals of one to four days days. (These are usually referred to as forgetting curves, even though they actually show how much was retained.) There is a large drop in memory performance initially, followed by further but smaller losses as the retention interval gets longer. The rate at which retention loss occurs is greatest early on but diminishes as time goes by. These basic facts about forgetting apply across shorter and longer time scales, the nature of the to-be-remembered experiences, and the kind of person doing the remembering.

The practical importance of these simple facts about the forgetting curve is apparent in the results of an experiment in which a group of factory and office workers were trained in the procedures for cardiopulmonary resuscitation until they had mastered the required skills. Three years later—a period during which few of the workers had any occasion to use the skills—retention tests showed that the skills and knowledge had deteriorated to about

15 percent of what they originally were, and the deterioration followed the classic curve of forgetting from three to 36 months.

John Anderson and colleagues at Carnegie-Mellon University have developed an interesting idea about why forgetting is sometimes useful or adaptive. The idea is basically that the longer information is stored in memory without being accessed or used, the less likely it is that *losing* that information will have any bad consequences. If you have not called on your once-upon-a-time knowledge of Latin declensions or your storehouse of information about baseball in the past five years, it is even less likely that you will in the *next* five years. Maintaining a large number of memory traces over long time periods has biological costs, which might be greater than the costs of allowing some traces to deteriorate.

Forgetting and Degree of Learning

Of all the things that influence whether or not you can successfully remember something when you need to, there's one that stands out: how well that "something" was stored in memory to start with. This is referred to as the influence of degree of original learning, and it has been demonstrated experimentally many times. As Figure 4-1 shows, subjects who had three learning trials recalled more at each retention interval than subjects who had one learning trial. You are probably not very surprised by this outcome. However, consider another result of this experiment that also appears in Figure 4-1: The rate of information loss over time appears to be the *same* for the two degrees of original learning (that is, the two curves seem to have the same slope).

Interestingly, this principle also seems to apply to "slow learners" and "fast learners." Test a group of 60 people in the word-learning experiment, giving everyone the same amount of time to commit the material to memory. Now divide the group into a subgroup of the 30 people with the highest scores on an immediate memory test and another subgroup of the 30 people with the lowest scores. Then retest them at different retention intervals from one to four weeks. Again, to no one's surprise, the fast learners will remember more than the slow learners—but both groups will have forgotten about the same amount. This surprising outcome has been found in comparisons of children and adults, younger adults and the elderly, schizophrenics and normal people, and people with and people without brain damage of various kinds. It is true that children, schizophrenics, and the brain-damaged *learn* much more slowly than do their respective comparison groups, but they do not appear to *forget* what they've learned any more rapidly.

Here's another interesting variation on this theme. Imagine another word learning experiment in which all of the subjects learned a list of 30 words perfectly—100 percent correct at the end of the learning phase. Of course, some people would require only a few learning trials to get to the point where they could remember all 30 words, while others would need many more trials. What would you find when you tested retention one month later? You would find that there isn't much, if any, difference in the amount recalled by the fast learners versus the slow learners.

In general, if you equate the initial learning for different people, you typically find that their later retention is about equal. As far as differences among people in memory are concerned, it seems to say that the differences reside in the encoding or learning phase of the memory process. People with "good memories" store information faster or more efficiently than people with "bad memories," but fast and slow learners do not seem to differ in how well their memory systems resist the forces of forgetting.

Massed and Distributed Practice

It has been known for many years that distributed practice in learning leads to better retention of the learned material than does massed practice. In a classic demonstration of this principle, Geoffrey Keppel at the University of California at Berkeley had two groups of subjects study a set of word pairs (such as tree–kitchen, bell–dream, and mark–shadow) so that they could recall

TABLE 4-1 The Effects of Massed Practice and Distributed Practice

	Monday	Tuesday	Wednesday	Thursday	Friday or one week later
Massed practice	—	—	—	Eight trials	Retention test
Distributed practice	Two trials	Two trials	Two trials	Two trials	Retention test

the second member of each pair when given the first word as a cue (a time-honored method known as paired-associate learning). Both groups were given eight learning trials, but how these trials were arranged over time was different (see Table 4-1). Subjects in the massed practice group experienced all eight trials on the same day. Subjects in the distributed practice group experienced two learning trials per day, spread out over four days. All subjects were then given a test of retention one day or eight days after the last day of learning. The results were very interesting, particularly for those of us who use a cramming approach to studying. At the one day retention interval, there was only a slight advantage for the distributed practice group. (This, of course, reinforces our cramming habit.) But at an eight-day retention interval, there was a very large difference (80 percent versus 30 percent), in favor of the distributed practice group, a difference of considerable practical significance.

What caused the difference? One explanation is that in the particular kind of learning task that Keppel used, the distributed practice subjects (but not the massed practice subjects) found out over the course of the experiment that some of the word pairs they had learned on Monday were forgotten by Tuesday and that this material needed additional study and strengthening.

The difference in the effectiveness of massed and distributed learning procedures is by no means limited to an artificial laboratory task involving forming associations between arbitrary word pairs. It is important for the more general issue of long-term maintenance of knowledge and skills. In a nine-year experiment Harry Bahrick had four heroic subjects learn sets of 50 English and foreign language pairs with 13 or 26 practice sessions occurring at two- or four- or eight-week intervals. Widely spaced sessions (eight-week intervals) led to much better retention over periods of up to five years than more closely spaced practice sessions (two-week intervals). In fact, 13 training sessions spaced at 56-day intervals were as good as 26 training session at 14-day intervals! Bahrick and other researchers argue that findings such as these need to be taken seriously by administrators of training programs, including the rather expensive one called education. It now seems possible to design instruction and training in ways that will maximize the retention and maintenance of skills and knowledge.

Forgetting: The Available and the Accessible

What causes the decline of memory performance shown in Figure 4-1? Does it reflect an actual loss of information from memory or a decrease in how readily a person can access information that is still preserved in memory? Some answers to these questions as well as a number of important facts about remembering and forgetting can be illustrated by the following simple example. Suppose you've been a subject in a psychology experiment in which the experimenter has shown you a list of 40 common English words, one every five seconds during which you rated the pleasantness of each word's meaning. A few minutes after you completed this task the experimenter told you that he wanted to test your memory of the words in the list, using a variety of testing procedures. The standard names for some of these procedures and the procedures themselves appear in Table 4-2.

Start with Free Recall 1. What this kind of memory test will typically show is that your recall is quite imperfect. For example, by the end of a 10-minute recall period you may have come up with only 16 words. Your rate of recalling new words slows from minute to minute, and at the end of the recall period the curve is far below the maximum of 40 words.

TABLE 4-2 Probing Episodic Memory

Test Method	Instructions
Free Recall 1	"Recall as many words as you can in any order they come to mind. You will have 10 minutes for this test."
Free Recall 2	"Try to recall the words again, including the ones you've already remembered as well as any new ones that come to mind."
Cued Recall 1	"One word that you haven't recalled was the name of an animal."
Cued Recall 2	"One word that you haven't recalled rhymed with "bother."
Recognition	"Here's a list of 20 words. Half of them were in the list you saw; half of them weren't. Which ones are the list words?
Implicit test	"Pronounce each of these words as fast as you can."

But has this recall effort actually exhausted your memory? Is it true that there's no more information in your memory store about what words were in the list? Almost certainly not. This basic fact about memory can easily be demonstrated by continuing this memory testing. The next type of test is simple: Just repeat the free recall test (Free Recall 2). What is typically found that some words will be recalled in the second test that were not recalled in the first test. This is called *hypermnesia*, a kind of growth (not loss) of memory over time. How many new words will typically be recalled on the second attempt? Generally, a relatively small percent of the remaining ones—for example, 4 out of 24, or 16 percent. By the way, a simple explanation of hypermnesia is that at the end of the first 10-minute recall period, the rate of recall is quite low, but it isn't zero. If you simply kept trying to recall for another 10 minutes, you will keep recalling more new words (though this can be a frustrating and headache-inducing task).

At this stage, suppose you've been able to remember 20 of the 40 words. How can we further test your memory for the remaining 20? One way is to provide *retrieval cues*. Table 4-2 shows two versions of such a test. These kinds of cues are generally effective when a free recall test—a memory search without cues—starts to come up empty. In our example, let's suppose that the retrieval cues lead to the production of six more words, so memory has now been demonstrated to exist for 26 of the 40 words.

We'll try a recognition test next, taking 10 of the remaining 14 words and also 10 new words that were not in the original list and make up a random ordering of them, and you have to select the target words from it. Once again, your performance on this test will most likely show further evidence of memory for words that were not initially accessible to your recall attempts.

Finally, we could use an implicit test of memory. All of the tests we've considered so far are classified as explicit tests of memory—you have been told to try to remember some specific information. For an implicit test we could take the four list words we didn't use for the recognition test, mix them with some new words, and have you try to pronounce each of them as quickly as possible. Notice that you're not being asked to remember anything. The idea is that if there are still some traces of information left in your memory about these four words, then it will probably show up in faster pronouncing of these words than of the four new words that were not in the list.

There are many other techniques that could be used to probe your memory for the word list (hypnosis, for example). The main point should be clear enough: More information is typically available in your memory than is accessible at a given point in time, in a given "retrieval environment." Cues for retrieval are crucial for some kinds of remembering, and many failures to remember may actually be cases of *cue-dependent forgetting.*

Once again, these conclusions and principles are not limited in their applicability to simple laboratory experiments with word lists or other artificial materials. They are demonstrably true for memory of life experiences over intervals of many years. In a study by Harry Bahrick and colleagues, "392 high school graduates were tested for memory of names and portraits selected from yearbook. The retention interval since graduation varied from 2 weeks to 57 years." For subjects in their seventies, free (unaided) recall of classmates' names averaged about 20 percent. When they were given graduation photos as retrieval cues, they were able to recall about 50 percent of the names. And when they were given a recognition test, they averaged about 80 percent correct—50 years after graduation!

The Causes of Forgetting

However effective various methods of prompting and cuing are, the basic fact remains that forgetting occurs. Once upon a time you could have recalled most of your classmates' names, and you certainly would have been able to recognize all of them. What happened as time went by? Why can you no longer do this, and why do you now need memory prompts?

The ideas that memory decays as time goes by or that memory weakens with disuse have long been common answers to these questions, but there are problems with them as explanations. As the psychologist John McGeoch famously put it many years ago, "In time, iron may rust and men grow old, but the rusting and the aging are understood in terms of the chemical and other events which occur in time, not in terms of time itself." McGeoch acknowledged that there were good reasons for thinking that over long periods of time, the biological basis of memory might deteriorate. His main argument against decay as a general explanation of forgetting was a simple and powerful one: Over a given period of time, the amount of forgetting that occurs can be increased or decreased *by varying the nature of the events that occur during that time interval*, particularly in ways that interfere with memory for a given event. The process is known as retroactive interference and is a basic and very general cause of forgetting.

Interference and Forgetting

Allan Baddeley demonstrated an interesting example of retroactive interference in everyday life events (see Table 4-3). He was able to arrange and control where people parked when making two successive visits to a clinic. The experiment went like this:

TABLE 4-3 An Experiment on Memory and Retroactive Interference

Monday	Wednesday	Next Monday
Park in location A	Park in location B	"Where did you park last Monday?"
Park in location A	—	"Where did you park last Monday?"

Some visitors came to the clinic on both Monday and Wednesday of a given week, while other visitors came only on Monday. The following Monday they were given a test of memory for where they had parked the previous Monday. The results of the experiment were clear: People who had visited the clinic twice had much poorer memory for this information than people who had visited the clinic only once. In other words, the experience of visiting the clinic on Wednesday somehow impeded remembering the Monday experience.

Retroactive interference can be created experimentally in many different ways. In one experiment with six-year-old children, the experimenters read either one or two stories to different groups of children and then tested their memory for the first story a week later. The children who had heard only one story were much better at answering questions about it than were the children who had heard two stories.

So it seems that Sherlock Holmes was right when he said that "there comes a time when for every addition of knowledge you forget something you knew before." However, he did leave out something important: the influence of similarity.

In experiments of the kind considered here, the amount of forgetting caused by events that occur after the creation of memory for earlier events is typically much greater when the two sets of events are similar. In the experimental condition of Baddeley's clinic visit experiment, the same situation (visiting the clinic) was associated with two different sets of information about parking. Under conditions like those in Baddeley's experiment, this results in loss of access to memory about the events associated with the first experience.

It seems reasonable to conclude that retroactive interference is an important cause of forgetting life experiences in general. For example, we've seen in Bahrick's research on memory of high school classmates' names over periods of many years, that unaided recall of names was quite poor. According to the Interference Theory of Forgetting, the principles of retroactive interference and similarity explain this in terms of the very large amount of information about other names and other people entered into memory between the time the subjects left high school and the time their memories were tested many years later.

Interference Theory also identifies a second kind of process known as *proactive interference*. Baddeley's clinic visit experiment included conditions that were intended to evaluate the importance of this second kind of interference, with the arrangement shown in Table 4-4. This experiment was designed to see what effects a prior experience (the Monday visit) would have on retention of a later experience (the Wednesday visit). The effect, it turns out, was a negative one: Subjects who visited the clinic only once (on Wednesday) were better at remembering where they had parked than subjects who had made a previous visit.

It is not known exactly how the process of interference works. The classical interpretation of retroactive interference is that it results from *associative unlearning*. In Baddeley's experiment we may suppose that information in memory about going to the clinic on Monday becomes associated with information about a parking location, and that this association is somehow weakened when another, later visit is associated with new information about parking location. This is perhaps something like the process of

TABLE 4-4 An Experiment on Memory and Proactive Interference

Monday	Wednesday	Next Monday
Park in location A	Park in location B	"Where did you park last Wednesday?"
—	Park in location B	"Where did you park last Wednesday?"

overwriting of information in a computer's memory. Michael Watkins has described this as the *cue overload principle*: A retrieval cue such as "visiting the clinic" loses its ability to access a memory when there is too much information attached to it.

Context and Remembering

In 1940 John McGeoch proposed that some amount of ordinary forgetting occurs because of differences between the circumstances existing at the time a memory is formed (the learning context) and the circumstances existing at a later time when a person needs to access the memory (the retrieval context). The key idea here is that change of context is detrimental to memory retrieval. This has been demonstrated in many different settings. One is reinstatement of environment context. Suppose you were able to return to your high school environment—to your old homeroom or cafeteria or gymnasium. Would this improve your ability to recall classmates' names? Experiments have shown that the original context does aid retrieval of memories—sometimes. Probably the best-known example of this is Allan Baddeley's experiment in which members of a diving club studied a list of words on land or while submerged and were later tested for word memory on land or while submerged. The important result of the experiment was that recall was better when the learning and testing environments matched, and recall was not as good when the environments had changed between learning and testing.

Many different kinds of experiments along these lines have been conducted. For example, it has been shown that congruency (sameness) of moods aids recollection. Research subjects who memorize material while in a negative mood state tend to recall the material better on a later test if they are again experiencing a negative mood. Happily, this is also true for positive moods.

The importance of context has also been found in studies of the effects of drugs on memory. Information learned in a drugged state is often better remembered when the person's memory is later tested while in a drugged state than when the person is sober (a change of state). The opposite also holds: Information learned in a sober state is remembered better when in a later sober state than in a drugged state. (Of course, the best state to be in when learning and when later remembering is the sober state.) Strong effects of this *state dependency effect* can be seen in addictions. For example, rats that have developed tolerance to large doses of heroin in one environmental context will overdose and die if the same dose is given to them in a very different environment.

In general, reinstating the context of learning can lead to improved remembering. However, there seem to be limits to the effectiveness of context reinstatement in human learning. One such limit was shown convincingly by William Saufley at the University of California at Berkeley. In a series of 21 experiments in seven different courses, students attended lectures in a given classroom throughout a semester, and then half of the students took their tests in the same classroom while the other half took tests in a different room. This had no effect at all on test performance, possibly because the kind of learning that occurs in lectures (when any does occur) becomes "decontextualized"—that is, a person's understanding and remembering of a calculus procedure is not tied in any important way to the physical context in which learning occurred.

Hypnosis: Does It Improve Recall?

Can people in a hypnotic trance recall a great deal of accurate information about events they've witnessed? Yes. Does hypnosis improve memory? Could we add it to the list of effective memory-recovering techniques we've considered? No. These questions and answers are a simple summary of current scientific understanding of the effects of hypnosis on memory retrieval. It's important to understand why they're not contradictory.

The use of hypnosis in witness questioning is well illustrated by an event in 1976 known as the Chowchilla (California) kidnapping, in which a school bus was taken over at gunpoint and hidden—bus, driver, and children—in an underground chamber. The driver and children eventually escaped, and the police questioned the driver to obtain a description of the culprits. The driver was initially able to recall some details, including two digits of a license plate. Then he was hypnotized, which usually involves instructions such as the following:

> Turn loose now, relax. Let a good, pleasant feeling come all across your body. Let every muscle and every nerve grow so loose and so limp and so relaxed. Arms limp now, just like a rag doll. That's good. Now, send a pleasant wave of relaxation over your entire body, from the top of your head to the tips of your toes. Just let every muscle and nerve grow loose and limp and relaxed. You are feeling more relaxed with each easy breath that you take. Droopy, drowsy and sleepy. So calm and so relaxed. You're relaxing more with each easy beat of your heart . . . with each easy breath that you take . . . with each sound that you hear.

The bus driver was then interviewed and was encouraged to try hard to recall and reexperience the original event. Under these conditions he did remember many more details, some of which were used to track down and arrest the culprit.

Is this proof of the efficacy of hypnosis? No, because there are problems with concluding from this incident that hypnosis improves retrieval from memory. One may have already occurred to you: hypermnesia! It's common to be able to recall things on a second recall attempt that you didn't remember on an earlier attempt. No hypnotic trance is needed for this to happen. The recovery of memory under hypnosis may be due to the instructions that encouraged the bus driver to spend more time trying to recall.

To demonstrate the special usefulness of hypnosis in memory retrieval, it must be shown that hypnosis promotes better recollection than the recollection that would occur without hypnosis. How should you go about determining what the special effects of hypnosis are on memory, if any? It's actually pretty straightforward (see Table 4-5). For example, arrange for a group of test subjects to witness a staged event. Then, at some later point, hypnotize a random half of the subjects and compare the accuracy of their recall or recognition to the nonhypnotized subjects (the

TABLE 4-5 How to Test the Effects of Hypnosis on Remembering

Experimental Group	Witness event	Induce a trance state	Test memory
Control Group	Witness event	No trance state	Test memory

control group). Make sure that the only difference is that the experimental group is in a trance state and the other isn't at the time of the memory test.

The recall instructions, the behavior of the interviewer, the encouragement given to the witness, and the amount of time allowed for recall are all the same. Under these conditions, with these controls, you typically do not find any difference between the two groups in the amount recalled. In some studies the hypnotized subjects actually do worse in the sense that they make more recall errors (confabulations) than do the nonhypnotized subjects.

Marilyn Smith at the University of Toronto reviewed many studies along these lines, some of them laboratory studies and some of them done under highly realistic conditions. She arrived at this conclusion: "When proper control subjects are used and they attempt to recall the same material as hypnotized subjects, with relevant variables held constant, performances for the two groups typically do not differ." The same conclusion seems to apply to the effects of a procedure called *hypnotic age regression* in which a person in a trance state is led to "regress" to an early time in their life (typically early childhood) and is encouraged to act as they did at that point in their lives. It is not difficult to get adults to act in a childish way—some of us do this occasionally without hypnosis—but the research on hypnotic age regression has not supported the sensational claims that were once made for it (that people could remember details of their fourth birthday party, or extensive details about a childhood illness, for example).

As Smith puts it, "there has developed among police and other investigative agencies an unshakeable belief that through the appropriate uses of hypnosis otherwise irretrievable memories may be recalled." Where does this belief in the efficacy of hypnosis come from? It's probably based on a cognitive illusion. From the fact that hypnotized witnesses *can* recall large amounts of information when they're hypnotized, it's concluded that this happens *because* of the hypnosis. But, as we've already seen, they don't recall any more than they would if they weren't hypnotized. You need a control group!

Perhaps you're thinking that this is an academic point. After all, a memory testing procedure that includes hypnosis does work. True enough, but hypnosis increases recall errors, the nature of hypnosis itself is not well understood, and there are equally effective and more scientifically respectable procedures available—such as the Cognitive Interview (see Box 4-1).

Aging and Memory

If you are in your twenties or thirties, depend on it: There will come a time (and it starts before "old age") when you simply can't rely on your memory the way you can now. The magazine or journal articles that you read last week and noted as interesting or important—you can't assume, as you once did, that you will remember them or that they will come to mind when they should come to mind. When these things start to happen often enough, you'll be experiencing what's euphemistically called *benign senescent forgetting*, a general but not pathological decline in memory (see Box 4-2). Senescent forgetting is sufficiently benign that it can be made light of in jokes, and even rationalized as having a positive aspect, as in the adage "everything old is new again."

Hebb's experiences, as described in Box 4-2, are typical of normal aging. The decline in memory ability with age can be relatively minor, even into the seventies and later and is not to be confused with senile dementia such as Alzheimer's disease—which, while far and away the most common form of senility, develops in considerably less than half of people in their early eighties.

BOX 4-1 The Cognitive Interview

Research demonstrating the important role of context in memory has led to an interesting and useful technology known as the Cognitive Interview, a procedure designed by Ronald Fisher, Edward Geiselman, and others to improve the results of witness interviews. The Cognitive Interview is based on Endel Tulving's Encoding Specificity Principle, which in most respects is an updated version of McGeoch's ideas about context and memory. This principle states that any information stored in memory along with information about some target event (a robbery, for example) can later aid recall of the target information. The Cognitive Interview consists of attempts by the interviewer to encourage the witness to think about (to mentally reinstate) the context of the event in question. It uses these specific procedures and instructions:

Reinstate the Context: Try to reinstate in your mind the context surrounding the incident. Think about what the surrounding environment looked like at the scene, such as rooms, the weather, any nearby people or objects. Also think about how you were feeling at the time, and think about your reactions to the incident.

Report Everything: Some people hold back information because they are not quite sure that the information is important. Please do not edit anything out of your report, even things you think may not be important.

Recall the Events in Different Orders: It is natural to go through the incident from beginning to end. However, you also should try to go through the events in reverse order. Or, try starting with the thing that impressed you the most in the incident and then go from there, working both forward in time and backward.

Change Perspectives: Try to recall the incident from different perspectives that you may have had, or adopt the perspectives of others who were present during the incident. For example, try to place yourself in the role of a prominent character in the incident and think about what he or she must have seen.

The Cognitive Interview has been found to be more effective than standard witness interview procedures and has been adopted by police and investigative agencies. The procedure is simple and inexpensive, requiring a training session of 30 minutes, and it is based on a solid science of memory.

BOX 4-2 Aging Mind and Aging Memory

Donald Hebb was a pioneering figure in the study of memory and brain processes. At the age of 47 he had a terrifying experience. He was reading a scientific article that was closely related to his own interests. He came upon a passage he thought was particularly important for his work and said to himself, "I must make a note of this." He then turned the page and found a penciled note about this passage in his own handwriting! He was shocked. He had never before forgotten anything that particularly interested him. He began to worry that perhaps he might be experiencing early signs of senility.

As it happens, Hebb was extremely busy at the time. He was director of a new laboratory, had major research projects going, was writing extensively, and was chair of his department. His memory was simply overloaded. He slowed down a bit, cut back on administrative activities, and took more leisure time. As a result, his memory for what he was reading came back to its "normal, haphazard effectiveness."

Hebb reported this experience in an article he wrote "On Watching Myself Get Old" when he was 74. Although he felt he was now experiencing some decline in his memory and thought patterns, he was still an active scientist and writer. Indeed, the editor of the magazine that published his article commented, "If Dr. Hebb's faculties continue to deteriorate in the manner he suggests, by the end of the next decade he may only be twice as bright and eloquent as the rest of us."

If we compare 75-year-olds with 35-year-olds today on tasks of memory and intelligence, the 35-year-olds will of course perform better, but this does not necessarily mean that all forms of memory and intelligence decline with age. Longitudinal studies in which the same individuals have been tested several times over their life span show that some forms of intelligence increase through the late seventies. Furthermore, people who are 60 today perform significantly better on memory tests than people who were tested at age 60 in 1942.

Age-Related Memory Changes

What do we know about the normal course of memory change with increasing age? Beginning in 1988, Lars-Goran Nilsson and colleagues at Uppsala University in Sweden conducted one of the most extensive studies yet of aging and memory. They gave a highly varied set of memory tests to groups of people from ages 35 to 80 (a cross-sectional comparison) and have repeated the testing on a yearly basis on these same people, adding new groups each year (a longitudinal comparison). The test battery included tests of immediate memory, working memory, memory for word lists, tests of episodic-declarative memory, tests of semantic memory, tests of language use, and tests of implicit memory. The study was notable for the extensive health information that was available as well.

One of the major findings of this study was that aging is associated with declines in almost any kind of test of explicit episodic memory for new information. (Older subjects also seemed more prone to false memory—see Chapter 6.) Moreover, these declines were not due to health problems. Age impairments showed up most dramatically in the learning of new material, that is, in trying to store new information in long-term memory. The episodic memory decline found with increasing age was not precipitous at any one age, and the extent of the decline was quite variable in any one age group. Interestingly, in the Swedish study, women's episodic memory was better than men's in all age groups, and this did not seem to be due to the women's better vocabulary scores.

The good news part of the research was that certain aspects of semantic memory, notably language comprehension, showed little or no decline up to at least age 75 when the influence of educational level was taken account of. Also, some kinds of implicit learning did not decline much, if at all, with increasing age. For example, both older and younger subjects displayed significant priming effects (benefits from previous exposure to an event).

Other research, however, seems to indicate that even semantic memory becomes problematic with increasing age. Possibly the most irritating and familiar one is difficulty in finding a particular word, or accessing one's "mental dictionary." This occurs at all ages but becomes more frequent as we age and also becomes harder to resolve by finally accessing the information..

What are the causes of aging-induced forgetting? There is fairly general agreement among those who specialize in aging and memory that the impairments observed in episodic memory tasks are to a considerable extent due to reduced speed of cognitive operations and reduced attentional resource, resulting in less information being encoded into memory. This seems to suggest that age-related memory problems are most likely to occur when events are brief or occur in quick succession, when attention must be divided or rapidly shifted. When elderly people are given a dual listening task , with two different messages presented to each ear, they do not perform as well as younger individuals. Elderly people must make a greater effort to attend to the task, and their ability (or possibly willingness to expend the effort) is somewhat reduced.

General cognitive slowing cannot be the whole story, though. For example, it does not seem to account for word-finding problems. Here we must consider the possibility that semantic memory is not so permanent after all and that actual degradation of semantic memory traces, or of the retrieval paths leading to them, or outright loss of information from semantic memory may occur with advancing age. This leads us to consider some of the biology of aging as it relates to memory and learning.

Brain, Aging, and Memory

We'll start with some general observations about the biology of aging. Life spans vary wildly in life forms. *C. elegans*, a little worm that lives in dirt and is a favorite of neuroscientists because it has only 302 neurons and 7,000 synapses, all of which have been identified, lives no longer than a month. At the other extreme, redwood trees live for thousands of years. Among animals, a type of clam called a quahog can live for more than 200 years, and lobsters can live for 100 years or more, as can sturgeon and turtles.

But these are the exceptions. Most animals live considerably less than the 100-year maximum life span of humans. The average human life span has, of course, increased dramatically in the past century thanks to improvements in medicine and nutrition. But the maximum human life span has always been about 100 years.

The fact that the maximum life span for humans has not increased despite better medicine, including elimination of many diseases, suggests that there may be built-in aging factors. For a long time it was thought that the organs were primarily responsible for aging; the heart, kidneys, and other organs simply wore out. It is now known that this is not the entire answer. Investigators grew cultures of normal body cells taken from people of different ages. Cells from a human embryo double about 50 times before they die, whereas cells taken from a middle-aged human divide only about 20 times before they die.

Is this control on cell aging in the DNA of the cell nucleus the "prime contractor," or is it in the cell bodies outside the nucleus, the "subcontractors"? The investigators exchanged the nuclei in human embryo cells and adult cells, and found that whether a cell body was from an embryo cell or from an adult cell, the cell divided only about 20 times if the nucleus was from an adult. If the nucleus was from the embryo, the cell divided about 50 times. These experiments suggested that part of the aging process is genetic, or under the control of the DNA in the cell nucleus. The only kind of human cell that is immortal is the cancer cell.

A genetic time clock that regulates the number of times a human body cell divides cannot, however, be the whole explanation of the aging process. The most important cells in the human body, the neurons in the brain, never divide after birth, although new neurons are formed from stem cells throughout life. Therefore, resetting of the genetic aging clock in body cells would not solve the problem of possible deterioration of the brain.

For many years it was thought that normal aging is accompanied by substantial losses of neurons in the brain, particularly in the cerebral cortex. Indeed, classical studies counting the number of neurons in particular regions led to estimates of something like a 50 percent loss of neurons in the neocortex by age 95. We now think that those findings are not correct but rather due to artifacts that influence the methods used to count cells. New and much more accurate procedures for determining cell numbers were developed by Mark West in Denmark and others. As a result of these new studies, many areas of the brain do *not* seem to have significant loss of neurons in aging. Some parts of the brain do show neuron losses. Three examples are the acetylcholine-containing neurons in the basal forebrain, a region of the hippocampus, and Purkinje neurons in the cerebellar cortex. The latter may account for the fact that it is more difficult for elderly people to learn new motor skills; in other words, you can't teach an old dog new tricks.

All of this is not to say that there are no major changes in the brain as we age. A basic one is a slow but steady decline in brain weight that appears to begin around age 25. Fergus Craik at the University of Toronto has argued that basic changes in the central nervous system that occur in normal aging—declines in brain size, metabolism, blood flow, and neurotransmitters—may be the causes of general cognitive slowing and reduced attentional powers and that impairments of these basic processes negatively impact how well information gets registered and stored in memory. This fits with the results of experimental demonstrations that, just like younger subjects, successful retrieval in older subjects will occur when steps are taken to promote effective processing of new information and when the retrieval environment provides good support—just as in Bahrick's demonstration that elderly people were able to match names and faces over retention intervals of 50 years or more.

Sleep, Dreaming, and Remembering

The role of sleep and dreaming in memory storage and retrieval has fascinated people for a long time. Why is it that our memories for dreams are so fleeting and fragmentary? Does sleep improve memory? Does dreaming improve memory? Can we learn while asleep?

Sleep

Sleep is an extraordinary mystery that we all take for granted. After nearly a century of research we still have no idea why sleep is necessary. Without sleep, animals die and normal humans go mad and, according to some reports, eventually die. As of this writing we have no understanding of why this is so. An early hypothesis was that sleep provided the body with rest so metabolic functions could recover after a period of waking activity. Actually, sleep is no better than reading a book as far as metabolic activity is concerned.

Virtually all animals with nervous systems are thought to sleep. We do know a great deal about the brain controls on the wake-sleep cycle, the so-called circadian rhythm. Humans and most other primates, and some birds of prey, rely heavily on vision and are active by day. Animals such as mice that serve as prey sensibly remain inactive by day. Unfortunately for mice, owls are active at night and have sonar "vision."

Patterns of sleep vary widely in animals. The opossum sleeps 19 hours out of every 24 and the giraffe sleeps only about 2. Some birds sleep with only one brain hemisphere at a time, with one eye closed and one eye open. It appears that dolphins also show a similar pattern of brain sleep; only one hemisphere sleeps at a time. Presumably if both hemispheres slept at the same time, birds might fall and dolphins drown.

When someone flies halfway around the world, it takes about a week to reverse the normal wake-sleep cycle to correspond to the new night and day. It used to be thought that the sleep cycle was controlled directly by the cycle of day and night. Indeed, exposure to bright light can speed this reversal. However, even people who have lived in caves with a constant low level of illumination for months show a normal wake-sleep cycle. Actually, they settle down to a 25-hour cycle rather than 24 hours.

The wake-sleep cycle is not directly controlled by the external light-dark (day-night) cycle but is influenced or entrained by it. There is a little group of neurons at the base of the brain just above the optic nerves from the eyes that serves as the master clock controlling our wake-sleep cycles. It has the rather forbidding name suprachiasmatic nucleus (SCN). Nerve cells there exhibit increased activity by day and decreased activity by night. They exhibit this circadian cycle independent of any control from other sources. The neurons have internal clocks. Some optic nerve fibers from the eyes project directly to the SCN neurons and entrain them to the external day-night cycle. But the wake-sleep cycle exists in the SCN neurons even if they are not activated by the optic nerve fibers.

There is one other aspect to this intriguing story: the third eye. All vertebrates, including humans, have a "third eye," the pineal gland. In lower vertebrates it is just under the skull at the top of the brain and has photoreceptors directly responsive to light shining through the skull. In higher vertebrates and humans it is buried in the depths of the brain. It still has remnants of photoreceptors, but they are vestigial. However, a circuit of neurons connects the SCN with the pineal gland. When darkness develops, or rather when the SCN goes into its darkness-sleep mode, it causes the pineal gland to release the hormone melatonin, which helps induce sleep.

Melatonin is sold over the counter at drug stores and health food stores and many people take it to help get over jet lag. Robert Sack, a physician at the Oregon Health Sciences University in Portland, is an expert on sleep and melatonin. He points out that if you take the hormone at a time when the pineal gland is releasing it, namely when you normally go to sleep, it will not be effective. Instead, take it when you would like to sleep at your destination. Suppose you travel from Los Angeles to London. You need to advance your clock eight time zones from Los Angeles to London. Take melatonin at 3 p.m. on the day of departure. On the next three days or so take the melatonin an hour or two earlier each day (10 p.m. on day 2, 9 p.m. on day 3). It should help. Interestingly, for most people it is easier to fly west than east. Since the natural SCN clock runs on a 25-hour cycle, it is easier to lengthen your day than shorten it.

Dreaming

Sleep occurs in two states: sleep with rapid eye movement (REM) and sleep with no rapid eye movement (NREM). REM sleep is deeper, and the eyes make rapid jerky movements behind the closed lids, as though the person is dreaming. Indeed, when people are awakened from REM sleep, they report typical dreams, including vivid and fantastic images and events. When awakened from NREM sleep, they also report dreams but ones that are pale and have more the quality of daydreams. The patterns of EEG activity, the brain waves recording from the surface of the scalp, also identify REM and NREM sleep. The NREM pattern consists of slow waves (anywhere from 1 to 12 hertz) which were earlier thought to be typical of all sleep. However, in the REM state, brain activity is identical to the waking state, with low-voltage fast activity, much faster and more irregular than the slow waves of NREM sleep.

Do animals dream? Mammals all show alternating periods of NREM and REM sleep. If you watch a dog sleeping, you will see periods when its paws start twitching and it makes little growling sounds. If you look closely, you will see its eyes moving rapidly under the closed lids (REM sleep). The impression that the dog is dreaming, perhaps having a good chase, is compelling. This raises again the issue of consciousness. Dreaming, after all, is another form of awareness. To believe that consciousness or awareness is the exclusive province of humans is a very parochial view.

Sleep and Learning

Memories of dreams are fleeting, but if awakened abruptly from REM sleep, people can give detailed descriptions of their dream experiences. What about people with severe amnesia like the patient HM? These people cannot remember their own experience in the waking state. But according to one report, when awakened from REM sleep, they can remember and report their dream experiences.

Can a person learn while asleep? Suppose you are trying to learn French. One approach would be to play taped lessons to yourself at night while you sleep. (It's been said that the best place to learn French is in bed, but that's probably because of something other than the effects of sleep on memory.) There have been many studies of this approach, with varying results. Some researchers report enhanced learning following sleep exposure to lessons and others are less positive. An important qualification in many of these studies is that no measures were taken of whether the person was actually asleep or instead had been wakened to some degree by the taped message. One recent experiment on learning during sleep eliminated these problems by monitoring the electrical activity of the brain while word lists were read repeatedly to sleeping subjects, and making sure that the subjects remained in REM sleep. The results of the experiment were clear: There was no evidence for any kind of memory formation for events that occurred during sleep, in tests of either implicit or explicit memory.

Two remarks about this experiment and its findings: First, note the contrast with the results of the anesthesia experiment described in Chapter 1, in which implicit memory traces were apparently formed by one of the memory systems of the brains of unconscious subjects. It's not obvious how to reconcile these two sets of findings, especially since patients under deep anesthesia are very much less responsive to external events than subjects who are merely sleeping. Second, keep in mind that this sleep learning experiment deals with memory for external events that occurred *during* sleep. Later in this chapter strong evidence is presented that sleep does, in fact, have major influences on memory for experiences that *precede* a period of sleeping.

Being repeatedly awakened before you would awake naturally would probably impair many cognitive functions. Depriving humans and animals of sleep definitely impairs performance on a number of learning tasks. This is particularly true if subjects are awakened repeatedly during REM sleep, leading to long-term REM deprivation. But is this due to lack of sleep or to stress? Being repeatedly awakened is a stressful situation. The impairment in learning is much greater when learning new tasks than when repeating older well-learned tasks. Interestingly, deprivation of NREM sleep is much less disruptive than REM deprivation.

There is evidence from the animal research literature that rats show increased REM sleep when they are being trained on various tasks. However, REM sleep levels return to normal once the animals have mastered the tasks. In control studies, animals that are given tasks not involving learning do not show increases in REM sleep.

One clear result of learning and sleep research is that material learned just before a night's sleep is better retained the next morning than material learned in the morning and tested for at the end of the day. Dramatic examples can be seen in learning motor skills. In one study a complex sequential motor task of finger tapping was trained before a period of normal sleep or waking. Sleep after practice enhanced the speed of performance by about 34 percent compared to being awake after practice. Perhaps there is a lesson here for athletes.

A simple explanation of the effects of sleep on remembering is lack of interference. As we stressed in our discussion of forgetting, learning new material interferes with the memories of earlier learned material. But there is more to this story. Some remarkable discoveries by Matthew Wilson at the Massachusetts Institute of Technology and Bruce McNaughton at the University of Arizona suggest that during sleep the brain actually rehearses material learned during the day.

We take a step back in time to describe the discovery of "place" cells in the hippocampus by John O'Keefe in London some years ago. He recorded the activity of single nerve cells in the hippocampus of the animals that were running through simple mazes. He found that a given neuron would increase its discharge frequency (action potentials) reliably at one and only one small place in the maze. Other neurons would code other places in the maze so that by recording from a number of such neurons, the entire space of the maze could be coded. Wilson, McNaughton, and others developed ingenious methods for recording from a number of single neurons in the hippocampus of the rat or mouse at the same time, as the animals were running in mazes. The results were remarkable. By looking at the patterns of activity in the "place" neurons being studied, they could tell exactly where the animal was in the maze.

They went one step further and recorded the activity patterns of neurons when the animals were learning the maze and when they were asleep. The patterns of neuronal activity that occurred while the animals were learning the maze were repeated during episodes of REM sleep! The brain, at least the hippocampus, appeared to be rehearsing and consolidating during sleep what was learned that day.

A human brain imaging study appears to support this idea of consolidation during sleep. People were first trained on a motor skill task. During REM sleep some brain areas were more active in trained subjects than in untrained subjects. Further, the activated brain areas were the same areas that were activated while the trained subjects were learning the task. Also, the trained subjects' performance on the task was improved following a post-sleep retest session.

All of these studies certainly argue that memories are retrieved better following sleep than waking. There is a clear message here for students studying for exams. This work also suggests that dreaming may be a mechanism for rehearsing material that has been experienced during the day. On the other hand, the actual content of dreams often does not seem to have much relationship to daytime experiences, and we don't yet have a science of the meaning of dreams.

Hypnagogic Images

Have you ever experienced hypnagogic images? These particularly vivid images are usually visual; we experience them just as we are falling asleep. They typically occur when people have engaged in novel physical or mental activities for extended periods of time. The existential philosopher Jean-Paul Sartre described them well:

> A radical distinction must be drawn between the way a face appears in perception and the manner the same face appears in hypnagogic vision. In the former case something appears which is then identified as a face . . . consciousness must focus on the object. . . .
>
> In hypnagogic vision this discrepancy does not exist. There is no focusing. Suddenly knowledge appears as vivid as sensory manifestation: one becomes aware of *being in the act* of seeing a face.

It does seem to be the case that such vivid images reflect the day's activities. Donald Hebb related the following:

> A day in the woods or a day-long car trip after a sedentary winter sometimes has an extraordinarily vivid aftereffect. As I go to bed and shut my eyes—but not till then, though it may be hours since the conclusion of the special visual stimulation—a path through the bush or a winding highway begins to flow past me and continues to do so till sleep intervenes.

Hypnagogic images are very similar to dream images experienced during REM sleep—vivid and fantastic. But there is one important difference. In dreams the person dreaming is always present in the dream, usually as an actor. This is not the case in hypnagogic images; they are images without the presence of the "imager."

Although exact data are lacking, it has been estimated that about 70 percent of adults report having experienced hypnagogic images. The actual incidence may be higher because some people are reluctant to admit to experiencing "visions" or hallucinations of any sort. Robert Stickgold and associates at Harvard Medical School were able to induce these images in normal subjects. The people were required to practice intensively a complex computer video game called Tetris. About 70 percent of people new to the game reported vivid hypnagogic images of playing the game as they were falling asleep, and about half of the people expert in the game reported such images. In addition to normal subjects, people with severe medial temporal lobe amnesia like the patient HM were trained and tested on the game. These patients also reported and described hypnagogic images upon falling asleep. But when asked about the game when they were awake, they had no memory of it.

Severely amnesic subjects can also remember and report their dreams. Since they cannot remember normal waking experiences, this seems to imply that different brain systems may be involved in remembering waking experience on the one hand and dreaming and hypnagogic images on the other (see Chapter 5). Specifically, the hippocampus—medial temporal lobe system essential for remembering normal waking experience may not be involved in memories for dreams and hypnagogic images. Instead, they may involve association areas of the cerebral cortex. Recall that visual priming memory involves visual association areas. Stickgold and associates argue that the lack of hippocampal involvement could explain many of the properties of dreams. "Without the anchor of temporal and spatial associations found in hippocampal declarative memories, much of the bizarreness of dreams, including their discontinuities and uncertainties would appear almost inevitable." The fact that our normal waking memories of most dreams are fleeting and fragmentary is consistent with this possibility.

5

Amnesia

Sudden memory loss has been an important plot element in many works of fiction. The film *Memento*, released in 2001, features a protagonist named Lenny who suffers brain damage in an assault. He is shown as being mentally normal in many ways: His language production and comprehension are normal, he has retained perceptual skills and knowledge (he knows the names of objects and what they are for), his social behavior is appropriate, and he remembers his personal past that preceded the brain damage. What Lenny has lost is his ability to form new, durable memories. He cannot remember the previous day's experience and he has to write notes to (sometimes onto) himself if he is to remember his plans, intentions, and recent experiences.

The Majestic is another movie that appeared about the same time as *Memento*. Its central character also suffers a head injury, this time in a car accident. Like Lenny, he retains his perceptual memory, language, and habits of social behavior but, unlike

Lenny, is still able to form and retain new memories. The problem is that he has lost most memories of his personal past.

Neither film is science fiction. *Memento* presents a generally accurate depiction of severe *anterograde amnesia*. *The Majestic* depicts a very severe case of *retrograde amnesia*, although in a somewhat improbable way, since retrograde amnesia caused by brain damage is usually accompanied by some anterograde amnesia. In this chapter we examine these two kinds of amnesia in detail, along with a discussion of other kinds of amnesia produced by disruption of the normal state or functioning of the brain.

Temporal Lobe Amnesia

Lenny's memory problems are very much like those of patient HM, described in Chapter 1. HM's story began in 1953 when a neurosurgeon named William Scoville performed a series of surgeries on a group of mentally disturbed patients in an attempt to treat severe and intractable psychotic behavior as well as on one nonpsychotic individual with severe epilepsy whose seizures were becoming more frequent and not controllable with medication. The surgical procedure consisted of making two holes in the forehead above the eyes, inserting a surgical tool to move the frontal lobes out of the way, and then removing brain tissue from the medial temporal lobes, including the hippocampus and amygdalae.

Scoville reported improvement in some of psychotic patients, but he also reported that the procedure had a terrible side effect for one psychotic patient and for the epileptic patient—"grave loss of recent memory," or what we have referred to as severe anterograde amnesia. These two patients (one of them HM) were now severely limited in their ability to form new (postoperative) memories of everyday events, and performed very poorly on tests of episodic learning and memory. The two patients did show some retrograde amnesia but it was relatively mild compared to the anterograde amnesia. Their abilities to recognize objects and their language skills were intact.

The memory problems of the epileptic patient HM have been studied for 50 years now, and many other similar cases have been identified since the 1950s. The surgical procedure that HM experienced was discontinued when the adverse side effects were discovered, but other cases of temporal lobe amnesiacs have occurred as a result of brain damage from accidents, encephalitis, or conditions that interrupt blood supply to the brain. Under some conditions, these kinds of events damage hippocampal tissue without much damage to other areas.

The findings of these studies have had an enormous impact on memory theory. To start with, they drew attention to the possible importance of the hippocampus for learning and memory. Figure 5-1 is a coronal (frontal cross-section) view of the hippocampus in the left hemisphere of the brain. It is about eight centimeters long and is located on the inner (folded) part of the temporal lobe in both brain hemispheres. ("Hippocampus" is Greek for "seahorse." With a little imagination, you can see why this brain region is so named by looking at the structures in Figure 5-1.)

A second major finding of temporal lobe amnesia research is that hippocampal damage impairs some kinds of learning and

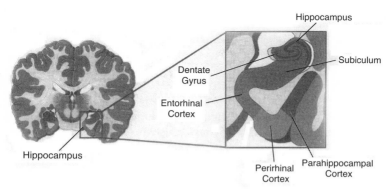

FIGURE 5-1 *The hippocampal complex in the temporal lobes of the human brain.*

memory functions while leaving others unaffected. For example, HM's memory has been described as consisting of the following sets of *spared* functions:

- Intact immediate or short-term memory (his memory span is in the normal range).
- Intact general mental functioning (his IQ did not decrease following the surgery).
- Intact ability to learn some new motor skills.
- Preservation of language skills.
- Preservation of perceptual skills (recognition of objects and their meaning).
- Intact implicit memory and priming (he is faster at pronouncing a word if he has seen or heard the word earlier).
- Retention of most personal or autobiographical memory, but with some loss of memory for events a few years before the surgery (time-limited retrograde amnesia).

HM's main memory problem is a severe anterograde amnesia, based on extreme difficulty in creating new episodic memories. He is described as being unable to remember peoples' names despite being introduced to them repeatedly, as having little memory for news events, and as not knowing the meanings of words that started appearing in everyday language long after 1954 (*jacuzzi, frisbee, mousepad, slamdunk*). This would seem to indicate that his semantic memory has also been affected. His performance on the battery of memory tests making up the Wechsler Memory Scale is very poor (a memory quotient of 64, compared to his IQ of 110). Many of the tests that make up the Wechsler Memory Scale are tests of explicit episodic memory in which new information must be retained in the face of distractions and delays.

The sparing of implicit learning abilities in temporal lobe amnesics was an important discovery. Temporal lobe amnesics *do* have the ability to store and retain new information as long as they are tested in ways that do not require explicit, conscious attempts at memory retrieval. This has been shown in studies of *repetition priming.* For example, when normal research subjects read a list of common words, pronouncing each one as quickly as possible, and then at some later time are given a second test with a word list that includes words from the original list as well as new words, they will pronounce the repeated words faster than the new words in the second test. (As we saw in Chapter 2, this can happen over intervals of several weeks or more between the first and second tests.) The same is true of temporal lobe amnesics. Some studies have found that these patients show as much priming (that is, benefit from a previous experience) as normal control subjects. Clearly, for there to be a priming effect in this experimental task, a subject must retain information from the first experience with the words. These same studies also show that temporal lobe amnesics have poor memory for the original word list when this memory is tested by an explicit test procedure ("Recall as many of the words as you can from the list you saw yesterday"). These combined results are referred to as the *dissociation of explicit and implicit memory systems.*

The anterograde amnesia that temporal lobe patients display is often described as a "complete inability" to remember, and their implicit memories are described as being "normal." but these descriptions appear to be somewhat exaggerated. HM, for example, can perform reasonably well in a memory experiment if he is given ample study time or many learning trials, and not all studies find that implicit learning is really as good in patients as in control subjects. Nevertheless, temporal lobe damage that includes the hippocampus and adjacent structures reliably leads to severe deficits of some kinds of memory, with a relative sparing of other kinds of memory. A relatively recent example of this involved three children who suffered early hippocampal damage. All of them seem like patient HM in that their episodic memory measured by explicit tests is very poor, but all of them had acquired language, world knowledge, and schooling. Some researchers take this to mean that "fact memory" formation does not require the hippocampus; only episodic memories of personal experience do.

Animal Models of Amnesia

In the years since his case was described, numerous unsuccessful attempts were made to re-create HM's massive memory impairment in animal models. It was only in 1978 that Mortimer Mishkin, working at the National Institute of Mental Health in Bethesda, Maryland, reported success. He worked with Rhesus monkeys, a popular animal model of human brain function. Although this animal's brain is considerably smaller than the human brain, it has a similar organization of the cerebral cortex and other higher brain regions. The Rhesus monkey has color vision that is identical to human color vision, and visual areas (30 or more!) in the cerebral cortex that are very similar to human visual areas. Indeed, humans and Rhesus monkeys are only separated by some 20 million years or so of evolution. The key to Mishkin's success came in the behavioral task he set for the monkeys. It is called delayed non-matching-to-sample and is very simple. The animal is first presented with an object (see Figure 5-2). He moves the object and obtains a reward of a peanut or raisin. He is then presented with two objects, the one he has seen before and a new object. If he moves the new object, he gets the reward, but if he moves the old object, he does not. New objects are used for each test, so the animal cannot form long-term memories of the objects in order to solve the problem. A delay is introduced between presentation of the single object and presentation of the two objects. Once the monkey has learned to do this task, he can remember the initial object for delays of many minutes. Monkeys greatly enjoy this task. As with humans, they like novelty and new experiences. Interestingly, if we reversed the task and required the monkey to choose the old object instead of the new one, it would take him much longer to learn the task.

Mishkin made extensive brain lesions in the medial temporal lobe on both sides that included the hippocampus and closely adjacent brain regions. These animals were markedly impaired on the tasks for delays beyond a minute or so; however, they performed normally for very short delays, showing that their percep-

Delayed Nonmatching to Sample

FIGURE 5-2 *The delayed matching-to-sample test of working memory.*

tions of the objects were normal. This is a simple form of recognition memory; rather than remembering *where* the object is, the monkey must remember *what* it is. This task seems to capture at least some aspects of HM's memory impairment.

Following Mishkin's discovery, other researchers repeated and extended this work, most notably Larry Squire and Stuart Zola at the University of California at San Diego. We now know that the hippocampus is critically involved, but closely adjacent regions of the cerebral cortex are also involved; the more of these that are damaged, the worse the impairment in the memory, in both monkeys and humans.

Where Are Permanent Memories Stored?

Mishkin's monkeys have something else in common with human temporal lobe amnesics: Damage to the hippocampal area does not result in the loss of all knowledge and skills that existed prior to the damage. That is, there is no massive retrograde amnesia. As Squire and Zola showed, these animals are impaired in remembering only things they had learned up to about two months prior to the brain lesion. As we've seen, patient HM shows a time-limited retrograde amnesia and no loss of language skills or IQ. All of this seems to say that long-term permanent memories are not stored in this temporal lobe-hippocampal system. But then where are they stored? The cerebral cortex is the main possibility.

The most compelling evidence for long-term storage of factual information like vocabulary in the cerebral cortex comes from patients for whom damage to the neocortex resulted in selective loss of certain categories of words. Damage to left temporal-parietal regions or left frontal-parietal regions (Figure 5-3) might impair knowledge of one category of words—for example, small inanimate objects such as brooms and chairs—but not knowledge of words from another category such as living things. On the other hand, damage to the ventral and anterior temporal lobes can have the opposite effect. Elizabeth Warrington and asso-

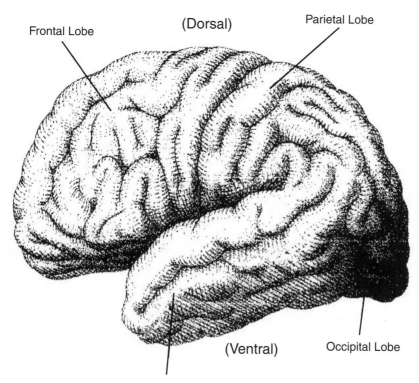

Frontal Lobe   (Dorsal)   Parietal Lobe

(Ventral)   Occipital Lobe

FIGURE 5-3 The four major lobes of the human cerebral cortex.

ciates, who discovered these patterns of brain damage and word category loss, suggested that the particular sensory and motor systems used to learn about the world influence where information is stored in the brain. For example, people learn about living things primarily through vision, and many aspects of vision are coded in the temporal lobe, whereas people learn about inanimate objects like hammers and furniture by manual and postural movements, involving the parietal and frontal lobes.

In part because animals cannot speak, we have less knowledge about where information might be stored in their brains. When monkeys are taught visual discriminations, where they have to learn about particular objects and store that information in long-term storage, damage to an intermediate region of the temporal lobe termed TEO can markedly impair these long-term visual memories. Remarkable studies by groups in Japan and at the National Institute of Mental Health in Bethesda, Maryland, report that when monkeys have learned to discriminate particular objects well, neurons in their temporal lobes seem to code these objects (and respond selectively to the sight of them). An unanswered question is whether this TEO region of the monkey cortex is where memories of objects are stored or whether TEO is just necessary to perceive the objects; in either case, damage to TEO impairs the animal's ability to recognize objects. Studies such as these are only the beginnings of the study of a major scientific question; at present relatively little is known about how neurons and patterns of neural activity actually represent and maintain specific memory information.

Memory Consolidation and Retrograde Amnesia

The concept of memory consolidation is very old and very simple. It is essentially the idea that, when memories are first formed, they are relatively fragile and easily interfered with. Over a period of time they become much more firmly fixed and resistant to decay and interference. Consolidation has been proposed as an explanation of time-limited effects in retrograde amnesias—of why forgetting experiences that occurred just prior to brain damage is more likely than forgetting older memories. Allan Brown of Southern Methodist University has performed detailed analyses of studies of retrograde amnesia in humans and concluded that there is strong evidence for such temporally graded retrograde amnesia as well as evidence for a consolidation process in human long-term memory that occurs over periods of several years at least.

One problem with the evidence from human studies is that very little of it comes from controlled experimentation. You cannot concuss human subjects, starve them of oxygen, create lesions in the cerebral cortex, or induce massive convulsions (with one exception, as we'll see). But such treatments are possible with nonhuman subjects. One in particular has been studied in detail: the effects of an electric current applied to the head that is strong enough to produce massive disruption of the normal electrical activity of the cortex, unconsciousness, and a convulsion.

The classic study of electroconvulsive shock (ECS) was done by Carl Duncan at Northwestern University. Rats were given one trial a day for 18 days in a simple learning task in which they had to run from one side of a box with a grid floor to the other side when a tone came on to avoid getting a foot shock. Normal animals learned this task well and remembered to avoid the shock on the last 12 or so days of the test. Duncan ran this experiment on several groups of animals. One group was given ECS 20 seconds after the learning trial, another group 40 seconds after, and so on up to an hour or more. The results were dramatic. Animals given the ECS very soon after the learning trial learned nothing—they acted as if they had not learned any association at all between the tone and the shock. But there was a pronounced gradient such that animals given the ECS an hour after learning were not impaired at all compared to controls given no ECS.

So began a large and fascinating field of science. Many alternate ideas were proposed: Perhaps the ECS hurt, so animals were being punished; perhaps they were learning fear. One by one these hypotheses were overturned, and the consolidation view survived. Key experiments showed that if the animals were anesthetized and the seizure activity was limited to the brain using in-dwelling electrodes, the same memory impairment occurred. Massive interference with normal brain activity can markedly impair the consolidation of memories.

If treatments like ECS can interfere with memory formation, perhaps it would also be possible to *facilitate* memory formation. Many years ago Karl Lashley, a pioneering scientist who studied the brain mechanisms of memory, did just such an experiment. He gave rats a powerful stimulant drug and found that they learned a maze better than did nondrugged animals. (Unfortunately, they also *ran* faster, so it was not entirely clear whether they actually learned faster or not. The drug affected their behavioral performance, but this was not necessarily due memory factors.) This issue was resolved years later in now-classic studies by James McGaugh and his associates at the University of California at Irvine. They introduced the post-trial treatment procedure. Animals were given a trial of training, perhaps in a maze. A stimulant drug was then administered right after the learning experience. The animal was tested the next day, after the effects of the drug had worn off. The results were striking: Stimulant-injected animals developed much better memories of the maze than did control animals injected with saline. The drug could not have affected performance during the learning experience because it was not injected until afterward. It must therefore have facilitated consolidation of the memories. Just as with ECS, there is a time gradient for memory facilitation. In rats, injections right after learning are most effective. Later injections are progressively less effective, and injections an hour or so after learning do not work in rats.

A number of chemicals and drugs can markedly enhance the formation of memories if injected after a learning experience. Most of this work has been done with animals, but similar results have been found with humans. Two of the most effective memory-enhancing drugs (in rats) are strychnine and amphetamine. Don't try this at home. Strychnine is a deadly poison; it blocks inhibition in the brain and in higher doses leads to epileptic seizures and death. Amphetamine is a powerful and addictive stimulant and repeated use leads to psychosis.

Actually the body and brain produce their own memory consolidation agents, particularly in times of stress or anxiety—for example, the arousal hormone adrenaline. For both animals and humans, adrenaline can enhance memory consolidation and thus improve later retention of a learning experience. There are many substances that can enhance memory consolidation, the safest being glucose. If you eat a candy bar right after a learning experience, it can enhance your memory of the experience.

Is there such a thing as a memory pill? The substances we

discussed here, such as adrenaline and glucose, can enhance memories somewhat, depending on the circumstances. But there is no pill that can make ordinary memorizers into supermemorizers. The memory pill has become the goal of a major search by the pharmaceuticals industry, primarily because of Alzheimer's disease, where the basic symptom is progressive loss of memory ability, due to brain tissue degeneration. There are now drugs on the market that can help memory a little in the early stages of the disease but as yet there are no really effective treatments.

To return to the idea of memory consolidation, the hippocampus and surrounding structures in the cortex are critically important for the formation of long-term memories. Patient HM and monkeys with damage to these structures cannot form long-term memories of their own experiences, even though their short-term working memory processes are normal. These cases are among the strongest evidence favoring the consolidation view and the hypothesis that *the hippocampus and other structures are necessary to consolidate working memories into long-term memories.* These cases also strongly support the distinction we have made throughout this book between short-term working memory and long-term memory.

There is another kind of evidence that supports the distinction between short-term and long-term memories. Studies with animals have shown that if drugs are injected that block gene expression and the manufacture of proteins, long-term memory formation is prevented, but short-term memory processes are not impaired. This strongly implies that long-term memory formation requires structural growth changes in neurons, changes that require proteins to be made.

Human Memory and Electroconvulsive Therapy

Electroconvulsive therapy (ECT) for the treatment of severe depression is a very common medical procedure in many countries. Its use is strongly endorsed by the National Institutes of Health: "Not a single controlled study has shown another form of treatment to be superior to ECT in the short-term management of severe depression." For many patients a series of two or more treatments a week for perhaps four weeks results in remission of the most severe symptoms of depression and reduction in the risk of suicide. It is not a cure, because recurrence of depression is quite common. The modern form of the treatment consists of inducing a convulsion by passing an electric current through the brain by means of electrodes applied to the head. The patient is first given a muscle relaxant, an injection of a fast-acting barbiturate that produces unconsciousness, and is then given the convulsion-inducing electrical current.

Here is a description of what it is like to undergo ECT, written by Norman Endler, a psychologist whose own depression was not responding to drug treatments:

> I changed into my pajamas and a nurse took my vital signs (blood pressure, pulse, and temperature). The nurse and other attendants were friendly and reassuring. I began to feel at ease. The anesthetist arrived and informed me that she was going to give me an injection. I was asked to lie down on a cot and was wheeled into the ECT room proper. It was about eight o'clock. A needle was injected into my arm and I was told to count back from 100. I got about as far as 91. The next thing I knew I was in the recovery room and it was about 8:15. I was still slightly groggy and tired but not confused. My memory was certainly not impaired. I knew where I was. I rested for another few minutes and was then given some cookies and coffee. Shortly after eight thirty, I got dressed, went down the hall to fetch my wife, and she drove me home.

This description of ECT bears little resemblance to the descriptions often found in films, magazine articles, and in statements by certain advocacy groups (including the Church of Scientology). These sources depict ECT as a barbaric practice that robs people of their emotions and autobiographical memories. The idea that severe memory loss commonly results from ECT is widely believed, at least outside the medical specialties that actually use the procedure.

What is actually known about memory and ECT? First, massive erasure of personal memory is simply not a risk with modern

ECT. As Max Fink, psychiatrist and longtime proponent of ECT puts it, "There is no longer any validity to the fear that electroshock will erase memory or make the patient unable to recall her life's important events or recognize family members or return to work."

At the same time, there is evidence that some impairments of learning and remembering can result from ECT. For example, retrograde amnesia may occur following the treatment. This was evident in the results of an experiment by Larry Squire in which patients were tested for their memory of the names of television shows before and after ECT. The names were selected from shows that had originally aired for one season from one to 15 years earlier. Prior to ECT, patients' memories for the names of the TV shows showed the usual forgetting curve, with memory accuracy generally decreasing the older the show. Following ECT, there was a selective impairment of memory for the more recently experienced shows only.

This result might be attributed to incomplete consolidation and increased vulnerability of the relatively recent experiences. However, there was another very important outcome of this experiment. On a later follow-up test, memory returned for the shows that could not be remembered immediately following ECT. This suggests that the memory failures in the first test were in fact only *performance failure,* reflecting the inaccessibility of otherwise intact memories. The ECT-induced memory loss and subsequent recovery in this experiment also resemble the pattern of loss and recovery often reported following a concussion.

Some of the most convincing evidence about ECT and memory loss comes from experimental studies in which depressed patients were randomly assigned to a real ECT treatment or a "sham" ECT treatment in which they underwent all the usual components of the ECT procedure (muscle relaxant, general anesthetic) but were not actually shocked and did not convulse. Experiments like these are very powerful from the standpoint of research design because they control for the effects that depression itself might have on memory, as well as the effects of drug-induced unconsciousness on memory functions. Some experiments along these lines have also used double-blind controls, meaning that the patients did not know what treatment they would receive and the people evaluating a patient's mood and memory functions after treatment did not know either.

What experiments like this have shown is that there appears to be no permanent loss of memories that existed prior to the ECT treatment, and no impairment of general cognitive functioning in the days following the procedure. In fact, memory functions sometimes seemed to improve following ECT. This is probably due to the effectiveness of ECT in alleviating many of the symptoms of major depression, which itself appears to interfere with memory functioning.

What are the risks to memory associated with ECT? They seem to be mild. ECT does seem to produce some retrograde amnesia, but this can be followed by memory recovery. It does seem to have some anterograde effects (for example, Professor Endler's grogginess following the procedure), but these do not persist. There is still some concern that an extended program of ECT might have negative effects on cognition in general.

Why then does ECT continue to be controversial in many quarters? There are several reasons. One is that the safeguards and specific procedures used in modern ECT evolved from earlier procedures in which neither the benefits nor the risks were well understood, and in which the procedures used were crude by today's standards. A second reason is that there is still no clear scientific understanding of *why* ECT works to alleviate symptoms of major depression, although there are many hypotheses involving hormonal changes, alteration of neurotransmitter activity, and possibly growth of new neurons in the hippocampus.

This may leave you wondering what the rationale for the ECT procedure was when it was first used 70 or more years ago. There are varying accounts. One is that it originated in the observation that patients suffering from both epilepsy and schizophrenia seemed to show a reduction in psychotic behavior following an epileptic seizure and that this rather naturally led to the speculation that deliberately inducing a seizure might have the same result.

In any event, as scientific understanding of memory progresses, newer and more sensitive forms of memory testing will become available, and there will be continuing evaluation of ECT's effects on memory and cognition. This is what Anne Donahue called for in a compelling personal account of her experience with depression and ECT. Although she thinks that ECT may have impaired her memory, she is thankful that she had a course of treatments: "I remain unflagging in my belief that the electroconvulsive therapy that I received may have saved not just my mental health but my life. If I had the same decision to make over again, I would choose ECT over a life condemned to psychic agony, and personal suicide."

Virtual Lesions

In the last few years a new technology has been developed that might be an alternative to ECT and that might also be a valuable research tool for the study of normal human memory. It is called transcranial magnetic stimulation (TMS) and it consists of generating a magnetic field in a coil held near the head (see Figure 5-4). The magnetic field penetrates the scalp and the skull and generates an electric field that can disrupt the normal electrical activity of neurons in the cerebral cortex. For example, when the coil is held near the motor cortex (a narrow band lying across the top of the cerebral cortex), it can cause the muscles of the thumb to twitch. Several studies of TMS as a treatment for depression, with sham treatment controls, have suggested that it temporarily reduces the symptoms and risks of major depression (but again for reasons that are not clear).

Unlike ECT, the TMS procedure is simple and apparently safe enough to use as a research tool to study brain function in normal subjects. In one study, subjects looked at pictures of familiar objects presented on a computer monitor, fixing their gaze on the midline of the display. A TMS coil was held over the visual pro-

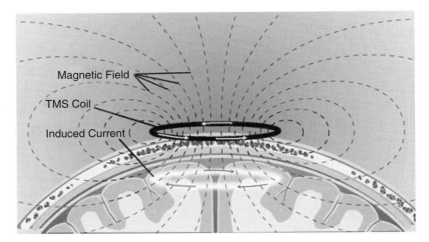

FIGURE 5-4 Transcranial magnetic stimulation of the brain.

cessing areas in the right occipital-parietal lobes. After a few minutes of stimulation, subjects reported that the left half of the visual display could no longer be seen. When the coil was deactivated, their perception immediately returned to normal.

Transcranial magnetic stimulation has also been used in the study of memory. In one experiment it was applied over the left and right frontal lobes while subjects were either studying a set of pictures, or being tested for their memory of the pictures. The experiment was conducted as a test of Endel Tulving's HERA theory (hemispheric encoding-retrieval asymmetry). This theory states that the left frontal lobes are more active during learning or encoding (trace formation), while the right hemisphere is more active during retrieval (trace access). The results of the experiment were consistent with the theory. Stimulation applied to the left-frontal lobes disrupted memory performance if applied during learning but not during testing, while stimulation applied to the right frontal lobes disrupted memory performance when applied during testing but not during learning. Interestingly, this seems to imply that if subjects were later retested without TMS, their "lost" memories would return. In any event, the TMS technology seems to provide something that until now has not been available for studying human memory: a way of producing safe and reversible "virtual lesions."

Dementia and Memory

Case histories like the one presented in Box 5-1 are all too common these days. There are several different conditions that consist of a steady, inexorable decline in the brain and its functions and lead to dementia. Alzheimer's disease is the most common of these, and it is equally prevalent in men and women. The affected initially have trouble learning new material and eventually cannot learn at all. Death usually comes after 10 years or so and is often caused by other factors such as pneumonia. By this point the patient is unaware of his surroundings, does not recognize anyone, and is unable even to care for his own bodily functions. Some 10 to 15 percent of people over 65 develop the disease, as will one in every four Americans over 85.

The decline in memory with Alzheimer's disease is dramatic, even in the early stages. Unlike normal aging, both short-term and long-term memory abilities are compromised and patients gradually lose their long-term semantic and personal memories. Eventually, everything goes. Simple tests show how marked the impairment can be even in moderately advanced cases. Patients have difficulty with such questions as:

- How many wings does a bird have?
- If two buttons cost 15 cents, what is the cost of a dozen buttons?
- In what way are a tiger and a lion alike?
- Draw the face of a clock set to 11:10.

This last question causes problems even in the early stages of the disease. Patients have difficulty placing the minute hand on the 2: instead they try to place it on the 10.

A number of tests have been devised to diagnose the initial stages of Alzheimer's disease. Most are simple memory tests like

BOX 5-1 Alzheimer's Disease and Its Victims

Harry seemed in perfect health at age 58, except that for a couple of days he had had the flu. He worked in the municipal water treatment plant of a small city, and there, while responding to a minor emergency, Harry became confused about the order in which the levers controlling the flow of fluids should be pulled. Several thousand gallons of raw sewage were discharged into a river. Harry had been an efficient and diligent worker, so after puzzled questioning, his supervisor overlooked the error. Several weeks later, Harry came home with a baking dish that his wife had asked him to pick up; he had forgotten he had brought home the identical dish two nights before. Later that month, on two successive nights, he went to pick up his daughter at her job in a restaurant, forgetting that she had changed shifts and was working days. And a week later he quite uncharacteristically became argumentative with a clerk at the phone company; he was trying to pay a bill that he had paid three days before.

By this time his wife had become alarmed about the changes in Harry's behavior. She insisted that he see a doctor. Harry himself realized that his memory had been failing for perhaps as long as a year, and he reluctantly agreed with his wife. The doctor did a physical examination and ordered several laboratory tests and an electroencephalogram (a brain wave test). The examination results were normal, and thinking the problem might be depression, the doctor prescribed an antidepressant drug. If anything, the medicine seemed to make Harry's memory worse. It certainly did not make him feel better. Then the doctor thought that Harry must have hardening of the arteries of the brain, for which there was no effective treatment.

Approximately eighteen months had passed since Harry had first allowed the sewage to escape, and he was clearly a changed man. He often seemed preoccupied, a vacant smile settled on his face, and what little he said seemed empty of meaning. He had given up his main interests, golf and working. Sometimes he became angry—sudden storms without apparent cause—which was

those given above. But these tests only identify probable Alzheimer's (or at least dementia) once the disease has progressed to the point where clear memory impairment and accompanying neuron loss in the brain have developed.

A test that shows promise in diagnosing the initial stages or quite unlike him. He would shout angrily at his wife and occasionally throw or kick things, although his actions never seemed intended to hurt anyone. He became careless about personal hygiene, and more and more often he slept in his clothes. Gradually his wife took over, getting him up, toileted, and dressed each morning.

Harry himself still insisted that nothing at all was wrong, but by now no one tried to explain things to him. He had long since stopped reading; he would sit vacantly in front of the television though unable to describe any program that he had watched. His condition slowly worsened. He was alone at home through the day because his wife's school was in session. Sometimes he would wander out. He greeted everyone he met, old friends and strangers alike, with "Hi, it's so nice." That was the extent of his conversation, although he might repeat "nice, nice, nice. . . ." He had promised not to drive, but one day he took out the family car. Fortunately, he promptly got lost and a police officer brought him home; his wife then took the keys to the automobile and kept them. When he left a coffee pot on the electric stove until it boiled dry and was destroyed, his wife, who by this time was desperate, took him to see another doctor.

Harry could no longer be left at home alone, so his daughter began working nights and caring for him during the day until his wife came home after school. Usually he sat all day, but sometimes he wandered aimlessly. He seemed to have no memory at all for events of the day, and he remembered very little of the distant past, which a year or so before he had enjoyed describing. His speech consisted of repeating over and over the same word or phrase.

Because Harry was a veteran, she took him to the nearest Veterans Administration hospital, 150 miles distant. Harry was set up in a chair each day, and the staff made sure he ate enough. Even so, he lost weight and became weaker. When his wife came to see him he would weep, but he didn't talk, and he gave no other sign that he recognized her. After a year he even stopped weeping, and after that, she could no longer bear to visit. He lived on until just after his sixty-fifth birthday when he choked on some food, developed pneumonia as a consequence, and soon died.

even predicting subsequent development of the disease has come from an unexpected source—classical conditioning—in studies by Diana Woodruff-Pak at Temple University and Paul Solomon at Williams College. An example of such a study of eye-blink conditioning is shown in Figure 5-5. Note the massive impairment in

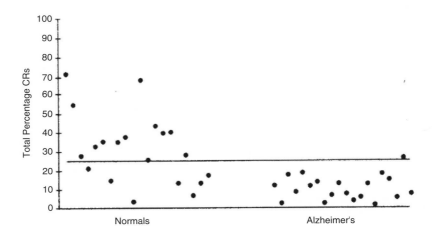

FIGURE 5-5 Eye-blink conditioning in normal control subjects and Alzheimer's patients. The graph shows the percentage of conditioned responses (CRs) in each group.

learning by early Alzheimer's patients compared to normal age-matched controls. Note also that a few of the normal subjects performed as poorly as the Alzheimer's patients. In a three-year follow-up study, several of these low-scoring normal people developed Alzheimer's disease but none of the high-scoring normal people did!

Before examining the causes of Alzheimer's disease we look briefly at another devastating form of dementia, Huntington's disease, where genetic factors are clear. Huntington's is a terrible disease with marked movement disorders, involuntary writhing movement of the limbs, together with rapidly developing brain degeneration, dementia, and death. It is due to an abnormality of a single dominant gene on chromosome 4. This means that 50 percent of all children of someone suffering from the disease will have the gene too and virtually 100 percent of these will also develop the disease. About half of those who have the gene will develop the disease before the age of 40 and the other half not until after 40. Someone with the gene may not be aware of this fact and have children, half of whom will be destined to suffer the disease.

The defective gene can be identified in a simple test done on DNA from cells in blood or saliva. Unfortunately, there is no treatment. This raises serious issues about genetic counseling. One person is reported to have committed suicide after learning of his genetic diagnosis of Huntington's disease by telephone without prior counseling.

As of this writing we do not know all the causes of Alzheimer's disease. A clear brain pathology definitely identifies Alzheimer's disease: senile plaques, BB-sized accumulations of debris left over from destroyed neurons surrounding a central core of protein called *amyloid*; tangles of neurofilaments inside neurons; and, ultimately, massive loss of neurons and brain volume. These are most prevalent in regions of the cerebral cortex critical for declarative and working memory: the medial temporal lobe–hippocampus and prefrontal cortex. Actually, normal elderly individuals may also develop some plaques and tangles.

A possible lead to genetic factors in Alzheimer's disease came with the discovery that people suffering from Down's syndrome also had plaques and tangles and loss of neurons in the brain, but at a much earlier age, always before the age of 10 years. Children with Down's syndrome are typically mentally retarded and have a collection of unusual symptoms, including folded eyelids. The genetic basis of Down's syndrome is well known. These individuals have an extra chromosome 21. Down's syndrome incidentally, is not inherited; it is caused by abnormality in the development of germs cells. Three copies of chromosome 21 means 50 percent more DNA and this means 50 percent excess protein product, possibly in the form of plaques and tangles.

The genetic factors in Alzheimer's disease are rather complicated. There is a particular form of Alzheimer's disease that involves at least three abnormal genes and is associated with early onset of the disease, before the age of 60. However those genetic factors account for only about 10 percent of Alzheimer's patients. Another gene termed *apoE* on chromosome 19 is implicated in a different way. There are actually three different forms of apoE—2, 3, and 4. It is only the apoE 4 that is associated with Alzheimer's disease. But the presence of apoE 4 does not cause the disease; it simply increases the likelihood that the disease will develop in old age. The apoE 4 gene is present in some 40 percent of people who develop Alzheimer's disease in old age. But this still leaves 50 percent of all Alzheimer's patients with no known genetic causal factors.

The neurotransmitter acetycholine (ACh) may have some involvement in Alzheimer's disease. Studies of the brains of a number of patients who died from Alzheimer's disease have indicated a marked loss of neurons in the basal forebrain, which contains ACh neurons projecting to the cerebral cortex, and much lower levels of certain chemicals associated with the ACh system. But some loss of ACh neurons in the nucleus basalis also occurs in normal aging.

It has been known for some time that anticholinergic drugs, which counter the effects of ACh, impair memory. Drugs that block this enzyme lead to increased actions of ACh at these synapses. Such drugs facilitate memory in animals and humans. More ACh is good for memory. It is not yet known whether loss of ACh neurons is the sole or even a major cause of Alzheimer's disease, or whether there is any causal relationship among the appearance of senile plaques, neuron loss in the cerebral cortex and hippocampus, and the marked loss of ACh neurons in the nucleus basalis.

There is clear evidence in studies of normal young adults that drugs that enhance ACh function in the brain enhance memory performance and drugs that antagonize ACh impair memory performance. Unfortunately, these memory-enhancing drugs have unpleasant side effects. But new classes of drugs that antagonize AChE have been developed to treat Alzheimer's disease.

Tacrine (Cognex) is one these drugs. It does have less severe side effects but may cause nausea and vomiting in some patients. Tacrine was evaluated in a series of clinical trials with Alzheimer's patients. It seems to be most helpful in treating the memory and cognitive impairments seen in the early stages of the disease. Patients on the drug show a modest but significant improvement on measures of basic cognitive skills. Tacrine does not prevent Alzheimer's; it seems to slow development of the debilitating symptoms somewhat. But this still has important consequences. If patients on the drug can remain at home for just a few months longer before going to a nursing home, it will save billions of dollars, not to mention enhancing the quality of life for the patients, at least for this period of time. Another new drug, Aricept, appears to be somewhat more effective in slowing progression of the disease.

There has been much interest in the possibility of predisposing environmental factors in Alzheimer's disease. An earlier hypothesis was the presence of aluminum. However, to date, no specific environmental villains have been identified.

So far we have considered ultimate causes about which little is proven beyond the genetic 10 percent. More is known about the immediate or proximal causes of Alzheimer's disease. A protein present in cells, beta-APP (amyloid precursor protein), may be directly responsible for the abnormal accumulation of fibrillar material that kills neurons, resulting in tangles and plaques. But we still do not know why it happens.

The general notion is that certain genes may suddenly begin expressing proteins that lead to plaques and tangles or may cease producing proteins that prevent these abnormal phenomena, or both. If this proves to be the case, chemical therapies may be possible. Thus, if genes start expressing abnormal proteins, drugs might be developed that would prevent the expression of these proteins. Perhaps the ultimate preventive treatment will involve some form of genetic engineering. The causes of and possible treatments for Alzheimer's disease are some of the most active areas of research today in neuroscience.

6

False Memory

In 1974 Elizabeth Loftus, then at the University of Washington, reported the results of experiments that showed how visual memory could be interfered with when the experimenter presented certain kinds of false information to research subjects. In one such experiment, subjects first watched a short film that included a brief segment showing a collision between two cars. Subjects were then immediately asked to write a description of what they had seen, and then were asked to estimate how fast the cars were going when they collided. The key part of the experiment was that different subjects were asked this question in slightly different ways. For some of them the question was, "About how fast were the cars going when they hit each other?" For other subjects the question was, "About how fast were the cars going when they smashed into each other?" For other subjects (the control group), no such question was asked. One week later, all subjects were asked if they had seen broken glass at the accident scene. Only 6 percent of the control subjects said they had, and only 7 percent of the *hit* subjects said they had—but 16 percent of the *smashed into* subjects stated they remembered seeing broken glass. In other experiments Loftus and her co-workers found that the verb chosen to describe the accident could increase their subjects' estimates of vehicle speed at the time of the accident.

Loftus proposed that these research results could be understood as resulting from the incorporation of information presented during the questioning period into the memory of the original event. This should remind you of the process of retroactive interference described in Chapter 4: Memory of an event occurring at one time can be interfered with by the memory processing of events occurring at a later time. Of course, retroactive interference was a well-known phenomenon long before Loftus's research. What she did was devise creative new ways of applying this concept to memory testing procedures that were quite different from conventional ones.

Loftus was aware of the possible relevance of her research to legal issues. The way misinformation was presented in her experiments seemed similar to *leading questions*—questions whose form or content implies or assumes something about an event. However, in 1974 Loftus could not have anticipated how, in just a few years, her research was going to become enmeshed with an incredible and appalling series of events involving child sexual abuse, criminal conviction, and imprisonment of the innocent. These events came about in part because of unfounded and inaccurate beliefs about human memory.

Child Sexual Abuse and Recovered Memory

You have probably heard cases involving allegations of childhood sexual abuse and "recovered memory" of abuse in adults. But you may not know the full story. It has been described this way by the psychologists Maggie Bruck and Stephen Ceci:

> In these cases . . . young children claimed that their parents or other adults had sexually abused them. The claims were often

fantastic, involving reports of ritualistic abuse, pornography, multiple perpetrators, and multiple victims. There was little medical evidence of sexual abuse in these cases, nor were there any adult eyewitnesses. Nonetheless, children's often fantastic and uncorroborated claims (e.g., of being forced to eat live babies) were believed by mental health professionals, by police officers, by prosecutors, and by parents. In the ensuing legal proceedings, the major issue before the jury was whether to believe the children. Prosecutors argued that children do not lie about sexual abuse, that the child witnesses' reports were authentic, and that their bizarre and chilling accounts of events—which were well beyond the realm of most preschoolers' knowledge and experience—substantiated the fact that the children had actually been brutally victimized.

The full details of some of these cases are sometimes difficult to believe. In 1994 in Wenatchee, Washington, the 11-year-old foster daughter of a police detective started to relate stories to her father and child care workers of how she and others had been sexually molested. This led to 2,300 charges of child molestation, the arrest of more than 40 people, the conviction of several of them, the separation of children from their parents, and an inestimable amount of human suffering—all on the basis of uncorroborated and unsubstantiated testimony from an 11-year-old and a few other children.

What did the children say they remembered happening to them? Here is a sample, as described by Dorothy Rabinowitz, a writer for the *Wall Street Journal*:

> Among those tried was 31-year-old Sunday school teacher Hanna Sims, accused of raping and molesting children during the group sex adventures at Pastor Roberson's church every Friday and Sunday night—charges of which she was later acquitted. Each accuser offered versions of these festivities, some of them wonderful to contemplate. One child said that he was so tired from having to engage in sexual acts with all the adults at the church on weekends that the pastor would write a note to the school to get him excused on Mondays. Another told of inflatable sex toys kept under the altar, of the pastor lying on-stage crying "Hallelujah!" while attacking young victims during services, of mass child rape (at the church and elsewhere) by men all in black wearing sunglasses and by ladies wielding colored pencils and carrots, and of crowds of adults so organized that everybody got

a turn with each of the children. Anyone who missed his turn with a child would, it was explained, get an extra visit that month.

Equally astounding are cases of *recovered memory* in adults with multiple personality disorder (MPD). MPD is supposed to result from attempts by a person to cope with early traumatic experience, childhood sexual abuse being the most important form of this. The person adopts a new personality (or "dissociates" from his or her real or current personality) and this somehow prevents or reduces stress, conflict, and suffering. This is said to be accompanied by a *functional amnesia* caused by the complete repression (unconsciously motivated forgetting) of memories of the abuse.

An important history of MPD and recovered memory can be found in a *New Yorker* article by Joan Acocella. The article's title is "Hysteria," a term that was in common use in the nineteenth century to describe disordered and abnormal behavior, almost always in women. One of the most widely known cases is described in the book and movie *The Three Faces of Eve*, which deals with a woman who had three distinct personalities. Another book, *Sybil*, which appeared in 1973, raised the stakes in describing a woman who, over the course of an 11-year period of psychotherapy, displayed 16 different personalities: "One could play the piano; another could install sheetrock; two had English accents; two were boys." (Acocella goes on to observe that "Sybil was more like a club than a person.") Sybil's emergent memories, "recovered" with the help of guided imagery, hypnosis, drugs, and relentless questioning by a psychiatrist, read like a movie treatment of a horror-fantasy story. It can't be proved that the popularization of multiple-personality case histories contributed to events such as those in Wenatchee, but the timing is certainly right.

Questionable Beliefs About Memory

Why many claims of abuse and recovered memory have been accepted without corroboration and without physical evidence are questions for students of law and society to ponder. Our concern is with beliefs about memory, what is actually known about memory accuracy, and how this knowledge could or should have influenced the acceptance of such claims. Loftus and others argue that a set of false beliefs about memory and other psychological processes has contributed to the recovered memory issue.

One of these beliefs is that memory is a high-resolution recording device that creates a continuous, detailed copy of experience from which memories can be "played back" with perfect fidelity. This belief is constantly strengthened by movies and television shows that depict people not just remembering something about the past but reexperiencing it in all of its original detail. It is true we have vast visual and auditory long-term memory stores that enable us to recognize objects, faces, scenes, voices, and music, but this does not require belief in a "videorecorder" model of memory.

A second mistaken belief is that there is a memory process known as *repression* (unconsciously motivated forgetting) that is capable of removing memories, even memories of prolonged or repeated experiences, from deliberate or conscious remembering. In Freud's theories, repression was the fundamental defense mechanism, a way of keeping disturbing and anxiety-generating thoughts and memories out of consciousness. In classical Freudian theory, repression was also an unconscious process that reduced the accessibility of information in memory and as such is an example of forgetting as a retrieval failure rather than a trace failure. Note that repression is quite different from *suppression*, which is more like the familiar process of consciously and purposely directing attention away from troubling thoughts or recollections, of not mulling over things (and thereby not strengthening the memories), and of letting time and the ordinary curve of forgetting do their work.

The idea that repressed memory of early abuse is an important cause of psychological and behavioral abnormalities in adulthood is familiar to all of us. We come across it in films, plays, and books such as *The Two Faces of Eve* and *Sybil*. It has been with us since the heyday of psychoanalysis. What is the status of repression as a scientific concept? The brief answer is that trauma-induced repression has not been validated as a fundamental cause of forgetting. A much more forceful statement appears in Richard McNally's book *Remembering Trauma*, a recent and detailed evaluation of the available scientific evidence:

> Events that trigger overwhelming terror are memorable, unless they occur in the first year or two of life. The notion that the mind protects itself by repressing or dissociating memories of trauma, rendering them inaccessible to awareness, is a piece of psychiatric folklore devoid of convincing empirical support.

This is not to say that memory is unaffected by conflict or anxiety, in conscious and possibly unconscious forms. (One of the present authors still winces at the recollection of being unable to remember his prom date's name when introducing her to his mother.) However, repression of the kind assumed to result from childhood sexual abuse and to result in multiple personality disorder has never attained the status of an experimental fact. As many memory researchers have pointed out, the memories of severe abuse and punishment are distinguished by the difficulty people have in *forgetting* the events, not the difficulty in remembering them. There have also been numerous experimental studies of emotion, memory, and the brain (see Chapter 7) but to date none of them have led to identification of the kinds of biologically plausible brain mechanisms that would be required for repression to operate.

Loftus and others suggest that a third contributor to the acceptance of abuse and recovered memory testimony is the failure to understand just how malleable memories might be. According to Bruck and Ceci:

> The defense tried to argue that the children's reports were the product of repeated suggestive interviews by parents, law enforcement officials, social workers, and therapists. However, because there was no direct scientific evidence to support the defense's arguments, and in light of the common belief of that time that children do not lie about sexual abuse, many of these cases eventuated in conviction.

The good news in all of this is that since recovered memory cases started appearing about 25 years ago, a rich experimental science of memory errors and a greatly improved understanding of human memory have come about, and much of the "direct scientific evidence" that Bruck and Ceci say was missing is now available.

The Science of False and Fallible Memory

The experiment by Loftus described at the beginning of this chapter has been followed by dozens of others that have extended the known set of conditions that can produce false memories. Some of this research is based on standard procedures in human memory labs, testing subjects' memories for lists of words, pictures, or events. This research has led to the identification of some basic characteristics of false memories. One such finding is that the effects of misinformation can be long-lasting; they aren't limited to a test at the end of a 15-minute session. Another important finding is that subjects can be very confident about the accuracy of their false memories.

Experimental Creation of False Memory

The classic Loftus experiment consists of presenting information to a research subject, following this with some misinformation, and then testing the subject's memory of the original event or information. But false memories can also be created without any false information being presented or experienced at all, as shown by experiments reported over 40 years ago by James Deese at the University of Virginia. Try it yourself: Read the following list of 15 words at a rate of about one word per second. Then, without looking at the list again, try to recall as many of the words as you can, in any order they come to mind. Keep trying for at least one minute.

Insect

Bug

Fright
Fly
Arachnid
Crawl
Tarantula
Poison
Bite
Creepy
Animal
Ugly
Feelers
Small

If you are like Deese's subjects, the odds are good that you will have recalled the word *spider*. But this word does not occur in the list! What the word list consists of are the 15 most common free associations to the word *spider*, and what Deese was doing in his experiments was exploring the influences of association among words on their recallability.

Many years later Henry Roediger and Kathleen McDermott repeated and extended Deese's experiments and showed how, under certain conditions, people would falsely recall such "critical words" more than 60 percent of the time. One reason for the high rate of false recall in these experiments is fairly obvious: The 15 words in the list are all associates of the critical word *spider*, and by the time the list of words has been read and processed into memory, it is likely that the mental representation (or trace) of the critical word has been activated or primed several times. This makes it difficult for the subject attempting to recall the list to distinguish between presented and nonpresented words.

There are some interesting but not well-understood findings with this simple experimental procedure. One is that false recall of critical words is greater—sometimes much greater—when the list of words is heard rather than seen. When research subjects see Deese's word lists, presented one at a time for 1 second each, the rate of false recall is no more than 30 percent. In contrast, rates of over 60 percent have been reported when the word lists are heard. And just as in Loftus's experiments, subjects can be very confident in the correctness of their false recalls and recognitions, even when they are warned not to recall words that were not in the list.

Creating a False Personal Past

Are the results of these simple experiments relevant to the child sexual abuse and recovered memory issue? What does remembering what you think you saw in a slide show or remembering word lists have to with everyday memory? Do these experiments tell us anything about memory in the real world? There is strong evidence that they do. The basic Loftus experiment has been elaborated and extended in many respects. A particularly important one is that false autobiographical (personal) memories can be created under certain conditions. This goes far beyond modification of the memory of small details of an impersonal event. In one such experiment Loftus and colleagues put together a set of descriptions of actual childhood events for their college student research subjects. Most of these events were actual experiences and were provided to the experimenters by parents and siblings. Some of the events were entirely fictitious but involved plausible and personally meaningful or emotional events, such as having been lost in a shopping mall, spilling champagne at a wedding reception, or being hospitalized. The subjects read the narratives, indicated whether they remembered the events or not, and wrote recollections of the events if they did remember them.

Several important outcomes occurred in such experiments. One was that subjects could recognize a high percentage (75 percent or more) of the true narratives, and this probably represents recall of material after something like a 15-year-long retention interval. The second important result was that about 25 percent of the subjects in these experiments also accepted the fictitious narrative and continued to do so in follow-up testing sessions. Are there limits to the kind of false memory that can be implanted? In some studies it has been shown that the plausibility of the false event can have a strong influence on how readily a fictitious event will be accepted as a real one. Kathy Pezdek demonstrated this in an experiment in which Catholic and Jewish adolescents read narratives which included events that could plausibly have occurred during religious ceremonies as well as implausible events (for example, an event that would be plausible for a Catholic ceremony but implausible for an event during a Jewish ceremony, and vice versa). Both groups of subjects could be induced to accept some false but plausible events but were much less likely to do so for implausible events.

However, other studies along these lines suggest that we don't yet know the limits of false memory formation. In a study by K. Wade and associates (entitled "One Picture Is Worth a Thousand Lies"), subjects were shown a genuine photograph of themselves as children accompanied by a relative, but with the photograph "pasted" digitally into a photograph of a hot-air balloon ride. This was an unlikely event that family members of the subject were sure never happened. At the end of a series of memory-probing interviews, up to one-half of the subjects recalled some or all of this nonevent as having actually happened.

The special power of pictures to induce false recollection has also been demonstrated in an amusing way. Subjects were first shown pictures of advertisements for Disneyland that included the usual cast of characters plus one who would never have appeared there—Bugs Bunny. (He is a Warner Brothers character and property.) By now you won't be surprised to hear that Bugs started showing up in the subjects' recollections of their trips to Disneyland.

False Memory and Personality

The original Loftus experiment and variations on it make a strong case that false personal memories can be created relatively easily and that this set of experimental facts bears directly on evaluation of claims of repression and recovered memory. The same thing can be said about the Deese experimental procedure, which may at first seem to have little to do with the analysis of real-life false memories. But it does because several studies by Richard McNally at Harvard have shown that there are correlations between personality characteristics and the rate of false remembering in the Deese experiment. In one study, three different groups of subjects were tested: people who reported having been abducted by space aliens but were unable to recall the specific events; people who reported having been abducted by aliens and who had recovered memories of it; and a control group of people who said they had never been abducted by space aliens. (We're not making this up!) The results were most interesting. First, the two groups of "alien abductees" made more recall and recognition errors than the control group. Second, all three groups recalled about the same number of actually presented list words, so that the alien groups were not just worse at learning and remembering word lists than the control group. Third, compared to the control group, the space alien victims were more hypnotically susceptible, had more symptoms of depression, and had more schizotypal characteristics. (*Schizotypal* refers generally to having odd beliefs and perceptions.) These results are completely consistent with Acocella's description of the many people diagnosed with multiple personality disorder who have a history of other kinds of psychological disorders as well.

Other studies of personality differences in relation to false memory have shown that IQ scores are negatively correlated with the propensity for false memory: the lower the IQ score, the more the false recollections in memory experiments.

McNally and associates have performed several laboratory-based assessments of claims about repressed and recovered memory. One experiment was intended to test the hypothesis that people claiming recovered memory are prone to forgetting of emotionally negative experiences. He studied three groups of women: those reporting abuse who also had signs of post-traumatic stress disorder (PTSD), women reporting abuse with no PTSD, and women reporting no history of abuse. One of the experimental tasks was called *directed forgetting*, in which subjects study a list of words and are told to either remember or forget each word right after studying it. Some of the words were neutral in emotional content (such as *desktop*) and some were emotionally negative (such as *assault*). One of the main results was that abuse-PTSD subjects recalled as many negative as neutral words, whether they were "remember" or "forget" words. The other subjects, in contrast, recalled more "remember" than "forget" words, neutral or unpleasant. In other words, subjects who were thought to be prone to forget unpleasant experiences in fact had good memories for such experiences.

McNally's findings could be dismissed by arguing that artificial and simplified laboratory tests are not going to show the true effects of abuse and PTSD. But what do you think recovered-memory theorists would say if the research *had* found the expected differences?

Accuracy of Preschooler's Memories

Studies of memory in children have contributed greatly to improved understanding of memory accuracy and memory fallibility. Many of these studies were conducted as experiments in which experiences of different kinds were arranged and observed by the investigator in realistic or naturalistic settings. One reason why these studies are so important for the false memory controversy is that an objective record of the actual events is available. Another reason is that these studies have consistently shown that *the manner in which a child's memory is tested strongly affects the accuracy of the child's recollection.*

The episodic memory system of preschool children is sufficiently developed to allow them to accurately recall experiences over relatively long retention intervals when they are tested in ways that do not bias their responses. This has been shown in numerous studies conducted in real-world settings (for example, a child's memory for events that occurred during a visit to a pediatrician). This fact should not come as a surprise, given what we saw in Chapter 3 about memory formation in newborns and infants, who clearly have the ability to form and retain memories. These abilities continue to develop into childhood and beyond. But preschool children sometimes seem more susceptible than older children, adolescents, and adults to false memory formation and retrieval.

Research by Bruck and Ceci and many others has shown that children readily form and express false memories about peripheral details of experienced events, just as in Loftus's original experiments. But what about more salient, personally meaningful, or emotional events? In one experiment by Bruck and Ceci, children visiting a pediatrician's office for inoculations were exposed to different kinds of statements made by the adults present about how painful their injections had been ("hurt a lot," "didn't hurt at all," or no statement). A week later, they were questioned about how painful the inoculation had been and about how much they had cried. There was no apparent effect of the adults' statements because the children told that their inoculations were very painful and those told that the inoculations did not hurt at all did not differ from the control group in terms of their memories of the level of pain or how much they had cried. As Bruck and Ceci observed, "5-year-old children are not sponges soaking up misinformation from the environment and incorporating it into their reports." The single exposure to biasing information was not enough to influence memory for a salient and emotional event.

However, the creation of false memories started to appear when Bruck and Ceci conducted a series of follow-up suggestive interviews about a year later. During these interviews, some of the children were given additional false information about their original reaction to the inoculations as well as misleading suggestions about events that had not occurred at that time. For example, some children were told that the research assistant had given them their shots. These children were more likely to recall this fictitious event than were children not given this (mis)information. Preschool children's recollections of salient events can be influenced by biased questioning and interviewing techniques.

Probing Memory

What kinds of questioning and interviewing procedures seem likely to promote false recollections in children? The main ones seem to be these:

• Prior beliefs and biases of the interviewers, especially when interviewers are seeking to confirm these beliefs rather than gather information.

• Repeated questioning: A child may respond accurately when first questioned but will start making erroneous responses when questions are asked repeatedly.

• Specific questions: If a child is simply asked "What happened?," false recollection is less likely than when the question posed is specific and leading.

All of these seem to apply equally well to situations in which adults are being treated for childhood sexual abuse and recovered memory. Elizabeth Loftus and Katherine Ketcham argue in their book *The Myth of Repressed Memory* that some therapists see it as their job to "probe" and "dig" for repressed memories over a long series of therapy sessions. They encourage patients to visualize ("guided imagery") and to free associate; they sometimes hypnotize patients; and many therapists are not at all reluctant to make repeated suggestions to patients.

Anyone who knows the psychological science of false memory creation would immediately recognize this as a prescription for the creation of false memories, and anyone who knows something of the early history of psychoanalysis will recognize something else too—history repeating itself. Some scholars argue that Sigmund Freud has a lot to answer for here. Frederick Crewes has studied the early career and writings of Freud most thoroughly. A brief history of it all starts with Freud's announcement in 1895 that certain adult psychological disorders had their origin in sexual molestation (or "seduction" as he put it) during infancy and young childhood and that he had discovered this through lengthy questioning and probing of his patients' memories. The next development was Freud's announcement a few years later that he had discovered that events related to him by these patients had probably never occurred, and were instead the product of their own repressed fantasies. As Crewes observes, Freud failed to take the next step and admit that *he* may have been responsible for creating the fantasies during the original treatment sessions.

False Memory: What Don't We Know?

Memory researchers are devoting a great deal of effort toward identifying the conditions that produce false memories and to integrate this information into memory theory in general. Here are two of the basic questions they're asking.

    1. How does false information affect memory? We have seen how misinformation following an experience can interfere with attempts to recall some aspects of the experience. But does this mean that memory of the original event itself has been "erased"? Isn't it possible that the misinformation instead blocks access to the original (and still-intact) memory? These questions are basically no different many from of the basic questions we considered in Chapter 4 regarding ordinary forgetting.

    Some research seems to indicate that the memory trace itself is *not* compromised by misinformation. Michael McCloskey showed this in experiments that used the basic Loftus procedures in addition to an important new procedure. In the standard part of the experiment (see Table 6-1), subjects watched a video that showed, among other things, a man entering a room and stealing an object. The man was shown carrying a hammer. In the next stage, misinformation was presented to one group while a control group experienced no misleading information. The misleading information was a statement such as "What color were the handles of the pliers the man was carrying?" The subjects were then given

TABLE 6-1 Standard Procedure in McCloskey's False Memory Experiment

Experimental group	View film with *hammer*	Misinformation: *pliers*	Test: *hammer* or *pliers*?	55% correct
Control group	View film with *hammer*	No tool misinformation	Test: *hammer* or *pliers*?	70% correct

the same kind of memory test in which they had to choose which of two objects (*screwdriver* or *hammer*) they had seen earlier. Subjects exposed to the misinformation were correct 55 percent of the time while the control group was correct 70 percent of the time.

So far, so good; this is just Loftus's basic misinformation effect. The critical part of McCloskey's experiment was what happened with a modified procedure (see Table 6-2) in which subjects were treated exactly as the subjects had been in the standard procedure, except that they were given a recognition test that involved selecting between *hammer* and *screwdriver*—that is, a choice between the originally seen object and a new object, *one that had not been mentioned in the misinformation stage*. The rationale for this experiment was that if the misinformation actually degraded the memory trace, there should have been an effect of the misinformation on memory accuracy in this group of subjects as well. The important result was that subjects in this condition of the experiment showed no effect at all of the misinformation on their memory for the original event, recognizing correctly 70 percent of the time in the control group and 70 percent in the

TABLE 6-2 Modified Procedure in McCloskey's Experiment

Experimental group	View film with *hammer*	Misinformation: *pliers*	Test: *hammer* or *screwdriver*?	70% correct
Control group	View film with *hammer*	No tool misinformation	Test: *hammer* or *screwdriver*?	70% correct

experimental (misinformation) group. McCloskey concluded that the impairment of memory observed in the standard misinformation experiment was due to some kind of interference process that occurred during the memory test itself, rather than any degradation or replacing of the memory trace. Loftus herself has replicated McCloskey's experiment and its main results.

McCloskey's experiments have led to intensive attempts to further analyze the cause of the misinformation effect. If misinformation does not alter the original memory trace, why is performance on tests using the Loftus procedure so strongly and reliably affected by misinformation? These research efforts have led to the kind of conclusion that is so common when any moderately complex psychological process is analyzed carefully: The process of misinformation interference with memory is complex. Under some conditions, there is no evidence of an impaired memory trace, just as McCloskey found; under other conditions, there is some evidence of trace impairment or at least alteration of the memory trace. False memory may in some cases be due to *source confusions* (remembering an event as occurring in a context or emanating from a source other than the original one); it may be due to the negative effects of similarity on memory; it may be due to a blending of true and false information.

2. Can you tell true from false memories? Researchers have compared many characteristics of true and false memories in order to answer this question. For example, depending on the details of the experiment involved, they have compared the confidence in the accuracy of true and false memories, the clarity of the memories, and the speed at which memory probes are answered to. Some studies have in fact found that true and false memories differ along these lines, at least on average. In the Loftus and Pezdek studies mentioned earlier, recollections of events that had never occurred contained fewer words than recollections of actual events. Subjects also rated their own false recollections as being somewhat less clear and had less confidence in the accuracy of these memories than they had in recollections of actual events. However, these results are true on average. In any experiment some subjects will sometimes be very confident that their false memory is actually true and report the memory as being quite vivid. At present, there is no generally reliable way of distinguishing between true and false memories.

One new approach to the problem is to measure brain activity during false memory experiments. In an experiment by Brian Gonsalves and Ken Paller, subjects were shown words and asked to "visualize" the object referred to by the word. Some of the words were immediately followed by display of a picture of the object and some were not (Figure 6-1). In a later test subjects had to decide if test words had been shown previously *as pictures* or not. Event-related potentials (ERPs: recordings of electrical activity in cortical regions of the brain) were measured during presentation of the words and pictures as well as during the test. One important finding was that the ERPs for correct test responses (for example, remembering that "apple" had been presented as a picture) were different from those for incorrect responses (a false memory that "hat" had been presented as a picture). Other studies have used magnetic resonance imaging to determine if true and false memories produce different levels of activity in specific brain regions, and they too have yielded evidence that true and false memories can be distinguished to some extent by these kinds of measurements of brain activity, although with considerably less than perfect accuracy.

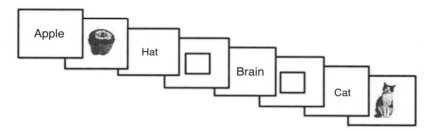

FIGURE 6-1 A stream of object names, pictures of objects, and imagined objects.

False Memory: Summing Up

You will be glad to hear that in the Wenatchee case, all those imprisoned have been released and the children returned to their families. The children (now young adults) who were most responsible for the false claims have retracted all the charges. There have been similar outcomes in other cases, but some of those accused, tried, and sentenced are still in prison.

Two more things need to be said about this issue. First, none of the research considered here and none of the conclusions reached are arguments against the existence of real childhood abuse. We also hope that our description of the psychological characteristics of people claiming to have recovered memories is not taken as a particularly cruel form of "blaming the victim." The important point is that there are reliable empirical facts about false memory that bear in important ways on genuine understanding of what recovered memory and false memory really represent.

Second, a great deal of suffering and wasted time and resources could have been prevented if those people conducting abuse and recovered-memory investigations had adopted the set of principles that the psychologist Robin Dawes argues should be expected of anyone applying psychology to important problems:

- I have studied the problem extensively.
- I have studied alternative hypotheses about the nature, causes, and possible amelioration of the problem.
- I have evaluated these hypotheses in light of the existing evidence.
- I have tentatively concluded that some of these alternative hypotheses are better supported than are others.
- Therefore, I understand something about the problem and how to address it, although new findings may always prove me wrong.

Finally, we want to stress the point that the creation of false memories is not a pathological process. The apparent ease with which existing memories can be modified and false memories created has to be put into the context of the overall function and purpose of the human learning and memory system. The formation of false memories seems to take place in much the same way as the formation of any kind of new memory.

7

Emotional Learning and Memory

Emotions are among the most powerful forces in human behavior. This is particularly true for learning and memory. The carrot and the stick, rewards and punishments, are the most effective ways of training animals and humans. Food rewards and unpleasant stimuli like loud sounds and electric shocks are extremely effective in training animals to learn anything they are capable of performing. Except in the laboratory, such direct rewards and punishments are not common for people. Instead, social approval and disapproval and more remote rewards like money are key to much human learning and behavior. Considerably more is known about the role of negative emotions and their brain systems in learning and memory than is true for positive emotions.

Fear

Fear and anxiety are compelling emotions (see Figure 7-1). Intense anxiety when remembering or reliving traumatic events can exert

FIGURE 7-1 The Scream.

disruptive effects on people for many years. Indeed, the problem is not so much being able to remember such traumas but instead being able to forget them.

One of the most famous (or infamous) experiments in psychology involved frightening a baby. John Watson, a pioneering psychologist, was convinced that most human behavior, including fear, is learned. He set out to demonstrate this in his experiment with "little Albert," together with his wife-to-be, Rosalie Rayner, in 1920. Little Albert was about 10 months old at the time. Luckily films were made of the experiment.

First, Albert was presented with a tame white rat. He petted the rat and showed no fear (see Figure 7-2). When the rat was given again to Albert, Watson stood behind him and made a very loud clanging sound by hitting a steel bar with a hammer. The loud noise greatly disturbed Albert and made him cry. Albert received seven such pairings of white rat and noise, an example of Pavlovian conditioning. Five days later Albert was presented with a variety of objects, including wooden blocks, Watson's actual

FIGURE 7-2 Little Albert being terrified by John Watson.

head, and a white rabbit. Albert showed intense fear of the white rabbit, a somewhat negative reaction to Watson's head, and no negative reaction to the blocks. Watson argued from this experiment that fear is learned, which was certainly true here, and that little Albert had developed a phobia to white furry objects. One wonders if little Albert went through life incapacitated by a fear of white furry creatures. Unfortunately, there was no follow-up study of Albert as an adult.

It seems that most human fears are learned, from the minor (or not so minor) fear of speaking in front of a group to incapacitating fears of horrifying events that can lead to post-traumatic stress disorder (PTSD). But are all fears learned? It seems clear that lower animals have genetically programmed innate fear responses to certain types of stimuli. A classic example is the effect of hawks on chickens. When chickens see a silhouette of a hawk flying overhead they run and hide and show every evidence of fear. But if that same silhouette is flown backward (in which case it resembles a goose) over the chickens, the chickens are not disturbed.

A very simple example of an innate behavior is bug catching by frogs. Frogs are programmed to strike out with their tongues at small buglike objects flying past, but only if they are moving. A frog will starve to death in a field of perfectly edible dead bugs. The decision to strike at bugs is made in the eye itself. The relatively simple neural networks at the back of the eye (retina) activate the brain tongue-strike reflex only when stimulated by moving bug like objects. There are neurons in the frog retina that serve as bug detectors, but they are activated only by small irregularly moving objects. It is not difficult to see how evolution could shape these simple neural circuits in the retina of the frog; they are genetically determined. Frogs that were not good bug catchers didn't survive long enough to reproduce. Judging by the size and shape of their eye sockets and brains, the same appears to be true for dinosaurs. These animals had no need to think about the appearance of the bug or other prey, no need to analyze the stimulus in the brain. The eye does it all. In these primitive animals seeing is indeed in the eye of the beholder.

Evolution took a very different tack in mammals and humans. The human eye codes only the simplest aspects of stimuli, basically the tiny light and dark spots, the pixels, that make up visual scenes. This simple information is projected to the brain, where it is synthesized into perceptions of objects. Decisions about the nature of stimuli, be they bugs or bears, are made in the brain. This was a profoundly important development. We can *learn* to perceive and recognize any visual stimulus because analysis of the visual world is done in the brain rather than the eye. We can learn to perceive letters and words, to read, which could never have happened if our perceptions were formed in the eye, as they are in the frog.

Are Fears Innate or Learned?

The famous psychoanalyst Karl Jung argued that humans do have genetically predetermined responses to certain types of stimuli and situations, what he termed *archetypes*. Snakes are a case in point. Most people are afraid of snakes, even though few of us have ever been injured by one. In the primate laboratory the standard fear-inducing stimulus is a realistic toy snake. For many years it was thought that monkeys' fear of snakes was innate, determined genetically. It turns out that most laboratory monkey colonies were started with monkeys caught in the wild. In the jungle, large snakes prey on monkeys and wild monkeys are terrified of them, presumably because of experience. Infant monkeys born in the laboratory apparently do not show fear of snakes upon first exposure in the absence of their mother. But if the infant is with his mother and the mother shows signs of fear, so will the infant and will do so in the future. It would appear that the fear of snakes by monkeys may at least in part be learned and passed from generation to generation.

When the daughter of one of the authors (RFT) was very young and just beginning to talk, one of her words was "bow-wow" for our dog. We were out on the lawn one day and a garter snake wiggled past. Kathryn smiled and pointed at the snake and said, "bow-wow." She was clearly not afraid (her mother was terrified of snakes and Kathryn quickly learned to become scared too). Interestingly, even though she didn't yet know the word for snake, Kathryn had the right idea; it was a living thing like the dog. This sort of reasonable overgeneralization is very common in toddlers who are just learning to talk.

But the fact remains that most people are afraid of spiders and snakes. Do humans have some sort of genetic predisposition to learn to be afraid of such creatures that in earlier times threatened the survival of our ancestors? If there is a genetic basis for these fears, then genetic variation must exist—some people must be more afraid of spiders and snakes than others, which does seem to be the case. Of course, this argument overlooks the possibility that people have different experiences with spiders and snakes.

Actually, phobias of objects and situations that would have posed serious threats to our early ancestors—snakes, spiders, heights, enclosed spaces, seeing blood, darkness, fire, and strangers—are much more common than phobias about equally dangerous items that our ancient ancestors did not have to deal with, such as stoves, bicycles, knives, and cars.

This notion that humans have predispositions to learn to fear certain types of stimuli has been tested in the laboratory. Volunteers were given fear training by pairing various visual stimuli with unpleasant (but not harmful) electric shocks. The stimuli included snakes, spiders, houses, and flowers. When pictures of these objects were paired with electric shocks, people developed conditioned (that is, learned) fear of the pictures, much as little Albert did with the white furry objects. Here the learned fear responses, such as increased heart rate and sweating of the palms, were emotional in nature. The volunteers (who by this time may have had second thoughts) were then given repeated exposures to the pictures without shock to see how quickly they would forget or extinguish the fear responses. The results were striking—people quickly stopped showing fear of objects like houses and flowers but did not stop showing fear of snakes and spiders. Once learned, these fears could not easily be forgotten.

It seems we do have some sort of predisposition to learn to fear certain types of creatures and to remember these fears. In a sense this would seem to support Jung's notion of genetically programmed "archetypes" in humans. As we saw in our discussion of memory development, newborn humans come into the world with many genetically determined predispositions—for example, to prefer faces to other types of stimuli. We have some beginning idea of how the brain codes faces but as yet no understanding of the brain bases of more complex predispositions or archetypes.

Flashbulb Memories

Older Americans will remember where they were when they learned that President Kennedy had been assassinated. For most of us it was an intensely emotional experience. Ten years after the assassination, *Esquire* magazine asked a number of famous people where they were when they heard the news. Julia Child, a well-known culinary expert of the time, was in her kitchen eating *soupe de poisson*, the actor Tony Randall was in his bathtub, and so on. As *Esquire* said, "Nobody forgets."

It is not just the fact that Kennedy was killed that is remembered. As Roger Brown, a distinguished psychologist at Harvard who coined the term "flashbulb memory" stressed, we don't need to remember this fact; it is recorded many places. What is remarkable about flashbulb memories is that we remember our own circumstances, where we were and what we were doing upon hearing the news. We remember the trivial everyday aspects of life at that moment in time; they are frozen in memory.

But how accurate are such flashbulb memories? A classic study by Ulrich Neisser involved the *Challenger* disaster. In January 1986 the *Challenger* space shuttle blew up just after liftoff. The event was particularly horrible because a schoolteacher was on board and her pupils were watching the lift-off on television. Neisser queried a group of college students the day after the disaster and again two and a half years later. Consider the following two quotes:

> When I first heard about the explosion I was sitting in my freshman dorm room with my roommate and we were watching TV. It came on a news flash and we were both totally shocked. I was really upset and I went upstairs to talk to a friend of mine and then I called my parents.

> I was in my religion class and some people walked in and started talking about [it]. I didn't know any details except that it had exploded and the schoolteacher's students had all been watching which I thought was so sad. Then after class I went to my room and watched the TV program talking about it and I got all the details from that.

The first report is from a college senior two and a half years after the event. The second report is from the same young woman taken the day after the event. Interestingly, at the interview two and a half years after the event, she was absolutely certain her memory was completely accurate, even though it was not.

Several other studies of flashbulb memories have similar findings. There seems to be little relationship between how accurate the memory is and how certain the person is that the memory is in fact accurate. But it does seem to be the case that the more closely a person is involved in a traumatic event, the better it is remembered. Neisser studied people who had been involved in the 1989 earthquake near San Francisco soon after the event and a control group from Atlanta who had heard about the earthquake on television. Several years later, those who had actually experienced the earthquake had much more accurate memories than did those of the Atlanta group.

Suppose we were to ask these two groups what they were doing 35 days after the earthquake. Assuming no special events had occurred on that day, the memories of the people in both groups would be virtually nonexistent. So flashbulb memories are especially well remembered, but distortions can alter these memories over time. The memories become less accurate, but the certainty of their accuracy does not.

A recent study measured college students' memories of the 9/11 tragedy at various times after the event. All students were initially tested the day after 9/11. Then one group was tested at a week, another group at six weeks, and a third group at 32 weeks after 9/11. As a control for nonemotional memories, each student was asked the day after 9/11 to pick an ordinary day between 9/7 and 9/11 and describe the events of that day. Each student picked a day when something ordinary like attending a party or a sporting event or even studying had occurred. In addition to measuring the accuracy of the memories, students were asked to indicate the vividness and emotionally arousing aspects of the memories. The results were surprising. Both 9/11 and everyday memories were remembered well and, most important, *equally* well over the 32-week period; however, the 9/11 memories were reported to be much more vivid and emotional. In this study, at least, flashbulb memories were remembered no better than ordinary memories but were thought to be much more vivid and accurate. But there is a problem with this study. The students rehearsed their memories for both days soon after. If the ordinary day had not been so highlighted in their memories, it might not have been remembered as well as the events of 9/11.

Emotionally charged memories can elicit extreme emotional responses even if the memories are completely false. In a Harvard study, people who claimed to have been abducted by space aliens observed videotapes of their earlier recorded stories of these events. As they watched the videos they showed markedly increased heart rate, sweating, and muscle tension—all signs of extreme emotion, particularly fear and anxiety. Recall our discussion of false memories in Chapter 5.

We think now that flashbulb memories are a milder aspect of learned fear and anxiety, a continuum of emotionally charged memories that range from minor to catastrophic. Even very mild emotional shading can influence memory. People were told a story with visual slides in two different ways. One version seen by one group of people was rather dull, indeed boring, but the version seen by another group of people was emotionally arousing. In both versions a mother and her son visit the father at his workplace and see him perform a task. In the neutral version the father is a garage mechanic working on a damaged car. In the emotional version the father is a surgeon operating on a severely injured accident victim. In one slide the surgeon is shown bending over the patient. Two weeks later the two groups were given a surprise memory test (they were college students). People who had seen the emotional version of the story remembered the basic plot of the story better than those who had seen the boring version.

Fear and the Amygdala

In recent years a great deal has been learned about how the brain operates to generate our experiences of fear and emotional memories. The key actor is a structure called the *amygdala* (Latin for "almond," for it is shaped like one) buried in the depths of the forebrain. Basic studies with animals years ago showed the critical role of the amygdala in fear. Rats are terrified of cats, seemingly an innate fear. Place a cat on top of a laboratory rat's cage and the rat will cower in the corner of the cage in abject fear, a behavior termed *freezing*. By remaining immobile the rat stands a chance of not being seen by the cat, an adaptive behavior shaped by evolution. Suppose we now destroy the amygdala on each side of the rat's brain. This operation does not appear to have much effect on the rat's normal activities. But present the rat with a cat and the now-foolish rat will climb all over the cat. Its innate fear of cats has been abolished. It has also been documented that direct electrical stimulation of the amygdala in humans elicits intense feelings of fear and anxiety.

The amygdala is also critical for learned fears. Place a normal rat in a cage with a grid floor, sound a tone, and then briefly electrify the grid with a current that will feel painful to the rat (but not strong enough to cause any damage to the rat's paws). After even one such experience the rat learns to associate both the cage and the tone with the unpleasant shock; it learns to be afraid. The next time the rat is placed in the cage or hears the tone, it will freeze in fear. But if the amygdala has been destroyed, the rat does not learn to be afraid in this situation.

The amygdala is ideally placed in the brain to serve as the arbiter of fear. It receives information from visual and auditory regions of the brain and information about pain (see Figure 7-3). In turn it acts on lower brain regions concerned with both the emotional and behavioral aspects of fear (see Table 7-1). It can control heart rate and sweating of the palms (in humans) and behaviors like freezing, flight, or fight, about the only behaviors available to deal with immediate threats.

Monkeys with damage to the amygdala also show lack of fear and like rats (and humans) cannot be trained to show fear of situations associated with shock. Perhaps more importantly, they develop severe social problems. Monkeys, like humans, live in social groups, but in monkeys the social hierarchies are much more extreme. One alpha male rules the group, and there is a strict pecking order all the way down to the lowliest monkey, who is picked on by everyone. If the alpha male's amygdala is destroyed, the

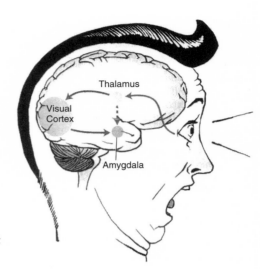

FIGURE 7-3 Visual input to the amygdala.

monkey quickly descends the social scale. Indeed, any monkey in the group whose amygdala has been damaged loses the ability to cope with social interactions and becomes an outcast or may even be killed. The amygdala thus plays an important role in social behavior. How this can occur became clear in recent years when humans with amygdala damage were studied.

There is an extremely rare hereditary disorder called Urbach-

TABLE 7-1 Biological Signs of Fear and Anxiety

Measures of Fear in Animal Models	Human Anxiety
Increased heart rate	Heart pounding
Decreased salivation	Dry mouth
Stomach ulcers	Upset stomach
Respiration change	Increased respiration
Scanning and vigilance	Scanning and vigilance
Increased startle	Jumpiness, easy startle
Urination	Frequent urination
Defecation	Diarrhea
Grooming	Fidgeting
Freezing	Apprehensive expectation— something bad is going to happen

Weithe disease in which, beginning in childhood, the amygdala progressively disintegrates. The brain tissue in the amygdala becomes calcified on each side of the brain, with apparently little damage to other brain structures. One such patient was studied in detail by neurologists Hanna and Antonio Damasio.

At the time of testing Miss A was about 30 years old, and her intelligence tested within the normal range. She was trained in a fear-learning procedure, in which neutral stimuli like colored slides and weak tones were paired with a very loud sound from a boat horn, a procedure much like the one Watson used on little Albert. Learned fear was determined by measuring the increase in skin conductance in the palm of the hand. The skin on the palm conducts electricity much better when the sweat glands are active. This is measured by applying a weak current to the palm, so weak that the person cannot feel it. Increased palm sweating (skin conductance) is a good measure of emotional arousal and fear.

Miss A and the control subjects were given a number of training trials pairing the neutral colored slides and weak tones with the boat horn. Both the control subjects and Miss A showed the same large increase in skin conductance (palm sweating) in response to the boat horn alone, as would the reader, for it is very startling. After training, the control subjects learned to give the same increase in skin conductance to the neutral stimulus, an example of Pavlovian conditioning. But Miss A showed no increased response at all to the neutral stimuli—no sign of learned fear. Unlike little Albert and normal adults, she could not be conditioned to show or experience fear.

Unlike monkeys with amygdala lesions, Miss A is more or less able to cope with life. She does have a history of inadequate social decision making and failure to maintain employment or marital relationships and depends on welfare, but she is not a social outcast and is a rather talented artist. Perhaps the most surprising aspect of Miss A is her complete inability to identify facial expressions of fear in others. Not only can she not learn to be afraid, she cannot perceive fear in others.

Miss A and normal control people were tested on their ability to identify pictures of faces displaying basic emotions: happiness, surprise, fear, anger, disgust, and sadness. The emotions displayed in the pictures of faces were all easily and correctly identified by the normal subjects. Astonishingly, Miss A correctly identified all the emotional expressions except fear. But she had no trouble identifying the fearful faces as faces; she just couldn't tell if they were showing fear. Indeed, she is able to draw pictures of faces showing all the emotional expressions except fear, as shown in drawings she made (see Figure 7-4).

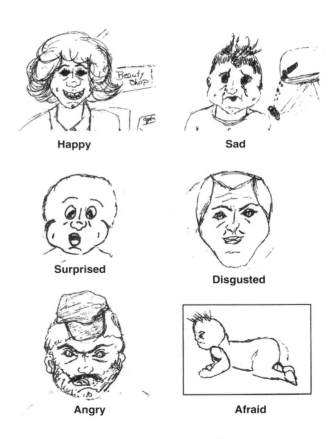

FIGURE 7-4 *Miss A could draw faces expressing all emotions except fear.*

Human brain imaging studies also show that the amygdala is selectively activated by viewing faces showing fear. We think that the degree of response to the fearful faces may in part be genetic. People with one variant of a particular gene show greater activation of the amygdala than those without this gene variant. It appears that some 70 percent of Europeans and North Americans have the gene variant. Perhaps these people tend to be more fearful and less likely to get themselves into threatening or dangerous situations. They may be more "law-abiding."

The selective role of the amygdala in fear would seem to make sense. It is a relatively old structure in the evolution of the brain. Fear is perhaps the most important emotion for survival of the individual in the primitive world. It was very important to detect cues to potentially dangerous situations. If you can't learn to be afraid of man eaters, animal or human, you won't survive. This would account for the key role of the amygdala for successful social behavior in monkeys. If you can't learn to be afraid of the alpha male or if you are the alpha male and can't detect fear in others, you are in trouble.

How does the visual information reach the amygdala? There are two visual systems in the brain, a primary system that leads to our awareness of seeing and a more ancient system that does not have access to awareness but does have access to the amygdala. We described the primary system and how it develops when we looked at critical periods in development (in Chapter 3). Information from the eye is sent (via the thalamus) to the primary visual area of the cerebral cortex and on to higher cortical areas. This is the system that allows us to see and identify objects in detail and be aware of doing so. If the primary visual cortex is destroyed, it causes complete blindness. Patients with such brain damage insist they are completely blind; they cannot "see" anything. But in fact they have "blindsight." From Chapter 2 you may recall that such patients could accurately point to a source of light even though they claimed they could not see it. The pointing behavior is guided by a much more ancient visual system that does not have access to awareness.

This ancient visual system is well developed in lower animals such as the frog. Information from the eyes is projected to a visual structure in the lower brain, the visual midbrain. The frog does not have much cerebral cortex; its highest visual brain is the visual midbrain. This is the structure that guides the frog to strike its tongue accurately at a moving bug, much as our "blind" patient points accurately to the spot of light.

This ancient visual system has projections to the thalamus and the amygdala. Brain imaging studies show that the amygdala can be activated by fearful faces even if the person is completely unaware of seeing the faces at all, let alone identifying them as fearful (see Figure 7-5). The amygdala controls emotional re-

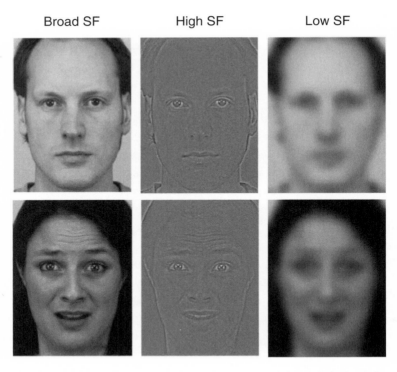

Broad SF   High SF   Low SF

FIGURE 7-5 Photographs of normal (above) and fearful (below) faces with normal (broad) spatial frequencies (left), high spatial frequencies (middle), and low spatial frequencies (right). Broad and low pictures of fear "speak" directly to the amygdala.

sponses like palm sweating, as we saw earlier, which can occur in response to fearful stimuli even if the person is unaware. Shades of subliminal perception! The advertising industry is well aware of this fact.

In higher animals and humans, the primary visual system involves the visual cortex and the cortical face area (fusiform gyrus) responsible for detail vision of faces. However, the ancient midbrain visual system responds to much fuzzier pictures of faces, particularly fearful faces. A neutral face and a fearful face are shown in the left panel of Figure 7-5. The middle panel shows just the detailed outlines of the faces, and the right panel shows the fuzzy versions. Brain imaging indicates that the cortical face area responds better to the left and middle pictures, regardless of expression. On the other hand, the amygdala response to the fearful face is much greater for the intact face on the left and the fuzzy face on the right than to the detailed outlines in the middle panel.

Photography buffs will probably realize that the middle panel shows only higher spatial frequencies of the photographs on the left and that the right panel shows only lower spatial frequencies of the photographs. The key point here is that the amygdala can be activated by rapid and crude representations of potentially dangerous situations from the ancient midbrain visual system. This can occur more rapidly than the highly evolved cortical visual system that is so adept at perceiving details. The difference is only on the order of milliseconds (there are 1,000 milliseconds in a second), but this can be a huge advantage when responding to danger. The amygdala is on guard for potential threats and can rapidly trigger defensive actions. Note that in the classic painting of *The Scream* by Edvard Munch, shown in Figure 7-1, lower spatial frequencies predominate. Perhaps one reason this is such a powerful painting is that it speaks directly to the amygdala.

To return to Miss A, in another study she was compared to patients with severe amnesia, due to a different type of brain injury of the hippocampus who are more or less unable to remember their own experiences, as was true of patient HM (see Chapter 6). Miss A and the amnestics were given the test of facial expressions of emotions. Again, Miss A was able to identify all the expressions except fear. On the other hand, the patients with amnesia correctly identified all the emotional expressions, including fear. After the testing was finished, Miss A and the amnestics were given a quiz to see how much they remembered about the faces. The amnestic patients were not able to remember much at all, but Miss A's memory was excellent. Indeed, she can verbally describe her cognitive knowledge of what the word "fear" means; she just can't experience it or perceive it in others. This raises a question: Are our *perceptions* of fearful faces due more to learning or more to innate genetic factors?

There are two different aspects to learned fears. One is the experience of being afraid, which involves the amygdala. Miss A is unable to experience fear. The other aspect is cognitive understanding of the meaning of fear. Miss A understands what the word "fear" means perfectly well. Amnestic patients also understand what the word means, but they can't remember the fearful experience. Amnesia of the sort so extreme in HM does not involve damage to the amygdala but rather damage to the hippocampus and related structures.

So when we experience a situation that is fearful, both the amygdalar and hippocampal brain systems become engaged. The same is true for the lowly rat. When it is shocked in a distinctive cage and becomes afraid of the cage, both the hippocampus and the amygdala are necessary for the animal to remember the fear. Damage to either structure, particularly soon after the fearful exposure, will abolish the fear memory.

Human brain imaging studies of normal people being shown faces expressing various emotions seem to indicate that different emotions involve different brain areas. As we noted, the amygdala is consistently activated when normal people view faces expressing fear. A perception of sadness involves the amygdala to some degree and a cortical region of the temporal lobe, and a perception of anger activates two frontal cortical regions (orbitofrontal and anterior cingulate). It seems that the amygdala is also sensitive to the direction of gaze. If the role of the amygdala is to detect threat of danger, it should respond more to a fearful expression directed to the subject rather than away, but the opposite might be true for anger. In one study, at least, the amygdala was activated much more by angry faces looking away from the subject than if looking directly at the subject.

Perception of disgust is particularly interesting. It selectively activates the striatum (also called the basal ganglia). This structure is severely damaged in some brain disorders, including Parkinson's disease and Huntington's disease. The latter is a progressive and severe genetic disorder leading ultimately to death. It is due to a single dominant abnormal gene (see Chapter 5). The sufferer typically does not show any symptoms until about age 40. For this reason a person with the abnormal gene may not know he has it unless he has been tested for it. People who have the abnormal gene but who have not yet exhibited any symptoms are termed *carriers*. Huntington's patients appear to be selectively unable to recognize facial expressions of disgust. Remarkably, even carriers also seem to be unable to recognize the expression of disgust. These rather surprising discoveries suggest that different emotions have very different evolutionary histories, as do the brain regions that seem to code them.

Interestingly, negative emotions display much more consistent patterns of brain activation than positive emotions. Results of brain imaging studies of people viewing happy faces have been inconsistent. Light was shed on this question in a study at Stanford University. People were rated on their degree of extroversion and then imaged while viewing happy faces. People who were rated high on extroversion showed much greater activation of the amygdala than did less extroverted individuals. The relationship of this finding to the well-established role of the amygdala in fear remains to be determined.

The amygdala indeed plays a special role in emotional memories. In a study done by Larry Cahill, James McGaugh, and colleagues at the University of California, Irvine, normal adults were exposed to a video composed of neutral film clips and one composed of emotionally arousing clips (animal mutilations and violent crimes). Brain images were taken during the viewing of the videos. Three weeks later the subjects were given memory quizzes. They remembered many more details of the emotional films, as expected. Importantly, there was a high correlation (positive relationship) between the amount of activation in the amygdala and the amount of material remembered from the emotional video but no correlation for the neutral video.

Studies like this one raise the possibility that the amygdala is the key structure in flashbulb memories. But what are the mechanisms and where are the memories stored? We must take a brief look at studies of emotional memory storage in animals. The basic association between neutral stimuli and fear-inducing stimuli, and the expression of this learned fear, as in freezing in rats and increased heart rate, sweating, and muscle tension in humans, critically involves the amygdala, as we saw earlier. But what about all the memories associated with fearful events?

Hormonal Effects on Fearful Memories

When animals and humans are emotionally stressed and experience fear, a well-understood series of hormonal events occur. The end result is release by the adrenal gland of adrenaline, the "arousal" hormone, and "corticosterone," the stress hormone. These hormones exert actions on the brain. We focus here on adrenaline. If rats are given fear training using electric shock, there is a marked rise in adrenaline following the experience. Later, where the rats are tested for their memory of the event, they typically show excellent memory. Indeed, the amount of increase in adrenaline release at training is directly related to the strength of the later memory.

In an important series of studies, James McGaugh and his colleagues showed that if rats were trained in a simple fear task using a moderately intense shock and were injected with adrenaline (into the bloodstream) after the learning experience, the rats later remembered the experience much better than control animals that received injections of a neutral salt solution. Since the drugs are injected after the learning experience, they can't act directly on the experience. Similarly, since they are injected well before the memory test, they can't act on the performance of the animals at the time of the test. The drug must somehow be acting on the brain to enhance or "stamp in" the memory of the initial experience.

This phenomenon, termed *memory consolidation*, is very general. As we saw earlier, emotions that occur in association with traumatic events can markedly enhance later memories of the events, as in flashbulb memories. The increased release and actions of the hormones occur well after the emotional event; they have a much slower time course than the actual experience of the events.

To return to McGaugh's studies, he and his colleagues were able to show that the actions of adrenaline and other memory enhancers are on the amygdala. There is a very high concentration of one type of adrenaline receptor in the amygdala, termed the *beta-adrenergic receptor*, which we will refer to as the beta A receptor. Receptors in the brain are tiny structures on the surface of nerve cells made of proteins. Only one kind of brain chemical or hormone can act as a given kind of receptor—the chemical molecule fits into the receptor like a key in a lock and causes certain reactions in the nerve cells. A particular hormone like adrenaline acts on several different types of receptors, each causing a different action on the neuron. Here we focus on the beta A receptor acted on by adrenaline on neurons in the amygdala.

If the brain form of adrenaline is injected directly into the amygdala after fear training in rats, the same enhanced consolidation of memory occurs as with injections of adrenaline into the bloodstream. Further, if a drug is injected into the amygdala that blocks the beta A receptors, so that the brain form of adrenaline can no longer act on this receptor in the amygdala, both the memory-enhancing effects of adrenaline injected into the bloodstream and the similar effects of direct injections into the amygdala are blocked. The blocking drug's molecules also fit into the beta A receptors, much like adrenaline, and remain on the receptors, so adrenaline can't attach to them. But when the block-ing drugs attach to the receptors, the receptors do not exert any actions on the neurons.

In a dramatic study, Cahill and McGaugh blocked the beta A adrenaline receptors in one group of human volunteers by inject-ing a beta A receptor blocking agent (called propranolol) into the bloodstream when the volunteers were experiencing a very emo-tional story or a neutral story. Control volunteers received an in-jection of an inactive substance (placebo). The two stories, accompanied by the same set of slides, are shown in Box 7-1. The placebo control group remembered details of the emotional part of the story much better than the corresponding part of the neu-tral story. But the subjects given the beta A blocker did not. They remembered both versions of the story at the same level as the placebo group remembered the neutral story. There was no memory enhancement of the emotional part of the story when the beta A receptors were blocked, presumably in the amygdala, judging by the animal studies.

These experiments provide us with a rather compelling expla-nation of the brain mechanisms involved in flashbulb memories. Following emotional experiences there is an increase in release of arousal and stress hormones that act on the amygdala to enhance the storage of memories in the amygdala and at various other places in the brain.

As a further validation of this idea, Cahill and McGaugh had the opportunity to study a patient in Germany suffering from Urbach-Weithe disease, which destroys the amygdala. They gave the German translation of the emotional story shown in Box 7-1 to him and also to normal individuals. The control people showed the expected memory enhancement of the emotional part of this story, but the patient did not.

Anxiety

We have all experienced feelings and symptoms of anxiety in this "age of anxiety." Indeed, we could not function adequately in our complex contemporary society without feelings of anxiety. But taken to the extreme, such feelings become anxiety disorders. In psychiatry there are three general categories of anxiety disorders: phobias, post-traumatic stress disorders (PTSD), and anxiety states. All three have similar emotional-physiological symptoms, which closely resemble the symptoms exhibited by animals trained in conditioned fear (Table 7-1). Indeed, much of what we have said about learned fear applies to human anxiety. Phobias and PTSD clearly involve learning. However, the picture is not so clear in anxiety states.

Phobias

Phobias, ranging from fear of crowds to fears of specific objects and animals, are thought to be due to traumatic learning experiences in childhood, examples of Pavlovian conditioning. Consider the following case history:

> A young woman developed during her childhood a severe phobia of running water. She was unable to give any explanation of her disorder which persisted without improvement from approximately her seventh to her twentieth year. Her fear of splashing sounds was especially intense. For instance, it was necessary for her to be in a distant part of the house when the bathtub was being filled for her bath, and during the early years it often required the combined efforts of three members of the family to secure a satisfactory washing. She always struggled violently and screamed. During one school session a drinking-fountain was in the hall outside her classroom. If the children made much noise drinking, she became very frightened, actually fainting on one occasion. When she rode on trains, it was necessary to keep the shade down so that she might not see the streams over which the train passed. (When she was 20 years old an aunt visited her and, upon hearing of her condition responded: "I have never told." This provoked a recall of the following events that took place when she was seven years of age.) The mother, the aunt, and the little girl . . . had gone on a picnic. Late in the afternoon, the mother decided to return home but the child insisted on being permitted to stay for a while longer with her aunt. This was promptly arranged on the child's promise to be strictly obedient and the two friends (aunt and niece) went into the woods for a walk. A short time later the little girl, neglecting her agree-

---

BOX 7-1 Narratives Accompanying Slide Presentation

Slide	Neutral Version	Arousal Version
1	A mother and her son are leaving home in the morning.	A mother and her son are leaving home in the morning.
2	She is taking him to visit his father's workplace.	She is taking him to visit his father's workplace.
3	The father is a laboratory technician at Victory Memorial Hospital.	The father is a laboratory technician at Victory Memorial Hospital.
4	They check before crossing a busy road.	They check before crossing a busy road.
5	While walking along, the boy sees some wrecked cars in a junk yard, which he finds interesting.	While crossing the road, the boy is caught in a terrible accident, which critically injures him.
6	At the hospital, the staff are preparing for a practice disaster drill, which the boy will watch.	At the hospital, the staff prepare the emergency room, to which the boy is rushed.

---

ment, ran off alone. When she was finally found she was lying wedged among the rocks of a small stream with a waterfall pouring down over her head. She was screaming with terror. They proceeded immediately to a farm house where the wet clothes were dried, but, even after this the child continued to express great alarm lest her mother should learn of her disobedience. However, her aunt reassured her with the promise "I will never tell. . . ."

This case is unusual in one regard—the traumatic event was identified. In many cases of specific phobias the initial learning experience cannot be identified. This is not so much a case of

Slide Neutral Version	Arousal Version
7 An image from a brain scan machine used in the drill attracts the boy's interest.	An image from a brain scan machine used in a trauma situation shows severe bleeding in the boy's brain.
8 All morning long a surgical team practiced the disaster drill procedures.	All morning long a surgical team struggled to save the boy's life.
9 Makeup artists were able to create realistic-looking injuries on actors for the drill.	Specialized surgeons were able to reattach the boy's severed feet.
10 After the drill, while the father watched the boy, the mother left to phone her other child's preschool.	After the surgery, while the father stayed with the boy, the mother left to phone her other child's preschool.
11 Running a little late, she phones the preschool to tell them she will soon pick up her child.	Feeling distraught, she phones the preschool to tell them she will soon pick up her child.
12 Heading to pick up her child, she hails a taxi at the number nine bus stop.	Heading to pick up her child, she hails a taxi at the number nine bus stop.

repression as it is interference by repeated experiences. How do you remember the first time you were scared by a snake (or running water) if it has happened many times?

Since phobias are in large part learned, they should be treatable by applying what is known about learning, particularly forgetting. Indeed, successful treatments of specific phobias involve procedures to induce extinction, to reduce and "extinguish" Pavlovian conditioned responses. When a rat is trained to fear by pairing a tone with a shock, the tone fear-freezing response is extinguished by presenting the tone over and over again with no shock. Eventually, the animal stops freezing. In treating humans for phobias, this process of extinction is called *desensitization*. But conditioned fear in humans to certain phobic objects like snakes does not extinguish readily.

Albert Bandura at Stanford University has developed procedures for extinguishing phobias that make use of desensitization but also emphasize the person's cognitive awareness of feelings. In a classic study he compared simple desensitization by repeatedly exposing the "clients" (suffering from snake phobias) to desensitization together with modeling (acting out) the behavior only by the therapist and by the therapist and the client, with a focus on personal feelings of efficacy.

> We conducted a series of experiments in which severe phobics received different types of treatments designed to raise their sense of personal efficacy. We selected adults who suffered from severe snake phobias. Virtually all had abandoned outdoor recreational activities. Some could not pursue their vocational work satisfactorily. The most pervasive effect of the phobia was thought-induced distress. Most of the participants were obsessed with reptiles, especially during the spring and summer, frequently dreaming of snake pits and being encircled or pursued by menacing serpents.

> To begin, we asked our clients to perform as many tasks as they could with a snake—looking at it caged, touching it, holding it, and so on. For each task, they rated their perceived self-efficacy, which was extremely low. Indeed, may clients refused to enter the room, let alone interact with the snake.

> During the treatment phase, one group of clients was aided through participant modeling to engage in progressively bolder interactions with a snake until they had mastered their fear. A second group merely observed the therapist modeling the same activities with the snake, relying solely on vicarious experience to alter their efficacy expectations.

> After their respective treatments, we measured the clients' perceived self-efficacy and behavior toward different types of snakes. We found that treatment based on performance mastery produces higher, more generalized, and stronger efficacy expectations than treatment based on vicarious experience alone. In both treatments, behavior corresponds closely to self-perceived

efficacy. The higher the sense of personal efficacy, the greater were the performance attainments.

Post-Traumatic Stress Disorder

This kind of anxiety stands in contrast to phobias in that the traumatic experience is too well remembered and cannot easily be forgotten:

Jim Griggs is a twenty-six year old married Vietnam veteran recently laid off from a job he had held for three years. He was admitted to the hospital for severe symptoms of anxiety, which began after he was laid off at work and found himself at home watching reports of the fall of South Vietnam on TV. When asked what was wrong with him, he replied, "I don't know. I just can't seem to control my feelings. I'm scared all the time by my memories." Jim described himself as well adjusted and outgoing prior to his service in Vietnam. He was active in sports during high school. He was attending college part-time and working part-time to pay his way when he was drafted to serve in Vietnam. Although he found killing to be repulsive initially, he gradually learned to tolerate it and to rationalize it. He had several experiences that he found particularly painful and troubling. One of these occurred when he was ambushed by a Vietnamese guerrilla, found his gun had jammed, and was forced to kill his enemy by bludgeoning him over the head repeatedly. Many years later he could still hear the "gook's" screams. Another extremely painful incident occurred when his closest friend was killed by mortar fire. Since they were lying side by side, the friend's blood spattered all over the patient.

Although he had some difficulty adjusting during the first year after his return from Vietnam, drifting aimlessly around the country in *Easy Rider* fashion and finding it difficult to focus his interests or energies, he eventually settled down, obtained a steady job, and married. He was making plans to return to college at the time he was laid off. At home with time on his hands, watching the fall of Vietnam on TV, he began to experience unwanted intrusive recollections of his own Vietnam experiences. In particular, he was troubled by the memory of the "gook" he had killed and the death of his friend. He found himself ruminating about all the people who were killed or injured and wondering what the purpose of it all had been. He began to experience nightmares, during which he relived the moments when he himself was almost injured. During one nightmare, he "dived for cover" out of bed and sustained a hairline fracture of the humerus (arm). Another time he was riding his bike on a path through tall grass and weeds, which suddenly reminded him of the terrain in Vietnam, prompting him to dive off the bike for cover, and causing several lacerations to his arms and legs when he hit the ground. He also became increasingly irritable with his wife, and was admitted to the hospital because of her concern about his behavior.

Jim's symptoms are common in PTSD: reliving, reexperiencing, and flashback episodes. In flashbacks the reliving may be so intense that the person is, in his mind, back in the stressful episode. In Jim's case a combination of antianxiety drugs and desensitization training, repeatedly recalling and reliving his traumatic experiences in Vietnam, proved helpful.

It has become standard practice in the United States to provide grief counseling to people immediately after extremely traumatic events such as high school shootings. In the wake of the terrorist attacks at the World Trade Center on 9/11/01, more than 9,000 counselors and therapists descended on New York City to offer aid and comfort to families and surviving victims. These therapists believed that many New Yorkers were at high risk of developing PTSD.

The most widely used method to counter the effects of a trauma is psychological debriefing, talking about the traumatic events as soon as possible. You may be surprised to learn that what evidence exists suggests that such interventions are of no help at all and may even interfere with normal recovery. People vary widely in their vulnerability to trauma. The vast majority of trauma survivors do not develop PTSD.

A remarkable new treatment for PTSD has been developed, based on basic research. We saw earlier that the drug propranolol which blocks the beta A receptor prevents the enhancement of memory of emotional or traumatic stories. A group in the psychiatry department at Harvard Medical School used this drug to treat PTSD. The drug (or a placebo) was administered to a large group of patients in the emergency room who had just experienced a traumatic event. The patients who received the drug showed a marked reduction in PTSD symptoms compared to those who received the placebo!

Anxiety States

Two major forms of anxiety states are panic attacks and generalized anxiety. With panic disorder, a person suffers sudden and terrifying attacks of fear that are episodic and occur unpredictably. The symptoms of a panic attack are dilated pupils, flushed face, perspiring skin, rapid heartbeat, feelings of nausea, desire to urinate, choking, dizziness, and a sense of impending death (see Table 7-1). Generalized anxiety disorder is a persistent feeling of fear and anxiety not associated with any particular event or stimulus.

Recent evidence suggests that both panic attacks and generalized anxiety have a significant genetic basis. Interviews of relatives of anxious patients in clinical studies indicated that up to 40 percent of the relatives also have had anxiety neurosis. It is tempting to postulate that anxiety states are learned: A person who grows up in a neurotic family seems likely to resemble the rest of the family in mental disposition. However, studies of twins show that if one identical twin has anxiety neurosis, the chances are greater than 30 percent that the other will too, whereas the chances of both twins having the disorder are only about 5 percent if they are not identical. Isolated cases in which one identical twin was adopted away from the family and the twins were raised separately show the same general result. But environmental factors (learning) also must be important.

In the mid-1930s dye compounds attracted the attention of chemists at the pharmaceutical company Hoffman-La Roche. The chemists were attempting to make a particular group of dye compounds biologically active. Unfortunately, the compounds they made did not seem to have any biological activity. The compounds were put aside, as were others. By 1957 the laboratory benches had become so crowded that a cleanup had to be instituted. As the chemists were throwing out various drugs and other compounds, one drug was submitted for pharmacological tests. It had extraordinary calming and muscle relaxant effects in animals. When the chemists analyzed the structure of the drug, it turned out to be a rather different compound than they thought they had made. It was, in fact, the substance that came to be known as Librium.

The discovery of Librium and other minor tranquilizing (antianxiety) drugs provided an intriguing new approach to understanding the anxiety neuroses. These drugs are all closely chemically related and are a class of compounds called the benzodiazepines (BDZ).

Antianxiety drugs are the treatment of choice for panic attacks and anxiety. In proper therapeutic doses they are relatively safe, have few side effects, and are not particularly addictive. In higher doses they are addictive, both in terms of tolerance that is built up (increasingly high doses are required to produce the same effect) and the variety of symptoms that follow withdrawal, including anxiety and emotional distress, nausea and headaches, and even death. Antianxiety drugs have also become drugs of abuse.

Antianxiety drugs ease anxiety and panic attacks. They are of little help in treating schizophrenia, even for treating the anxiety symptoms associated with the disease, and they may even make depression worse. Interestingly, they are not particularly helpful in the treatment of specific phobias, although they may be helpful in PTSD. These antianxiety drugs act very specifically on the brain. They enhance inhibitory processes in neurons, leading to a general decrease in brain activity.

There are many different chemical forms of BDZs. Indeed, the tranquilizer of choice varies from year to year. They all act to enhance inhibition of neurons in the brain. Hence, it might be expected that they can impair memory formation and indeed they do. Specifically, they interfere with long-term encoding of new episodic information—memories of our own experiences—but not with already established memories. They have little effect on memories for general knowledge (semantic memory) or on nondeclarative types of memory. Interestingly, the amnestic effect is not correlated directly with the sedative effects of these drugs.

Some BDZs have particularly powerful effects on episodic memory formation. Rohypnol, sometimes referred to as the "date rape drug" is a case in point. It induces drowsiness and sleep and is powerfully amnestic. Furthermore, it is water soluble, colorless, odorless, and tasteless. It can be slipped into a drink and afterwards the victim may be completely unable to remember anything that has occurred, including sexual assault. A number of such unfortunate cases have been reported. Fortunately, the drug is now illegal.

The Brain Reward System

Identification of the "reward system" in the brain is one of the most important findings yet about the brain and learning. It was discovered by a brilliant psychologist, James Olds, at the beginning of his career when he was working as a postdoctoral fellow in the laboratory of Donald Hebb, a pioneer in the study of the brain and memory, in Montreal. As Olds said, he arrived at Hebb's laboratory, only to be given a key to a storage area in the basement where pieces of wood and old equipment were kept. He had the impression Hebb would return a few months later to see what he might have discovered.

In a series of experiments, Olds and a graduate student, Peter Milner, discovered the brain reward system. They implanted small electrodes in different regions of the brains of rats under anesthesia and later, when the animals were awake, delivered mild electric shocks to the brains. When the electrodes were in certain places in the brain, the rats liked it. If they hooked up a lever so that a rat could deliver a shock to its own brain, the rat would press the lever as fast as it could to get those "fixes" (shocks). In a particularly "hot" spot in the brain, the rat would press the lever as much as 2,000 times in an hour! Electrodes have been implanted in this same brain system in a few human patients. They find it difficult to describe the sensations, except that the brain stimulus feels intensely pleasurable and they want more of it.

The brain reward system is a neuronal pathway from neurons in the brain stem that projects to forebrain structures, particularly the prefrontal area of the cerebral cortex and a structure called the *nucleus accumbens* in the brain (see Figure 7-6). The neurons in this reward pathway use dopamine as their chemical synaptic transmitter; that is, they release dopamine to act on neurons in the forebrain. Electrical stimulation of this pathway in animals by the experimenter to elicit pleasure causes the release of dopamine on neurons in the cortex and accumbens.

Stimulation of this brain reward system in rats serves as a powerful reinforcement for learning. Such brain stimulation can be even more effective than food or water in teaching the animals any particular task. They will learn and do almost anything to get their electrical brain fix.

This reward system in the brain is, of course, strongly activated by normal rewards. Thus, food for a hungry rat, water if thirsty, or a sex partner causes marked release of dopamine from the brain reward pathway on to neurons in the accumbens. The great unknown in this story of reward learning is how the associations between neutral stimuli and situations and appropriate behaviors become greatly strengthened with activation of the brain reward system, that is, how reward learning occurs. This is an important question for future research since so much of the learning people do involves rewards.

Drug Abuse

A remarkable fact about addictive drugs is that, to the extent studied, they all strongly activate this brain reward system. Cocaine and amphetamines (speed, crack) act primarily on this brain system but also on the amygdala. The opiates (morphine and heroine) act on this brain reward system, on the amygdala, and on other brain systems. Alcohol acts on this brain reward system and on a number of other brain systems as well.

Cocaine and Amphetamines

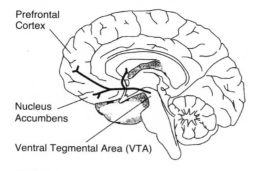

Opiates

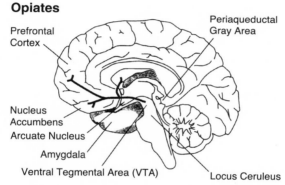

Alcohol

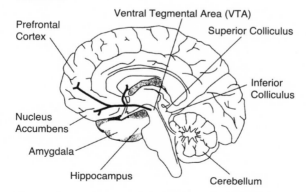

FIGURE 7-6 *Brain substrates activated by addicting drugs.*

There are three major aspects to drug addiction: addiction it-self, tolerance, and withdrawal. *Addiction* is really a behavioral term—the user seeks out and takes a substance with increasing frequency. Cravings, which increase after repeated use, are a large part of the reason for this behavior. We use the term *tolerance* to mean that increasing doses of the drug must be taken to achieve the desired effect. Finally, *withdrawal* refers to the very unpleas-ant symptoms, including intense cravings, that develop when the user stops taking the substance.

These phenomena of drug addiction profoundly involve learn-ing. Behavioral tolerance is a good example. Substantial tolerance develops with repeated use of heroin. In rats, tolerance is so ex-treme that a dose that would kill a rat new to the drug is easily tolerated by addicted rats (yes, rats can become just as addicted as people). Furthermore, much of this tolerance is actually learned to be associated with the environment where the drug is given. A dose of heroin that is safe for the addicted rat in the environment where the drug normally is given will kill the same rat in a differ-ent environment. This phenomenon of learned tolerance may ac-count for some human overdose deaths—for example, if an addict takes the high dose to which he has become tolerant in a different and unusual environment.

Craving is learned. It appears that the memories relating to the effects of the drug are transformed into craving for the drug in the amygdala. Imagine a drug user who usually buys cocaine at a particular subway stop. This stop is normally a neutral part of the environment. But it becomes linked in the mind of the user to the positive rewarding effects of cocaine. Even long after rehabilita-tion, sight of this subway stop can bring on a powerful craving for cocaine. The same is true for nicotine addiction. Circumstances where the smoker usually lit up, like with the first cup of coffee in the morning, can elicit cravings for cigarettes a year after quit-ting. In animal studies, lesions of the amygdala appear to block cravings. Recall that the amygdala is critically involved in learned fear and anxiety, feelings not too different from the unpleasant aspects of cravings experienced by the addict.

Alan Leshner, then director of the National Institute of Drug Abuse, stresses the fact that drug addiction is a disease:

> Scientific advances over the past 20 years have shown that drug addiction is a chronic, relapsing disease that results from prolonged effects of drugs on the brain. . . . Recognizing addiction as a brain disorder characterized by . . . compulsive drug seeking and use can impact society's overall health and social policy strategies and help diminish the health and social costs associated with drug abuse and addictions.

The addict is not simply a weak or bad person, but rather a person with a brain disease.

EMOTIONS AND ETHICS

Many people believe that science has no place in moral and ethical matters. Indeed, many moral philosophers and ethicists maintain that moral decisions must be based on pure reason. However, it seems obvious that the moral and ethical views that people hold are learned. Factors that underlie moral values include brain systems involved in learned feelings and emotions. Indeed, recent imaging studies of brain regions involved in emotions seem to cast light on some aspects of moral decisions.

Consider the following moral dilemma:

> You see a streetcar careening out of control, headed toward the edge of a cliff. There are five terrified people on board, and all will be killed unless you do something. As it happens, you are standing beside a switch that will send the streetcar onto another track and all will be saved. But, unfortunately, there is someone standing on the other track who would then be killed. (We know, it's a little unrealistic, but philosophers seem to like such scenarios.) So the question is, should you sacrifice one person to save five people? Most people think you should. But suppose now that there is no other track, and the only way you can stop the streetcar is to push a very heavy person onto the track in front of the on-rushing vehicle. This person would, of course, be killed. Most people think it would be wrong to stop the streetcar in this manner.

There is no logical reason why one outcome should be preferred over the other. Why is it OK to kill one person to save five in some circumstances but not others? A group at Princeton University imaged brain activity in people who read and reasoned their way through a number of scenarios of each type. In the body-pushing situations, areas of the brain particularly involving sadness and other emotions showed increased activation, but this did not happen in the switch-pushing situations. People felt much more emotional distress in the body-pushing situations, due in turn to learning, which accounts for their moral judgments. The outcomes are identical in that five people are saved and one is killed, but they differ in that only one course of action feels really wrong. So perhaps psychology and neuroscience will someday supplant philosophical approaches to morality and ethics.

8

Language

Language is the most astonishing behavior in the animal kingdom. It is the species-typical behavior that sets humans completely apart from all other animals. Language is a means of communication, but it is much more than that. Many animals can communicate. The dance of the honeybee communicates the location of flowers to other members of the hive. But human language permits communication about anything, even things like unicorns that have never existed. The key lies in the fact that the units of meaning, words, can be strung together in different ways, according to rules, to communicate different meanings.

Language is the most important learning we do. Nothing defines humanity so much as our ability to communicate abstract thoughts, whether about the universe, the mind, love, dreams, or ordering a pizza. It is an immensely complex process that we take for granted. Indeed, we are not aware of most aspects of our speech and understanding. Consider what happens when one person is speaking to another. The speaker has to translate thoughts into spoken language. Brain imaging studies suggest that the time from thoughts to the beginning of speech is extremely fast, only 0.04 seconds! The listener must hear the sounds to figure out what the speaker means. He must use the sounds of speech to identify the words spoken, understand the pattern of organization of the words (sentences), and finally interpret the meaning. This takes somewhat longer, a minimum of about 0.5 seconds. But once started, it is of course a continuous process.

Spoken language is a continuous stream of sound. When you listen to a foreign language you do not know, the speakers seem to be speaking extremely fast, indeed producing a continuous stream of incomprehensible sounds. Yet in our own language we hear words. We actually learn to perceive sounds and words from the continuous stream of speech. A classic example is the r and l sounds. In the Japanese language these two sounds do not exist as separate sounds. Patricia Kuhl and her colleagues showed that while all young babies, including Japanese babies, easily distinguished between r and l sounds, Japanese adults are unable to tell the difference.

Early Learning of Speech and Language

Imagine that you are faced with the following challenge. You must discover the internal structure of a system that contains tens of thousands of units, all generated from a small set of materials. These units, in turn, can be assembled into an infinite number of combinations. Although only a subset of those combinations is correct, the subset itself is for all practical purposes infinite. Somehow you must converge on the structure of this system to use it to communicate. *And* you are a very young child.

This system is human language. The units are words, the materials are the small set of sounds from which they are constructed, and the combinations are the sentences into which they can be assembled. Given the complexity of this system, it seems improbable that mere children could discover its underlying structure and use it to communicate. Yet most do so with eagerness and ease, all within the first few years of life.

The rate of language learning by infants (from *infantus*, "without language") and young children is quite amazing. Somewhere between 10 and 15 months of age the first word is spoken. But infants recognize and remember words well before then. Six-month-old infants shown side-by-side videos of their parents while listening to the words "mommy" and "daddy" looked significantly more at the video of the named parent. But when shown videos of unfamiliar men and women, they did not look differentially to "mommy" or "daddy." By age 2 children know about 50 words, and by age 8 the average child has a vocabulary of about 18,000 words. So between the ages of 1 and 8, the child is learning an average rate of eight new words a day!

It appears that learning the meanings of new words by young children can be extremely rapid. Children ages 3 and 4 were given just one exposure of a new word. At a nursery school the children were told to "bring the teacher" the chromium tray, not the blue one (there were two trays, an olive one called "chromium" and a blue one). Upon later testing the children remembered that the word "chromium" represented a color, and some even remembered what color (olive). This extraordinarily rapid learning of new words by children has been termed "fast mapping" and has been demonstrated in children ages 2 to 11. How many words do you think a two-year-old is exposed to every day? The average is between 20,000 and 40,000! But, of course, most of this is repetition of common words the child already knows.

Babbling, a Universal Language

Babies the world over begin to babble between four and six months of age. Early on, babbling is the same in all languages and cultures. "Skilled" babbling sounds very much like language, but so far as we know it conveys no meaning. Infants of deaf parents babble normally. It appears that early babbling is largely innate, but by about 10 months of age babbling begins to become differentiated. English-speaking babies begin to babble differently from

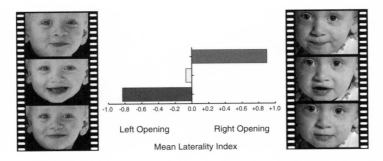

FIGURE 8-1 When smiling the left side of the baby's opened more (left) and when babbling the right side of the mouth opened more.

French babies, who babble differently from Chinese babies, and so on.

It appears that the left hemisphere of the brain is more involved in the control of babbling. The left hemisphere is specialized for language function in most adults, whereas the right hemisphere is more concerned with emotions. The evidence for hemispheric control of babbling comes from very simple video recordings of babies' faces made while they were babbling and smiling (see Figure 8-1). When babbling, the right side of the mouth is more opened and moving (left hemisphere), and the left side of the mouth is more involved with smiling (right hemisphere). These results would seem to argue that the neural determinants of babbling are fundamentally linguistic, that left hemisphere control for language function exists from birth.

In a striking recent study an optical method of measuring brain activation was used to compare activation of the left and right hemispheres of the brain when newborn infants (two–five days old) were listening to speech. This ingenious optical method is completely harmless—lights are shined on the scalp, and the light reflected back from the surface of the brain (cortex) can be measured. The newborns were played language spoken in "motherese" (see below) versus the same recordings played backward. The left brain hemisphere posterior speech areas (see below) showed much greater activation for forward than backward speech. No such differences were seen in the right hemisphere. Indeed, in the first few months of life, speech elicits greater electrical activity in the left hemisphere and music in the right hemisphere, as is the case with adults. However, the right hemisphere is also much involved in language in young children.

Motherese, Another Universal "Language"

How do you speak to a young infant? You may not be fully aware that you are speaking motherese. The pitch of your voice rises, you drag out vowel sounds, you use very simple words, and you speak in a sing-song tone ("Heellooo, baaabeee"). Motherese is not limited to English. Groups of English, Swedish, and Russian mothers were studied when speaking to their infants and to adults. In all three languages motherese had exactly the same characteristics. Speaking to babies in this manner emphasizes the basic characteristics of vowels and syllables, providing the infant with a simplified example of the language. Adult speech is extremely variable, with many subtle variations from person to person. As someone said, "When it comes to understanding language it's a phonetic jungle out there." How is the infant to learn language correctly? Motherese helps provide a more uniform speech. But why do we speak motherese to infants? It is certainly not with deliberate intent to instruct them. It turns out that babies pay much more attention to motherese than to adult language. It would seem they are training us to speak motherese to them, an example of infants operantly conditioning adults!

Infants are able to discriminate speech sounds and words when as young as four days old and are sensitive to the rhythms of speech but not nonspeech sounds. Thus, newborns can discriminate sentences from Dutch and Japanese but not if the sentences are played backward. Very young infants are able to do this equally for all languages; they show a categorical perception of speech sounds. Adults do not have this ability. We are much better at discriminating critical speech sounds in our own language than in other languages. Infants begin to lose their ability to discriminate speech sounds in all languages between the ages of 6 and 12 months, the very time when they are beginning to learn their own language.

Until recently it was thought that this ability of young infants to handle speech sounds in all languages was unique to humans. It now appears that this ability may be common to all primates. In a most intriguing study, it was found that cotton-top tamarin monkeys are able to distinguish between Japanese sentences presented normally or backward. It seems to be a basic ability of the primate auditory cortex.

What Is Language?

The basic elementary sounds of a language are called *phonemes*. They roughly correspond to the individual sounds of the letters. The total number of phonemes in all language is about 90. English uses 40, and other languages use between 15 and 40. Babbling infants can say most of them. This production of the basic sounds of language is called *phonetics* and it is clearly innate. All normal babies the world over do it in the same way.

The English language has rules for how these basic sounds can be combined into words. We have learned these rules but are not usually aware of them, only how to use them. In English the word "tlip" cannot exist—you can't begin a word with a *t* followed by an *l*. You knew that but you were not aware of the rule. On the other hand, "glip" is fine; it just doesn't happen to exist, as a word. As one linguist put it, if a new concept comes along and it needs a name, "glip" is ready, willing, and able.

Words are the next step, formed from combinations of phonemes, called *morphemes*. Morphemes are the elementary units of meaning. "Cars" is a combination of two morphemes, "car" and "s," meaning more than one. Again, English has rules for combining morphemes, even though most of us cannot state them. You know that the plural of "glip" is "glips" and the past tense of "glip" is "glipped," even though you have never encountered this word before. English has more than 100,000 morphemes combined in various ways to yield the million plus words in the English vocabulary. A typical educated adult English speaker will have a vocabulary of about 75,000 words. Talk about memory storage!

But there is much more to language. The way words are arranged in sentences following rules is called *syntax*. Many rules have been spelled out, as in the grammar parsing some of us suffered through in school. But the rules existed long before any of them were described or written down. Finally, we come to the whole point of language, to convey meaning, termed *semantics*. Both the words and the ways they are combined into sentences convey meaning. "John called Mary" is not the same as "Mary called John."

Interestingly, languages show little sign of evolution. All languages from English to obscure dialects of isolated aborigines have the same degree of complexity and similar general properties. They all have syntax—rules for making sentences—and although the particular rules differ for each language, in a general sense syntax is universal. This point may seem somewhat academic, but it is crucial, as in trying to determine whether apes can really learn language.

King James the first of England was a scholar and philosopher. Among other matters he was responsible for the King James version of the Bible. During his reign in the early part of the seventeenth century a hotly debated issue concerned the original human language. Some favored Greek; some favored other languages. But most scholars were convinced that there was an original language. King James devised an experiment to settle the matter. A number of newborn infants would be transported to an uninhabited island and cared for by Scottish nannies (he was Scotch) who were totally deaf and unable to speak. King James was convinced that the children would grow up speaking Hebrew. History doesn't record whether the experiment was actually carried out. We know of course that there is no "original" language. But some authorities argue for a fundamental commonality in all languages, determined by the structure of the human brain.

Brain and Language

Since language is so important to our species, it is not surprising that substantial areas of the cerebral cortex, the "highest" region of the brain, are devoted to language functions. One of the great mysteries about the human brain is hemispheric specialization. For most humans, language functions are represented in the cerebral cortex of the left hemisphere, corresponding to the fact that most of us are right-handed (the left side of the cortex controls the right side of the body). Indeed, the original sign of hemispheric dominance was handedness. About 90 percent of us are right-handed in all societies and throughout history. Even our most remote ancestors that could be called humanlike, the australopithecines who lived in Africa several million years ago, may have been mostly right-handed. Australopithecines walked upright and apparently used crudely chipped stone stools, although their brain was only about the size of a modern chimp's. Judging by how they bashed in the skulls of the animals they ate, they were right-handed.

The first hint that language might be localized in the brain came about 140 years ago when the French neurologist and anthropologist Paul Broca reported the case of a patient who had lost the ability to produce language except for a single syllable "tan." But he was able to understand simple questions and indicated *yes* or *no* by different inflections of "tan." The patient died two years later, and Broca was able to obtain the brain. As it happened, he did not dissect the brain but preserved it whole. Luckily, the brain resurfaced 100 years later in an anatomical institute in Paris, and it is available for study today (see Figure 8-2). Actually the damage was extensive. It does not appear so while looking at the surface of the left hemisphere, but when a CT (computed tomography) scan was done, the damage was clearly much greater. Broca's case was extreme. Patients with smaller lesions in the same general area of the frontal lobe of the left hemisphere have less severe symptoms. They are able to speak but have some difficulty doing so, have poor grammar, and omit many modifying words. This is the classic Broca's aphasia.

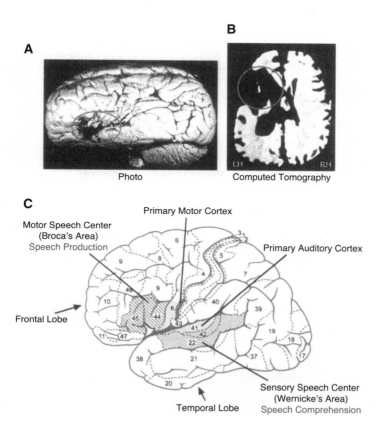

FIGURE 8-2 (A and B) The brain of Paul Broca's patient deceased in 1865. (C) Broca's and Wernicke's speech areas on the human cerebral cortex.

Several years after Broca's patient was reported, the neurologist Carl Wernicke reported on a series of patients who produced speech that conveyed little meaning. Also, they could not understand speech. Their common area of damage was in the temporal lobe (Wernicke's area; see Figures 8-2 and 8-3). Patients with damage to this region suffer from Wernicke's aphasia. They speak fluently and grammatically but convey little meaning and cannot understand spoken or written language.

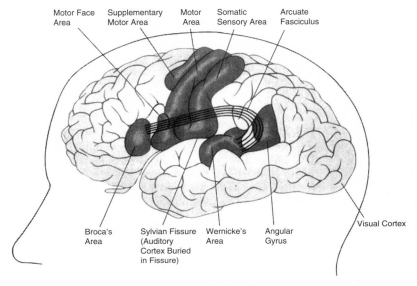

FIGURE 8-3 Language areas in the human brain.

Wernicke's and Broca's areas are interconnected by large bundle of nerve fibers (Figure 8-3). When this fiber bundle is damaged, as in a particular kind of stroke, a characteristic speech disability termed *disconnection syndrome*, occurs. You should be able to guess what this would be like. Wernicke's area is spared, so language comprehension is fine. Broca's area is spared, so speech production is also fine. But the patient's speech is exactly like that of the patient with damage to Wernicke's area—fluent but meaningless. It is no longer possible for Wernicke's area to "transmit" meaningful speech to Broca's speech production area. This must be very frustrating since the patient has good speech comprehension.

Figure 8-3 depicts the classical picture of the brain language areas. A frontal region (Broca's) just anterior to the motor cortex is concerned with speech production, phonology, and syntax, and a posterior temporal-parietal area (Wernicke's) is concerned with semantics and meaning. But it is oversimplified. Thus, meaning is given by syntax as well as words. Consider the following two sentences:

> The apple that the boy is eating is crunchy.
> The girl that the boy is chasing is tall.

In the first sentence, syntax is not needed to understand the meaning; boys eat apples, but apples don't eat boys, and apples can be crunchy, but boys are not. But in the second sentence, either the girl or the boy could be chasing the other and either could be tall. Syntax—that is, word order—tells us the meaning. Patients with damage to Broca's area have no problem understanding the first sentence but have great difficulty with the second sentence.

The classical view of brain substrates of language was based on patients with brain damage and was developed well before the days of brain imaging and only for patients who came to autopsy. With the advent of brain imaging, it was possible to determine the extent of brain damage while the patient was still alive and, even more important, to identify brain areas that become active in various language tasks in normal people. The story is now more complex than the classic view, although the Broca's and Wernicke's area notion still has some validity.

Evidence now indicates that Broca's area actually includes subareas concerned with all three of the fundamental aspects of speech: phonology, syntax, and semantics (meaning). This last aspect came as something of a surprise. Wernicke's "area" also seems to involve subregions. One area is concerned with auditory perception of both speech and nonspeech sounds; another area is concerned with speech production, and a more posterior area responds to external speech and is activated by recall of words. It does appear that this last region is critical for the learning of long-term memories for new words. The total area of this posterior speech region is larger than the classical Wernicke's area and includes parietal as well as temporal association areas of cortex.

Brain imaging studies indicate that the cerebellum, the ancient "motor" system, is also much involved in language. It is, of course, involved in the motor aspects of speaking but also in the meaning aspects of language, as in retrieving words from memory. A final complication from current brain imaging studies is that the right hemisphere is also involved in some aspects of language.

There does indeed appear to be some degree of localization for different categories of words in the posterior language area, judging by studies of patients with brain injury, thanks to work by Elizabeth Warrington in London and others. One patient, JBR, suffered extensive brain damage as a result of encephalitis. His aphasia was such that he was impaired for names of living things and foods but not for names of objects. Another patient, VER, following a major left-hemisphere stroke, had almost complete loss of comprehension of words for objects, even common kitchen items thoroughly familiar to her, but her memory for living things and foods was good. Patient KR, with cerebral damage, could not name animals but had no difficulty naming other living things and objects. Actually, she could not *name* animals regardless of the type of presentation (auditory or visual). When asked to describe verbally the physical attributes of animals (for example, what color is an elephant?) she was extremely impaired, but she could correctly distinguish colored animals from those that were not so colored when presented visually. Her symptoms suggest that there are two distinct brain representations of such properties in normal individuals, one visually based and one language based.

Brain imaging studies agree in showing a surprising degree of differential localization of different types of objects in the temporal area of the cerebral cortex. In addition to the face area, there appear to be differentially overlapping areas representing houses, chairs, bottles, and shoes (see Figure 8-4). It would seem obvious that there cannot be a separate area of cortex for each different object, there being billions of different objects in the world. Furthermore, it is difficult to see how a "shoe" area could have evolved since humans did not wear shoes until well after the brain had achieved its fully modern form. This represents yet another fascinating puzzle about the brain.

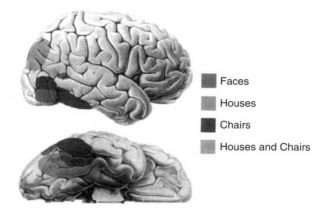

FIGURE 8-4 Faces, houses, and chairs activate different areas of the ventral temporal cortex.

Perhaps most extraordinary are studies of bilingual patients—for example, those who are fluent in Greek and English. Localized inactivation (a technique used in surgery) in central regions of Broca's or Wernicke's areas tended to disrupt language functions for both languages, but inactivation in the posterior language area outside classical Wernicke's area could disrupt only Greek or only English, depending on the locus of inactivation. Yet another example is Japanese writing. There are two forms of written language—picture words (Kanji) and alphabetic writing (Kana). Brain damage can have differential effects on the ability to read and write these two forms of writing, depending on the area of damage.

All these data would seem to argue that our long-term memories for words and their meanings are stored in the posterior language area and that there is some degree of differential localization of word categories. But we have no idea yet of how words and other aspects of language are stored in terms of the actual circuits, the interconnections among neurons. There is much to be done.

An intriguing hint comes from work by one of the world's

leading neuroanatomists, Arnold Scheibel of the University of California at Los Angeles. He and his associates measured the degree of dendritic organization for neurons in Wernicke's area in a number of cadavers whose brains had become available and compared the anatomical data to the degree of education the people had had (see Figure 8-5). You may recall from Chapter 3 that dendrites (from the Greek for "tree") are the fibers extending out from

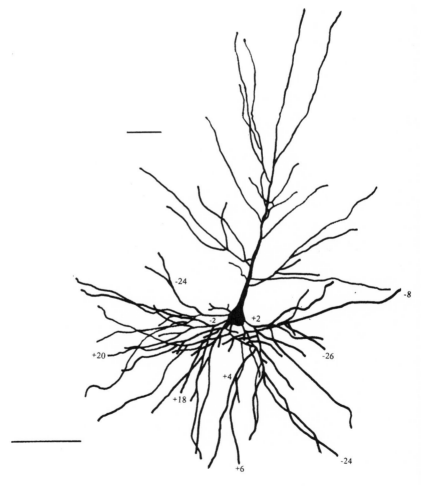

FIGURE 8-5 The multitude of dendritic branches of a neuron.

the neuron cell body that receive input from other neurons via their axons. Dendrites are covered with little spines, each one a synapse receiving input from another neuron. The more dendrites a neuron has (its dendritic material), the more synapses it has from other neurons. The Wernicke's area neurons from the brains of deceased people who had had a university education had more dendritic material than those from people with only a high school education, who in turn had more dendritic material than those with less than a high-school education. There is, of course, the usual chicken and egg issue here. Did the dendrites expand because of education or did the brains of those people with more dendrites seek more education? In some sense, increased connections among neurons may equate to increased knowledge.

The Critical Period in Language Learning

There is no question that children are more adept at learning language than are adults. Consider the following anecdote from Harvard neurobiologist John Dowling:

> We brought our daughter to Japan at the age of five for a seven-month period and in just four months she became fluent in Japanese. Her pronunciation of Japanese words was generally superior to that of my wife, who had been studying the language for the previous three years!

It seems that there is a critical period in language learning but it is long, ranging from birth to adolescence. We are all aware of the fact that it is very difficult for adults to learn a second language to the point where they can pass for native speakers. There have been many studies of people's initial efforts to learn a second language but not of their ultimate proficiency as a function of the age at which they began to learn it.

Elissa Newport of the University of Rochester answered this question in some ingenious studies. She selected people who had come to the United States from China or Korea at ages ranging from 3 to 39 and studied English as a second language for at least 10 years. They were all students or faculty members at the University of Illinois. Newport and her colleagues developed a test of English grammar competence. The results were striking. Those people who had come to this country before the ages of 3 to 7 performed as well as native English speakers. Thereafter there was a steady decline in performance, the worst being among people who began speaking English at ages 17 to 39.

Language is represented in both hemispheres of the brain in infants. Over the years leading up to adolescence, language representation shifts to the left frontal and temporal speech areas for most of us. Consistent with this, if the speech areas in the left hemisphere are damaged in childhood, there is good recovery. Unfortunately, with the same damage after the age of about 17, there is little recovery. In terms of synapse formation there is a steady increase in the number of synapses in the cortical speech areas in childhood that peaks around ages 3 to 5 and then declines to stabilize in adolescence. Similarly, brain energy utilization increases until about age 4, at which time the child's cerebral cortex utilizes over twice as much energy as occurs in adults. This high-energy use persists until about age 10, after which there is a gradual decline to adult levels. So the critical period for language learning is very real; it is in the first several years of life and then gradually declines.

Reading

The human brain evolved to its fully modern form well over 100,000 years ago. No changes in brain structure or organization have occurred for a very long time. Yet written language, and hence reading, was invented only about 10,000 years ago. Reading, after all, is a very unnatural act. There was no evolutionary pressure to develop reading ability in the brain. Learning to read is a slow and difficult task for children, unlike learning to speak, and it is especially difficult for those who learn to read as adults. Our cultural evolution has forced us to use certain areas of our brain in tasks for which nature never intended them. Spoken language, on the other hand, evolved along with the evolution of our species and brain and is natural and adaptive.

An interesting question is: What areas of the brain are used or misused in learning to read? It appears that certain higher regions of the visual and association areas in the cerebral cortex may be enlisted, particularly a region called the *angular gyrus* (see below). There is tantalizing evidence that aboriginal peoples who have no written language have almost photographic visual memories. Such abilities would seem to be adaptive for survival. "Are the leaves bent a little differently than they were earlier along this place in the path?" Perhaps reading has co-opted these visual areas of the brain. There is a suggestion that children have better visual memories before they learn to read. Brain imaging studies indicate that wide regions overlapping both the posterior and anterior speech areas are engaged when we read.

The neurosurgeon George Ojemann has succeeded in recording the activity of single neurons in the human cerebral cortex during learning of word associations. The patients were undergoing neurosurgery to treat epilepsy. They were, of course, anesthetized during exposure of the brain and also given local anesthetics. They were then brought to awareness while the nerve cell recording was done (the brain itself has no sensation of pain). They had to learn associations between word pairs. A unique sample of neurons were found in the temporal lobe in the general region of Wernicke's area (but in both hemispheres) that showed substantially increased activity only for associations that were learned very rapidly during initial encoding. These neurons could be distinguished from other neurons because they showed decreased activity during word reading (no learning involved) and increased activity during remembering of words just learned. These results are among the few examples showing single-neuron correlates of verbal learning.

Dyslexia

The aphasias are the major deficits in language caused by extensive brain damage. Dyslexia is a much more common language disorder and can range from mild to severe. Dyslexic children have trouble learning to read and write. An unfortunate case of a dyslexic child who was killed in an accident and came to autopsy has been described. There was a clear abnormality in the pattern of arrangement of the neurons in a part of Wernicke's area. Although this is only one case, it raises the possibility that dyslexia may be due to brain abnormalities. Dyslexia is five times more common among boys than girls.

Dyslexia also tends to run in families. It is to some degree heritable, indicating that it has a genetic basis. Just recently, a gene was discovered that appears to be involved in dyslexia. Called DYXC1, it is located on chromosome 15. The chromosomal region containing DYXC1 had earlier been associated with dyslexia by studies of families with the speech impairment. There appear to be at least two different mutations of this gene that are involved in dyslexia. This gene, incidentally, is different from the recently discovered language gene (FOX p2) described later in this chapter. It seems likely that more than one gene will be found to be involved in dyslexia. After all, the condition ranges from very mild to severe.

A study by the National Institute on Aging examined the degree of activation of the angular gyrus relative to visual regions during reading in normal and dyslexic men (see Figure 8-3). This is a brain area above Wernicke's area thought to be an auditory-visual association area critical for reading. In normal subjects there was a strong correlation between activation in the angular gyrus and visual regions. In marked contrast, in the dyslexic subjects there appeared to be a disconnection between the angular gyrus and the visual regions. There was no correlation between activities in the two regions. Additional studies of reading done at Yale University found decreased activation in the angular gyrus in dyslexics. Also found was decreased activation in Wernicke's area and in the primary visual cortex in dyslexics relative to controls in a reading task.

In addition to problems with reading, many dyslexic or language-impaired children have trouble understanding spoken language. Ingenious studies by Michael Merzenich at the University of California at San Francisco, Paula Tallal of Rutgers University, and their colleagues showed that such children have major deficits in their recognition of some rapidly successive phonetic elements in speech. Similarly, they were impaired in detecting rapid changes in nonspeech sounds. The investigators trained a group of these children in computer "games" designed to cause improvement in auditory temporal processing skills. Following 8 to 16 hours of training over a 20-day period, the children markedly improved in their ability to recognize fast sequences of speech stimuli. In fact, their language functions markedly improved.

A group at Stanford University imaged the brain activity of a group of dyslexic children before and after the training treatment noted above. Before treatment there was a virtual lack of increased brain activity in the language areas when the children were reading. Remarkably, after training, activity in these areas increased to resemble that of normal children, in close association with improvement in reading skills in these children.

Stuttering

Stuttering is a language-speaking difficulty that plagues many people. It occurs much more frequently in males than females and clearly has a genetic basis—it runs in families. Analysis of the inheritance patterns indicates that it does not involve a single gene defect but rather several genes, as yet unidentified. Brain imaging studies show differences in the language areas (Broca's and Wernicke's) between stutterers and nonstutterers. However, as William Perkins of the University of Southern California, an authority on the subject, points out, this cannot be the cause of stuttering. Stuttering is an aberration of very high speed synchronization of producing speech sounds and is involuntary. The cortical speech areas, on the other hand, process information at a slower rate—syllables and thoughts occur at about the same rate, much slower than the rate of syllable production. Perkins thinks the cerebellum may be the critical structure for stuttering. It is specialized for very rapid timing, and its activities are "involuntary"; they do not rise to conscious awareness.

Evolution of Language

There are tantalizing hints from studies on monkeys of how human speech areas may have evolved. In the general region of the anterior cortex, where Broca's area is located in humans, an entirely new premotor area appeared in monkeys, new in that it does not exist in other animals. It is just ahead of the primary motor area and is called the *ventral premotor area* (see Figure 8-6). In the monkey it serves as an additional cortical area for control of the muscles of the body. Neurons in this new motor area are activated when the animal performs visually guided reaching and grasping movements, as when the monkey reaches out and grabs something. In studying this area, the neuroscientist Giacomo Rizzolatti and his colleagues made an astonishing discovery. When the experimenter reached out and grabbed an object in front of the monkey, the neurons responded just as though the monkey had done the reaching. They termed these neurons *mirror cells*. This area seems to be involved in observational learning of visually guided tasks in monkeys.

Note that these ventral motor area neurons were able to establish a correspondence between seeing an act and performing it. As it happens, brain imaging studies in humans show that Broca's area is also activated by hand movements. So perhaps in early prehumans Broca's area-to-be was involved in matching observed vocal and hand gestures in communicating. As John Allman of the California Institute of Technology notes, these mirror neurons may be active when a human infant learns to mimic speech.

But this monkey area also receives visual input. Actually, in

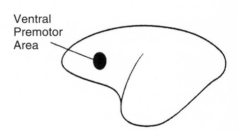

FIGURE 8-6 The location of the ventral premotor area on the monkey cerebral cortex.

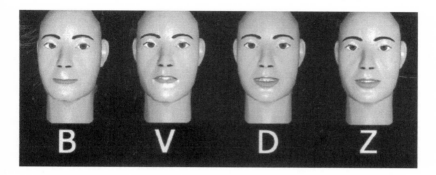

FIGURE 8-7 The McGurk effect.

normal human speech the appearance of the speaker's face while speaking is important. Enter the "McGurk" effect, first described by a scientist named McGurk. The shape of the mouth while speaking helps determine the sound perceived. This is illustrated in dramatic movies of Baldi, a computer-generated face created by Dominic Massaro at the University of California at Santa Cruz. In the movies, Baldi is seen pronouncing various sounds while either the same or different sounds are heard. The illusion is compelling. If the image of the speaker's face when pronouncing *D* is presented together with the acoustic sound *B*, the observer will hear an intermediate sound *V*, even though the actual sound is *B* (see Figure 8-7). The "McGurk" effect even seems to occur with infants only 18 to 20 weeks old. They look longer at a face pronouncing a vowel that matched the vowel sound they heard rather than a mismatched face.

As noted earlier, both young human infants and monkeys are able to distinguish the boundaries between similar speech sounds, such as *ba* and *ga*. In the temporal lobe of the monkey's cerebral cortex, in the general region where Wernicke's area exists in humans, there is a specialized auditory association area. Neurons in this area respond selectively to the vocalizations typical of the species. As it happens, these neurons are also very sensitive to the acoustic boundaries between speech sounds, as are monkeys and human infants.

Below this "speech" area on the temporal lobe is the monkey "face" area, where neurons respond selectively to monkey (and human) faces. Damage to this region in monkeys impairs their ability to respond appropriately to eye contact, a critically important social signal in monkeys and indeed humans. So it would appear that the beginnings of the human language areas were already developing in monkeys, in regions of the evolving brain that are critical for social interactions.

There is anatomical evidence that the region including Wernicke's area is larger in the left hemisphere than in the right in most humans. Evidence of this enlarged left speech area can even be seen in our remote ancestors. The temporal lobe leaves a clear marking on the inner surface of the skull, which is different on the two sides because of the enlarged speech area on the left side in modern humans. The same enlarged left temporal area was found in the skull of our brutish-looking distant cousin, the Neanderthal. The Neanderthal skull that was studied is more than 30,000 years old and was found in France. Even more remarkable is the same enlarged speech area reported in one study of the left hemisphere of a skull of Peking man in Asia, our much more remote ancestor *Homo erectus*.

The astonishing quadrupling in size of the human brain over the past 3 million years must have been molded powerfully by natural selection. Language marks a major difference between humans and apes, and much of the human cerebral cortex is involved in language. It seems likely that improving communication with developing language gave a competitive edge in survival to big-brained social animals. Some great apes, chimps and orangutans, also have an enlarged area of the left hemisphere in a region analogous to the human language area, although it is nothing like the human asymmetry. Monkeys, however, do not have this type of cerebral asymmetry. Incidentally, the brains of our early modern ancestors (Cro-Magnon) were significantly larger than our brains, judging by skull sizes. It may have taken more "brain power" to survive in the primitive world. Thus, dogs have smaller brains than wolves. But we stress that evolutionary arguments are always somewhat speculative.

A handful of African peoples speak by clicking their tongues. The two groups of Africans who speak this way are the !Kung (Bushmen) of Namibia and the Hadzabe of Tanzania. Genetic analysis suggests to some researchers that these clicking sounds may be vestiges of a language spoken by a common ancestor 112,000 years or so ago. Today, the click language is only spoken by the !Kung when hunting, perhaps in order not to scare their prey. In any event, even the click language has structure and syntax.

The Language Gene

Complex aspects of humans like intelligence and personality are influenced jointly by genes and experience. Such complex traits are generally thought to involve many genes. We noted earlier that autism, which is strongly heritable, is believed to involve somewhere between five and 20 different genes. Given the great complexity of language, it would seem likely that many genes are involved. Imagine the excitement in the field when a "language gene" was identified.

The discovery of this gene is a fascinating detective story in science. A few years ago a large family (called KEs) of several generations was discovered in which half the members suffered from a speech and language disorder. The fact that it was exactly half the members suggested that a single gene effect was involved. The affected members have problems articulating speech sounds, particularly as children, and in controlling movements of the mouth and tongue. But they also have great trouble identifying basic speech sounds and understanding sentences, and trouble with other language skills. They completely fail such tasks as "Every day I glip; yesterday I _____." The answer is, of course, "glipped," as any four-year-old will tell you. They are particularly impaired in syntax. Sound familiar? In many ways this resembles the classic Broca's aphasia.

More recently, a group of British scientists were able to show that the gene was on chromosome 7, over a region that contained 50 to 100 genes. Then an unrelated individual was found who had exactly the same language disorder. This person had what is called a *chromosome translocation*; chromosome 7 broke at a certain locus. It turned out that this locus was the region where the defective gene for the KEs family was thought to be. Making use of the results of the Human Genome Project, the investigators were able to localize and identify the actual gene, which they named FOXp2. In all of the affected members of the KEs family, but none of the unaffected members, this gene is defective. The gene is *not* defective in 364 chromosome 7 in unaffected people studied.

A brief word about genes. They are long strings made up of four different compounds called *nucleotides*. The four components are: adenine, thymine, guanine, and cytosine. Genes are "simply" long strings of these compounds, typically hundreds long, arranged in double strands—the famous double helix. These in turn determine the synthesis of proteins, which are long strings of amino acids. The coding is precise. A change in just one of the hundreds of nucleotides in a gene can markedly alter or impair the functioning of the gene. In the case of the language gene, a single guanine nucleotide at a particular locus is replaced by an adenine. This results in synthesis of an abnormal protein. (The normal protein is 715 amino acids long.) The normal FOXp2 gene is strongly expressed in fetal brain tissue and plays a critical role in the development of the cerebral cortex. Only one copy of the gene is defective in the KEs family, but this is apparently enough to impair normal brain development, at least for language functions.

But the story doesn't end there. Two teams of scientists, in Germany and England, set about to sequence the FOXp2 gene in the chimpanzee, gorilla, orangutan, Rhesus monkey, and mouse. The last common ancestor of mouse and human lived some 70 million years ago. Since then there have been only three changes in the FOXp2 protein. Two of these changes occurred since the time that the human and chimp lines split, about 6 million years ago. Strikingly, the third change, when all humans harbored the modern gene, occurred 120,000 years or so ago, the time when fully modern humans appeared on the scene.

A word of caution. This gene and its protein product seem particularly involved in the normal development, articulation, and other presumed functions of Broca's area, including some aspects of language understanding. But there is much more to language. Other genes must also be involved.

Enter the Neanderthals

The Neanderthals had large heads, massive trunks, and relatively short but very powerful limbs. They evolved in Europe from an earlier hominid form about 350,000 years ago and emerged in their fully "modern" form about 130,000 years ago. Their bones are found throughout Europe and Western Asia. Then, between 50,000 and 30,000 years ago they disappeared from the face of the earth, at the time when modern humans swept through Asia and Europe from their origins in Africa.

The Neanderthals were a fascinating but now completely extinct side branch of humanity. They were more brutish looking than modern humans, with jutting brow ridges. But their brains were fully as large or larger than those of modern humans. Their skulls were differently shaped, with a lower frontal area, large bulges on the sides, and a larger area in the back.

There has been much speculation over the years about whether we killed them off or simply interbred with them. Actually, modern genetic analysis from tissue extracted from Neanderthal bones indicates that the last shared ancestor of Neanderthals and modern humans lived between 500,000 and 600,000 years ago. Furthermore, there appears to have been little Neanderthal contribution to the living human genome.

It would be inaccurate to describe the Neanderthals as simply primitive. They shared with our early ancestors the ability to flake stone tools, bury their dead, and to use fire, and they had a heavy dependence on meat. Skeletal remains of both types of humans sometimes show severe disability, indicating they cared for the old and the sick. As one anthropologist put it, "There could be no more compelling indication of shared humanity." It isn't necessarily the case that we killed them off. Our early culture was much more complex and more adaptive to varying conditions. Our minds were better equipped to survive.

The discovery of the FOXp2 language gene suggests an answer to why we survived and Neanderthal did not. As was noted, this gene only appeared about 120,000 years ago in modern humans. Modern speech would seem to give our ancestors an enormous adaptive advantage in all aspects of survival. Although it is a bit of a guessing game as we improve our ability to analyze the genetics of tissues extracted from fossil bones, perhaps we can actually determine when the modern FOXp2 gene appeared and its impact on early human culture.

Learning and Language

The role of learning in language is a matter of some dispute. As noted, phonetics—speaking speech sounds—seems to be innate. All babies everywhere do it at the same stage. At the other extreme, the words of a given language are learned, as are the rules for putting words together. But perhaps the fact that all languages have this kind of structure, a syntax, could also be innate. Noam Chomsky, a pioneer in the modern analysis of language, argued that there is a "deep structure" to language that is universal and innate. Languages have to develop in a specific way in accordance with a genetic program controlling brain development. The discovery of the FOXp2 gene certainly lends credence to this view.

A common example of the innate view is the way children learn the rules for the tenses of verbs. At a certain age children use the regular past tense for irregular verbs: "I digged a hole." No one ever taught them "digged," only dug. But "digged" is the way it should be according to the rule for regular verbs. How can a child have learned this rule without having been instructed in it?

Cognitive and computer scientists have constructed artificial neural networks in computers, actually complex computer programs that learn language. One such network was given the task of learning the past tenses of verbs. A very large number of correct past tenses were fed into the network. As the network learned, it began to generate "digged" for "dug," regular past tenses of irregular verbs. It did this on a statistical basis. In the early stages of learning it experienced many more regular past tense verbs. Only with much additional experience did it master irregular past tenses.

So neural networks can learn the rules of language by experience, but what about children? In a most intriguing study at the University of Rochester, eight-month-old infants learned the segmentation of words from fluent speech solely on the basis of the statistical relationships between neighboring speech sounds. Furthermore, the infants accomplished this after only two minutes of training exposure. The investigators concluded that infants have access to a powerful neuronal mechanism for computation of the statistical properties of language. Shades of neural networks! The infant human brain is, of course, vastly more complicated than the most advanced computer neural networks.

Language in Animals?

There are some interesting examples that come close to language in monkeys. Most monkeys are social animals, living in groups, and they make sounds that clearly convey various meanings to the members of the group. Some neurons in the auditory cortex of a species of monkeys responded selectively to certain of their species-typical sounds but not to any pure tones. They responded like feature-detector neurons to sounds that conveyed meaning, as noted above.

An extraordinary example of a tiny "language" in monkeys was described by Peter Marler and his associates, then at Rockefeller University. They were studying vervet monkeys living freely in their natural state in Amboseli National Park in Kenya. Vervet monkeys make alarm calls to warn the group of an approaching predator. All the adult animals make the same three different sounds to identify three common enemies: leopards, eagles, and pythons. The leopard alarm is a short tonal call, the eagle alarm is low-pitched staccato grunts, and the python alarm is high-pitched "chutters." Other calls also could be distinguished, including one given to baboons and one to unfamiliar humans but not to humans they recognized.

The Rockefeller group focused on the leopard, eagle, and snake alarms. When the monkeys were on the ground and one monkey made the leopard alarm sound, all would at once rush up into the trees, where they appeared to be safest from the ambush style of attack typical of leopards. If one monkey made the eagle alarm, they would all immediately look up to the sky and run into the dense bush. When a python alarm was made, they would all look down at the ground around them. The investigators recorded these sounds and played them back to individual monkeys, with the same results. Perhaps most interesting were the alarm calls of the infant monkeys. The adults were very specific. The three alarm sounds were not made to the 100 or so other species of mammals, birds, and reptiles seen regularly by the monkeys. The infants, on the other hand, gave the alarm calls to a much wider range of species and objects—for example, to things that posed no danger, such as warthogs, pigeons, and falling leaves. When an infant would make such an error, a nearby adult would punish the infant. Even the infants, however, understood the categories; they gave leopard alarms to terrestrial mammals, eagle alarms to birds, and python alarms to snakes or long, thin objects. As the infants grew up, they learned to be increasingly more selective in the use of alarm calls. Why a given monkey would sound an alarm call is an interesting question. By doing so this monkey places himself in greater danger because the predator can notice him. Why then this altruistic behavior in monkeys?

The alarm calls are perhaps similar to phonetic expressions in humans; they are innate. But the objects of the calls—leopards, eagles, and so on—must be learned, just as humans must learn the meanings of words. Of course, this tiny "language," consisting of one-word sentences, has no syntax.

"Hurry!" "Gimme toothbrush!" "Please tickle more!" "You me go there in!" "Please hurry!" "Sweet drink!" No one would be surprised to learn that the speaker of these utterances was a small child. The intended meaning is clear, but the grammatical structure is primitive. But it may surprise you to learn that the "speaker" was a chimpanzee. Beatrice and Robert Gardner obtained Washoe, a one-year-old female chimpanzee, from the wilds of Africa and raised her in a trailer "apartment." During her waking hours, Washoe was constantly with human companions. She did not learn to speak English; in fact, Washoe did not learn to "speak" at all. The chimpanzee was taught American Sign Language. Many other experimenters had attempted verbal language training of chimpanzees and had failed. The Gardners reasoned that such failure was not due to an innate intellectual inability to learn language. Instead, it was due to the limitations of the animal's vocal apparatus. There is good reason to use the chimp as an animal model of language learning. The chimp is the closest living relative of the human species; 97 percent of the DNA in chimps and humans is identical.

From the very beginning, the Gardners "talked" to Washoe only in sign language. They started with a very limited vocabulary of the most important or meaningful objects in Washoe's environment, such as concepts of self and food, and gradually built the vocabulary. Washoe was rewarded first for trying to manipulate her fingers in imitation of the Gardners and then for making signs that were successively more like the desired ones. Finally, Washoe was rewarded only for making the desired signs. She learned rapidly. After several months of training, she had mastered 10 syllables. In three years her vocabulary increased to more than 100 words. Even more important, Washoe showed an amazing ability to generalize the signs to many situations other than the teaching situations. Gradually, she began to combine the signs into rudimentary phrases and sentences, using the signs spontaneously and appropriately. For example, when she wanted to go outside and play, she would make the appropriate sign with her hands. Another sign, pantomiming "peek-a-boo," indicated that she wanted to play a particular game. In the end, she was forming sentences of up to five words.

Was Washoe exhibiting "real" language? She certainly was communicating her wants, needs, desires, emotions, and reactions. She was able to carry on two-way communication with her experimenters. However, her language behavior was not at all like that of a child. Washoe was just as likely to say "Hurry! Gimme! Toothbrush!" as she was to say, "Gimme! Hurry! Toothbrush!" She did not seem to exhibit grammar and syntax.

So the key issue with Washoe (and Kanzi; see Box 8-1) is whether she will exhibit syntax. To date, the jury is out. On the other hand, Washoe, Kanzi, and other chimps have learned to communicate with humans very well. Indeed, such "talking" chimps provide a fascinating window on the mind of another species. Chimps, incidentally, may have some degree of self-awareness, judging by their behavior in front of a mirror.

BOX 8-1 Enter Kanzi

A discovery that may prove to be extremely important has been made by Sue Savage-Rumbaugh and Duane Rumbaugh, working at the Yerkes Primate Center in Atlanta, Georgia. Researchers there used a simple language (called Yerkish) made up of symbols to communicate with chimpanzees; the chimps can communicate by pressing the symbols on a large keyboard. As in other studies, the chimps learned to do this very well; they could communicate their wants and feelings, and they pushed the correct symbols showing pictures of objects. As in other chimp studies, the Rumbaugh chimps did not learn to respond to spoken language.

The Rumbaugh's previous work had all been done with the common chimp (*Pan troglodytes*). The pygmy chimp (*Pan paniscus*) is a different species found only in one region of Africa. The pygmies are not actually much smaller than the common chimp but have longer and more slender bones, tend to walk upright on their feet more of the time, and have a much wider range of natural vocalizations. They seem more humanlike. Indeed, they differ so much from common chimps that a separate genus has been proposed: *Bonobo*.

Matata was one of the first pygmy chimps the Rumbaughs studied. She was caught wild and her son, Kanzi, was born at Yerkes. In contrast to common chimps, at six months of age Kanzi engaged in much vocal babbling and seemed to be trying to imitate human speech. From this time until age $2\frac{1}{2}$ Kanzi accompanied Matata to her Yerkish training sessions. He was then separated from his mother for several months while she was being bred and was cared for by humans. The Rumbaughs decided to try to teach Kanzi Yerkish in a manner more like that of natural language learning in humans (no food reward for a correct response, no discrete trial training). He began using the keyboard correctly and spontaneously, which no common chimp had ever done. And quite by accident, it was discovered that Kanzi was learning English! Two of the experimenters were talking together. One of them spoke a word to the other and Kanzi ran to the machine and pressed the correct symbol for that word. Upon testing, Kanzi proved to have a vocabulary of about 35 English words at that time.

More recently, it was reported that Kanzi has begun speaking "words." The chimp started making four distinct sounds corresponding to "banana," "grapes," "juice," and "yes." Mind you, the sounds Kanzi made were not at all like the sounds of English words. But according to the experimenters, he used the four distinctive sounds reliably to refer to the appropriate objects. As far as we know, this is the first report of a chimp "speaking" discrete sounds to refer to objects.

9

Mechanisms of Memory

In an espionage movie an American secret agent discovers a horrendous terrorist plot to destroy a U.S. city. With this discovery he knows how to stop the terrorists. Unfortunately, before he can tell anyone else about it, he is killed. Government scientists extract protein memory molecules from his brain and inject them into the movie's hero. He acquires the memories from the dead agent's brain molecules and stops the terrorists.

Sound far-fetched? Actually experiments have been done that gave some credence to this sort of scenario. The initial studies involved little flatworms called planaria that have a very primitive nervous system. These little creatures are able to regenerate after being cut up. Planaria were "trained" using electric shocks to make a certain movement. When "trained" planaria were cut up, the regenerated worms remembered the task. As it happens, planaria are cannibals. So the experimenters then ground up trained worms and fed them to untrained worms. It was reported that the untrained worms then performed the learned response.

Memory Molecules

Studies like this gave rise to the notion of "memory molecules," the possibility that particular memories could be stored in protein molecules. This rationale led to further studies with rats, which were trained to approach a food cup. The brains of the trained rats were ground up and injected into untrained rats, who were then reported to have acquired the learned response.

Unfortunately, these dramatic experiments were not well controlled. Attempts by other laboratories to repeat these findings on planaria and rats failed completely. Indeed, a Nobel Prize–winning biochemist, hoping to identify memory molecules, devoted some 20 man-years of his laboratory's efforts to training planaria, with complete lack of success.

Donald Stein and his students at Clark University did a critical experiment that shed much light on this puzzling situation. They trained rats in a simple task where they had to remember not to step forward in a little box (if they did, they got shocked). Brains and livers from these trained animals were ground up and injected into untrained rats. Both the brain and liver recipients showed some degree of "memory," but the liver group did better than the brain group!

How could this happen? No one believed that memory molecules were stored in the liver. The answer is that injecting foreign protein tissue into an animal causes an immune response and other problems and can be very stressful for the animal. Stress can markedly influence activity and performance in simple learning situations. The untrained recipient animals did not "remember" the task at all; they were simply less active in the situation and didn't step forward in the box.

Other studies involved extracting RNA from the brains of trained animals and injecting it into untrained animals. There was a bit more logic here. RNA is the messenger molecule that takes information from DNA and uses it to make proteins. So if memory involves changes in the genome, the DNA, the extracted RNA should have this new information. Unfortunately, none of these studies could be replicated. As with the planaria, proper control conditions had not been used.

We now know that such experiments could not work. Proteins and RNA are large complex molecules and cannot pass the blood–brain barrier, a very special structure that prevents many harmful chemicals and large molecules for passing from the blood into the brain tissue. It is a kind of connective tissue lining all the blood vessels in the brain. We also know that when large foreign molecules are injected into the blood, they are generally broken down, so even if they could cross the barrier, the "memories" in the molecules would have been destroyed. Attempts to transfer memories from one brain to another by means of "memory molecules" did not work. But these studies encouraged *Time* magazine to suggest a solution for what to do with old college professors.

The possibility that memories could be coded in DNA and RNA raised yet again the old notion of inheriting acquired characteristics, the idea that memories could be coded by changes in the DNA of the genome as a result of experience. As far as we know, this does not happen. But the genome is very much involved in memory formation, particularly long-term memories. Studies on animals ranging from invertebrates to goldfish, rats, rabbits, and other mammals all agree that synthesis of proteins is necessary for the formation of long-term memories. The specificity of memories is in the connections among networks of neurons.

Synthesis of Proteins

Genes, DNA, are simply long chains or sequences of four different forms of a type of molecule called *nucleic acids*: adenine (A), guanine (G), cytosine (C), and thymine (T). A given gene may be hundreds of molecules long and has a specific sequence of these four nucleic acids. These sequences determine the protein made from the genes. Basically, all that genes do is generate proteins. RNA molecules transfer these genetic instructions from the DNA to make proteins in cells. Proteins, of course, can do many things.

Some form actual biological structures like neuronal synapses, and others serve as enzymes, controlling chemical reactions in the cell. Consequently, blocking this process of making proteins, which prevents long-term memory formation, means blocking the activity of the genes.

Many studies in which long-term memories were prevented by blocking protein synthesis involved injecting these blocking drugs systemically (that is, into the body and ultimately the bloodstream). These are powerful drugs, and they make animals sick, which might account for their effect on memory. However, infusion of these drugs into places in the brain where long-term memories are being formed can also prevent the memories from being established. One of the present authors (RFT) infused such a drug, actinomycin, into the cerebellar nucleus in rabbits, where long-term memory for the learned eye-blink response is formed. This procedure completely prevented learning of the eye-blink response. However, if the drug was infused in this location in trained animals, it had no effect. It only prevented *learning* of the conditioned response. Interestingly, a new protein was formed in this region as the rabbits learned the task. This protein is an enzyme that is normally involved in cell division. Since neurons do not divide after birth, perhaps such enzymes do other things in neurons.

One possibility of why gene expression—making proteins—is necessary for the formation of long-term memories is that new structures must be formed in the neurons to store the memories. Synapses, the connections between neurons, are an obvious candidate for new structures in neurons.

Synapses and Memory

The number of *possible* synaptic connections among the neurons in a single human brain may be larger than the total number of atomic particles in the known universe! This probability calculation assumes that all of the connections are random, and indeed many do seem to begin at random in the developing brain. But the actual number of synaptic connections in a typical adult human brain, is of course, very much less, roughly a quadrillion (1 followed by 15 zeros), still an impressive number.

The human genome contains a great deal of information, perhaps the equivalent of an encyclopedia set. However, the information capacity of the genome is orders of magnitude less than the number of synaptic connections between the neurons in the brain. So these connections cannot all be determined genetically. Instead, experience must shape the patterns of nerve cell connections in the developing brain. To be sure, the organization of major structures and areas of the brain and their patterns of interconnections are determined genetically. It is at the finer grain, the details of synaptic connections on the dendrites of neurons, where experience comes into play. In Chapter 3 it was noted that brain synapses increase dramatically in number over the first few years of life, the same period when much of our learning occurs. This is particularly true for the brain systems critically involved in memory formation, the cerebral cortex, the hippocampus, and the cerebellum. Synapses form, alter, and disappear throughout life.

We have a good understanding of how the patterns of synaptic connections form in the primary visual cortex. The axons from the visual thalamus conveying information to the cortex terminate on primary receiving neurons. Initially, each neuron has equal synaptic connections of input from each eye. Then as a result of visual experience after birth, input synapses from one eye or the other dies away, so each of these primary neurons is activated by only one eye or the other.

The key is visual experience. Covering one eye results in all the input from that eye dieing away from all the primary neurons, so the eye, actually the visual cortex, becomes blind. Seeing is necessary for normal development of the visual cortex. But how? It turns out that nerve cell activity, spike discharges, or action potentials are necessary. When seeing the world, the neurons projecting information from the eye to the visual cortex are very active, conveying many spike discharges per second to the primary receiving neurons in the visual cortex. Covering the eye prevents these action potentials from occurring. Suppose both eyes are functioning normally and the neurons projecting information from one eye to the cortex are inactivated, perhaps by infusing a drug that reversibly shuts down neurons, preventing them from generating spike discharges. The result is the same as if we cover one eye. The development and maintenance of the normal visual system is dependent on normal activity of the neurons in the visual brain.

Recall the rich rat–poor rat studies. A normal stimulating environment is necessary for normal development of the cerebral cortex. A poor environment results in many fewer synaptic connections. A similar type of process is thought to occur in the brain when we learn.

A typical neuron in the cerebral cortex is shown in Figure 9-1, the same one shown in Chapter 3. The dendrites receive connections from hundreds or thousands of other neurons via axons forming synaptic connections on these dendrites. Each little bump or spine on each dendrite is a synaptic connection from another nerve cell axon terminal. As you can see, the dendrites are covered with these little spine synapses. Rich rats have many more dendritic spine synapses than poor rats. Indeed, people with college degrees have more spine synapses on dendrites in certain areas of the cortex than do people with only high school degrees, who in turn have more synapses than people who did not finish high school. The memory trace, the physical basis of memory storage in the brain, may simply be more synapses. But this begs many questions—for example, how and where are they formed? We return to these questions later.

Does the proliferation of cortical synapses in the rich rat and well-educated human reflect specific memories or simply more general factors like intelligence and well-being? It has been difficult to answer this question, in part because for most kinds of memories it is not known exactly where they are stored in the brain. Indeed, some neuroscientists think that complex memories like those of our own experiences (declarative memory) may

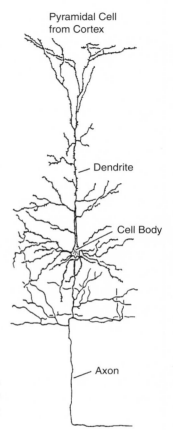

FIGURE 9-1 The dendrites of a neuron are covered with thousands of little bumps or spines, each of which is a synapse receiving information from another neuron.

be stored in widely distributed networks of neurons, probably in the cerebral cortex. The jury is still out on this question. But there are a few examples of where particular memories are thought to be stored in particular places in the brain.

Mark Rozenzweig of the University of California, Berkeley, and William Greenough of the University of Illinois pioneered the rich rat–poor rat studies. The first studies simply showed that the cerebral cortex was thicker in the rich rats. Greenough showed that this was due primarily to the growth of more synapses and more nonneural supporting cells called *glia*. (But remember that the rich rats were really normal rats, and the poor rats had fewer than normal numbers of synapses and glia.)

Greenough and his associates have provided a clear example of where a type of memory may be localized. When rats are trained to reach with a forepaw through a small hole in a piece of clear plastic to retrieve a bit of food, the region of the cerebral cortex that represents movements of the forepaw becomes critically engaged. After the animals have been trained, damage to this small region markedly impairs their performance in this task. As animals learn the task (no damage) there is a dramatic increased growth of synaptic connections among the neurons in this region.

Pavlovian conditioning of the eye-blink response provides an example of associative memory (see Chapter 7). As noted one of the present authors (RFT) and his many associates have been able to localize the basic memory trace for this form of associative learning to a particular place in the brain, a group of neurons in a cerebellar nucleus. Lesions of this small region completely and permanently abolished the learned eye-blink performance.

Studies by Jeffrey Kleim at the University of Lethbridge and John Freeman at the University of Iowa demonstrated that there is a dramatic increase in the number of excitatory synapses in this localized region of the cerebellum as a result of learning the conditioned eye-blink response. This particular memory appears to be stored by the increased number of synapses in this nucleus.

New Neurons and Memory

For a long time it was believed that people are born with the full compliment of neurons in their brains and that no neurons are formed afterward. We now know this is not the case. New neurons are formed in some limited regions in the brain throughout life. But they are not formed from other neurons. Once formed, neurons never divide. Instead new neurons are formed from stem cells adjacent to brain tissue. Stem cells do divide and in fact can form many different tissue cell types. Some stem cells migrate into brain tissue, becoming neurons. This process is now well established for a region of the hippocampus. Indeed, it is estimated that up to 5,000 new neurons form every day in the rat hippocampus! Pioneering work establishing this heresy was done by Fred Gage at the University of California, San Diego, and Elizabeth Gould at Princeton University. However, there is considerable disagreement about the extent to which new neurons form in regions of the cerebral cortex. In the hippocampus it appears that new neurons may actually become functional in circuits of neurons.

In a series of elegant experiments, Tracey Shors at Rutgers University showed that new neurons in the hippocampus play a critical role in learning and memory. She used eye-blink conditioning as her basic procedure. In the standard procedure, a tone is presented that lasts about half a second. At the end of the tone an air puff is delivered to the eye. Initially the air puff, of course, elicits an eye-blink response, but the tone does not. After repeated presentations of the tone and air puff, the tone comes to elicit the eye blink, a conditioned response.

There is another procedure, initially developed by Pavlov, called *trace conditioning*, in which the tone stimulus ends before the air puff begins. This trace interval can extend as long as a second or more and learning can still occur. Pavlov called it a trace procedure because a trace of the tone must be maintained in the brain to become associated with the occurrence of the air puff. The cerebellum is the essential structure for the standard procedure, as we saw earlier. However, both the cerebellum and the hippocampus are critical for trace learning.

Remember HM? After hippocampal surgery he was unable to learn and remember his own new experiences and could not remember events that occurred in the year or so before his surgery. But his memory of his experiences and knowledge before that time was normal. Exactly the same is true for animals (rabbits, rats) trained in trace eye-blink conditioning. If the hippocampus is removed before training, the animals are unable to learn trace eye-blink conditioning, but they have no trouble learning the standard procedure. If the hippocampus is removed immediately after training, the trace memory is abolished, but if it is removed a week or two after training, the trace memory remains intact (unlike the hippocampus, appropriate cerebellar damage always completely prevents learning and abolishes the memory for both trace and standard procedures).

Robert Clark and Larry Squire at the University of California, San Diego, worked with human patients with severe amnesia due to hippocampal damage similar to that of HM. These patients are completely unable to learn the trace eye-blink conditioning procedure with a trace interval of one second. But they learn the standard procedure (not hippocampal-dependent) normally. Some normal humans have difficulty learning the trace procedure, and others do not. Remarkably, those people who were aware that the tone would be followed a second later by an air puff to the eye learned well, and those who were unaware of what was happening had difficulty learning. You may remember that conscious awareness is a key feature of declarative memory. So it would appear that trace conditioning provides a simple model of declarative memory in both humans and animals.

Returning to the work of Tracey Shors, she trained rats in eye-blink conditioning using both the trace and standard procedures. Remember that removing the hippocampal prevents trace but not standard learning in rats. She discovered a substantial increase in new neurons in the hippocampus in rats that had learned the trace procedure but no increase in rats that learned the standard procedure. In a dramatic follow-up study she injected rats with a chemical that prevents cell division, including the formation of new neurons. Treated rats were unable to learn the trace procedure but learned the delay procedure normally. It seems that formation of new neurons in the hippocampus was essential for trace learning. This raises the intriguing possibility that other forms of new learning also may involve the formation of new neurons.

Plasticity of the Cerebral Cortex and Memory

Suppose you had a serious accident and lost a finger. What would happen to the brain area that represents your finger? The body skin surface is represented precisely on a region of the cerebral cortex called the *somatic sensory area*. We will refer to it here as the skin sensory area. Representation of the body surface on the cortex is indeed precise but very distorted and is determined by use and sensitivity. The more sensitive the skin is to touch, as in the fingers, the greater the amount of cortex that is devoted to it. Indeed, judging by the area of cortex devoted to each area of the body, humans are largely fingers, lips, and tongue. Each finger has its own little area of representation in the cortex.

To return to the hypothetical accident, after you lost your finger, the area of cortex representing this finger gradually shrunk. The areas representing adjacent fingers spread over the missing finger area and gradually took it over. Michael Merzenich and his associates at the University of California, San Francisco, have demonstrated this in a series of elegant experiments with monkeys. They also showed that if a finger was stimulated for a long period of time, perhaps by a vibrator, the skin cortical area for the finger expanded and spread into adjoining finger areas.

A dramatic example of this "takeover" of skin sensory cortex has been described for some patients with arm amputations. Long after the amputation, the patient may experience sensations of the nonexistent hand being touched when a region of his face on the side of the amputation is touched! It would seem that the face area of the skin cortex adjacent to the area for the missing arm has "taken over" this area. But the sensation is still of the hand being touched, not the face. By the same token, if we were to electrically stimulate the missing arm area of the skin cortex, the sensation would be localized to the missing arm.

Musicians provide a ready source of people with extreme overuse of their fingers. This is particularly so for violinist. The little finger of the left hand (for a right-handed violinist) works particularly hard. The area of representation of the left little finger on the skin sensory cortex is relatively small. In brain imaging studies, the extent of the left little finger representation in the skin cortex was determined for string instrument players. As expected, there was a major expansion of the left little finger area in the cortex. Indeed, the degree of expansion of this left little finger area increased in close association with years of experience as a violinist!

Regions of the cerebral cortex of adult humans can expand and contract with experience just as they do in an infant's brain as it grows and develops. It is plastic and dependent on experience throughout life. Part of this is probably due to changes in the number of synapses, but other kinds of processes occur as well.

Although it seems possible that growth of new synapses and even new neurons could be the physical basis of the memory trace for all forms of memory, this is known with some degree of certainty for only a few types of learning. But making new synapses takes time and new memories seem to be formed rapidly. As we experience events the initial memories are formed.

The First Stage in Memory Formation

When you experience any event, from items you hear on the morning news, to something a friend or loved one says, to a dream, you experience it only once, yet you remember it. If the event is not special, you do not rehearse it—keep thinking about it—but it remains to some degree in your memory for some time. Something must happen very rapidly in the neurons of the brain, in milliseconds to seconds, to form this initial memory. And whatever this process is, it must persist at least for days.

Long-Term Potentiation and Memory

Two scientists working in Oslo, Norway, in the laboratory of Per Andersen discovered the phenomenon of long-term potentiation (LTP). Tim Bliss, from England, and Terje Lømo, from Norway, were electrically stimulating a nerve pathway projecting to the hippocampus in an anesthetized rabbit. After giving a brief train of stimuli at a rate of 100 per second to this pathway for one second, they found to their astonishment that the neurons in the hippocampus activated by this pathway increased their responses substantially and that the increase lasted for hours—for the duration of the experiment. The neuron response was potentiated following brief high-frequency stimulation. This finding assumed particular importance because the hippocampus is critically involved in experiential or declarative memory.

We learned earlier that the hippocampus is not the repository of permanent long-term memories. HM can remember his life up to a few years before his surgery; monkeys remember up to about two months before hippocampal removal. Rats and rabbits remember events up to a week or two before surgery. Hippocampal-dependent memories are time limited. The hippocampus acts like a buffer memory system. It is necessary to hold memories for some period of time but not permanently. The final repository for long-term declarative memories is thjought to be among the neurons of the cerebral cortex, but the data are not clear.

In freely moving animals with electrodes permanently implanted in their brains, LTP can be measured for days or weeks. In rats, at least, LTP decays slowly over weeks. Neurons in the cerebral cortex also show LTP, and this may be a way that memories are initially stored in the cortex.

The mechanisms responsible for LTP in hippocampal neurons are well understood (see Box 9-1). The key actor is the chemical neurotransmitter glutamate. Molecules of glutamate are released from the terminals of the nerves that connect to (synapse on) hippocampal neurons. Glutamate, incidentally, is the workhorse excitatory transmitter for neurons in the brain. It increases the excitability of neurons and appears to be the key "memory" neurotransmitter wherever memory processes occur, in the hippocampus, cerebral cortex, and cerebellum.

Much of our understanding of the mechanism of LTP has come from a special procedure developed in Per Andersen's laboratory in Oslo—the hippocampal slice. Animals, usually rats or

BOX 9-1 The Mechanism of LTP

In hippocampal neurons, glutamate acts on several receptors on the neuron cell membrane at synapses. Two receptor molecules are critical for LTP: AMPA and NMDA (abbreviations for very long clinical names). Under normal circumstances where the pathway to the hippocampus is active only a little, AMPA receptors are activated and hippocampal neurons respond in a normal not a potentiated manner. However, when the pathway is stimulated at high frequency, the NMDA receptors are also activated. They in turn permit calcium ions (charged atoms) to enter the neuron. Calcium activates biochemical processes that result in more AMPA receptors becoming responsive to glutamate. Hence, the next time glutamate molecules act on the AMPA receptors, the activity of the neuron will be greatly increased. So the basic mechanism is an increase in the AMPA receptor response to glutamate in hippocampal neurons.

How it was discovered that high-frequency activation of the NMDA receptors causes them to become active, to pass calcium ions into the neuron, is a fascinating story. With normal low-frequency activation of the pathway, glutamate attaches to the NMDA receptors, but it is not enough to activate them. Why? Because there is another kind of ion, magnesium ions, in the calcium channels of the NMDA receptors that blocks the channels. If the pathway is now strongly activated by high-frequency stimulation, the magnesium ions are removed from the NMDA channels in the neuron permitting calcium to enter. This in turn increases the number of functional AMPA receptors, resulting in LTP. The actual mechanism causing the magnesium ions to be removed from the NMDA channels is a change in the neuron membrane voltage level. It becomes more positively charged or depolarized. This removes the magnesium ions from the channels.

mice, are anesthetized and painlessly killed; then the hippocampus is removed from the brain and cut into slices. The anatomy of the hippocampus is arranged so that each slice contains the key circuitry of the hippocampus, from input to output. The slice can be maintained alive and functional for many hours in its nutrient bath. Under these conditions the complete environment of the slice can be fully controlled, which is simply not possible when the hippocampus is in the brain. LTP can easily be induced in the hippocampal slice.

Some years ago a young neuroscientist anmed Timothy Teyler spent a year in Per Andersen's laboratory learning the slice technique and its use to study LTP. He then joined one of the present authors (RFT) at Harvard, where he set up his slice laboratory and taught several American scientists the method. Another young neuroscientist, Philip Schwartzkroin, also spent a year in Oslo and brought the method to the West Coast at the University of Washington in Seattle.

The form of LTP we have described is NMDA-dependent LTP (see Box 9-1). The NMDA receptor is one type of receptor for the chemical transmitter substance glutamate. A great deal is known about the biochemistry of the NMDA receptor. For example, substances have been developed that completely block its functions. One such drug, APV for short, completely blocks the development of LTP and has been used to study the role of hippocampal LTP in memory. In a pioneering study, Gary Lynch and Michel Baudry, at the University of California, Irvine, and Richard Morris, from Scotland, infused APV in the hippocampus of rats while they were trying to learn a maze. This completely prevented learning, suggesting that LTP in the hippocampus was key for this form of memory.

There are other forms of LTP as well. Teyler discovered a kind of LTP in the hippocampus that does not depend on NMDA receptors. Instead, calcium is moved into the neurons by channels that are activated when the neuron cell membrane becomes depolarized (voltage becomes positively charged). These are called voltage-gated channels. Teyler found that this voltage-gated form of LTP is widely present in neurons in the cerebral cortex and may be critical for the formation of long-term memories.

Other kinds of changes not involving synapses may also serve to code memories. John Disterhoft and his associates at Northwestern University discovered that changes in neurons in the hippocampus occurred within the neurons themselves, following eye-blink conditioning in rabbits. These changes did not involve synapses but made the neurons more responsive to synaptic activation.

A Tale of Snails, Flies, Mice, and Memory

Evolution is exceedingly conservative. If something works, it persists. The way a nerve cell sends information out its axon from the cell body to the synaptic terminals to act on other nerve or muscle cells—the action potential—is basically the same in all animals, from the most primitive animals with neurons, the jellyfish, to humans. Perhaps many other ways of conveying information were tried at the beginning of multicellular creatures. But once the action potential appeared, it worked so well that it was kept throughout the next billion or so years of evolution. The action potential, incidentally, is simply a rapid, localized change in the voltage across the neuron cell membrane that begins at the cell body and travels out the axon.

The speed of the action potential is slow relative to the speed of electricity, from about 1 mile per hour to something under 200 miles per hour. But distances are short, at least in the brain.

Habituation

The process of habituation—a decrease in response to repeated stimulation—is a clear case of conservation in evolution. To take a human example, if you hear a sudden, loud sound, you will be startled and jump briefly. If the sound is repeated often, you will stop being startled; you will habituate. Suppose you are then given an unexpected and unpleasant or fearful stimulus, perhaps an electric shock. The next time you hear the sound you will be startled, perhaps even more than you were initially. You have become sensitized.

The mechanism underlying this rapid or short-term habituation appears to be the same in all animals with nervous systems from simple invertebrates to mammals. The basic process is synaptic depression as shown in work by Eric Kandel, one of the present authors (RFT), and others. As a result of repeated activation of nerve axons, the amount of chemical neurotransmitter released from the axon terminals decreases. The chemical neurotransmitter molecules in the nerve axon terminal become less available for release. They are not simply used up. Following a strong stimulus like a shock, they now release much more transmitter than they did to the first presentation of the habituating stimulus. The circuit becomes sensitized.

Rats are startled by sudden loud sounds just as people are. But not all the synapses in the circuit from hearing the sound to jumping habituate. Instead, habituation occurs primarily at the synapses connecting the sensory system neurons, here the auditory system, to the motor system that controls the startle response. The same appears to be true for humans. Indeed, the same is true in simple invertebrates where the sensory neuron connects directly to the motor neuron.

Some years ago, one of the present authors (RFT), together with a graduate student, Philip Groves, developed a "dual-process" theory of habituation. The basic notion is that stimuli that elicit responses (like startle to a loud sound) induce both habituation processes in synapses and also sensitizing processes, and these yield the final behavior. This simple theory was able to predict a wide range of behaviors.

So the basic mechanism for habituation, at least for relatively short-term habituation, is well understood, perhaps the best-understood example of a "memory trace": synaptic depression. However, even for this simple form of learning, the mechanisms underlying long-term habituation occurring over days or weeks are not well understood.

Long-Term Memory

Snails

Eric Kandel and his many associates at Columbia University have used a relatively simple invertebrate, the sea snail *Aplysia* as an animal model to study the basic processes of memory. The nervous system of this animal has only a few thousand neurons, many of which are large and can be identified individually. Kandel focused on a simple circuit where a sensory neuron conveying information about touch connects directly to a motor neuron that activates a muscle. This piece of the nervous system is very hardy. It can be removed from the animal and kept alive in a dish. In fact, a tissue culture can be prepared with just the sensory neurons synapsing on the motor neurons. This system shows habituation—that is the response of the motor neurons to repeated stimulation of the sensory neurons decreases.

Strong and persistent activation of this system can result in long-lasting sensitization, an increase in synaptic transmission that can last for hours. Actually, the best way of inducing this long-lasting sensitization is by adding a chemical neurotransmitter, serotonin, to the system. This method provides a simple model of persistent use–dependent increase in synaptic activation, which they use as a simplified model of long-term memory.

Eric Kandel and his associates analyzed the biochemical processes that occur in neurons as a result of long-term sensitization in great detail. Indeed, Eric was awarded a Nobel Prize in 2000 in part for this work. A particular molecule in the neuron is critical for this process of long-term sensitization, CREB (*cAMP* responsive *element* *binding* *proteins*). When strong and persisting synaptic activation occurs on a neuron, a chemical inside the neuron called cAMP becomes activated and in turn activates CREB. CREB now acts on the DNA of the genome to change the expression of certain genes. Among other things, expression of these genes can result in structural changes at synapses and even the growth of new synapses.

This work on CREB was an elegant analysis of how long-term memories might be formed in neurons, but the model system was after all a rather simple invertebrate nervous system. How general might this possibility be? As it happens, CREB has been implicated in memory function in flies and mice, as well as *Aplysia*, and therefore must also be involved in memory formation in humans, or so we think.

Flies

It used to be thought that flies lived from birth to death without ever learning anything. Now we know better. The fly actually has a rather complex little "brain," as do bees, ants, and other higher insects. A geneticist at the California Institute of Technology, Seymour Benzer, decided to explore the genetic basis of complex traits like memory using the fruit fly, *Drosophilia melanogaster*. You have probably seen these little flies on fruit that is becoming spoiled. They die of old age about a month after they are hatched, making them particularly useful for genetic studies. Benzer treated the animals with procedures that induced mutation in the genes of the parents, resulting in mutant offspring. Many of these mutants had clear structural abnormalities, for example, different colored eyes.

Chip Quinn, a young neuroscientist working in Benzer's laboratory, developed a method for teaching the flies to discriminate odors, by pairing certain odors with electric shock, an example of Pavlovian conditioning. In these initial studies Quinn and a young scientist from Israel, Yadin Dudai, discovered a mutant they christened "dunce" that was unable to learn the odor task.

Tim Tully developed an ingenious procedure by which he could train large numbers of flies at the same time. He placed the flies in a central chamber with two side chambers, each having a different odor. One side chamber odor was paired with electric shock and the other was not. After several trials of training, the flies were placed in a new set of chambers with the same odors as before. Most of the flies congregated in the side chamber with the odor not associated with shock.

An important outcome of this work was the discovery that flies, like mammals, appear to have both short- and long-term forms of memory, at least for this olfactory task. One mutant called "linotte" could not learn the task at all. Dunce and "rutabaga" did show some learning but forgot immediately; they could not even form short-term memories. On the other hand, "amnesiac" and some other mutants were able to form short-term memories but could not form "long-term" memories (a relative term since the flies live for only a month).

A key point in this work is that the conversion from short-term memory to longer-term memory involves CREB. If CREB function is impaired, so is long-term memory. On the other hand, in a genetically altered fly with amplified CREB function, the fly forms long-term memories more rapidly than a normal fly.

Mice

An extraordinary new genetic approach to the study of memory in mammals is the gene "knockout" technology. It is possible to block the functioning of a particular gene by manipulating the DNA. The technical details are rather complicated, but the end result is mice with a particular gene being nonfunctional. Actually, it is even possible to create a mouse whose gene functions normally until the animal is given a certain chemical. The animal's genome has been so modified that this chemical temporarily shuts down (or turns on) the functioning of the gene.

This approach to the study of memory in mammals was pioneered in the laboratory of Susumu Tonegawa at the Massachusetts Institute of Technology. Tonegawa had earlier won a Nobel Prize for his work in immunology and now focuses on memory. A young scientist in his laboratory, Alcino Silva, prepared a mutant mouse with a gene for CREB deleted. These animals showed markedly impaired ability to form long-term memories in several types of learning situations, including learned fear and a form of maze learning. In normal mice, hippocampal damage also causes marked impairment in these learning situations.

One other set of discoveries brings the story full circle. LTP is easily induced in the hippocampus, as noted earlier. Some researchers have argued that LTP has two phases, a short time period of one to two hours after the one second high-frequency stimulation and a long time period of more than seven hours after stimulation. It is reported that inhibiting protein synthesis does not affect short-duration LTP but prevents long-duration LTP, as is true for the formation of long-term memories. CREB knockout mice do not develop the long-duration LTP.

Space, Place, LTP, and the Hippocampus

Rats and mice live in a world that is made up of complex spaces, a mazelike world. They have developed impressive abilities to construct internal representations of the spatial features of their worlds, and in recent years a great deal has been learned about how this is done in the brain.

One of the most intriguing discoveries about the hippocampus was the identification of "place" cells by John O'Keefe, working in London, as noted briefly in our discussion of dreaming. He was recording the activity of single neurons in regions of the hippocampus in freely moving rats. He noted that, when the animal was traveling along a runway, a given neuron might start firing only when the rats moved past a particular place on the runway. Other cells responded to other particular places on the runway. It takes only a few place cells to "fill" any environment. That is, each cell responds to some part of the spatial environment that the animal is in and perhaps 15 cells will code the entire particular environment.

Perhaps the most extraordinary recent studies on hippocampus place cells have been done by Bruce McNaughton and Carol Barnes at the University of Arizona, and Matt Wilson (now at MIT). They developed a system for recording the activity of many single hippocampal neurons at the same times, as many as 120, using sets of movable microelectrodes implanted in the animal's head (see Figure 9-2).

When the animal is in a particular environment, perhaps on the floor of a square box, different neurons in the hippocampus respond (fire action potentials) at different places on the floor of the box as the animal moves to these places. The activities of those neurons that respond to the different places in the box actually form a "map" of the box floor. By looking at the patterns of activity of these neurons at any given moment in time the experimenter can accurately tell exactly where the animal is in the box.

Are place cells learned? In rodents they appear to form rapidly, almost instantaneously, when the animal is put into a new environment. This contrasts markedly with the many trials and

*FIGURE 9-2 A mouse with an implanted microdrive to record simulta-
neously from a number of single neurons in the hippocampus while the
animal is freely moving about.*

long periods of time it takes a rodent to learn a complex maze.
The relationship between place cells, learning, and memory is
unclear, but hippocampal lesions do impair spatial learning and
memory performance in rodents. A common hypothesis concerning place fields is that they are initially formed by a process like
LTP.

Susumu Tonegawa, Matt Wilson, and their collaborators at
MIT developed a most interesting mouse whose gene that makes
a subunit of the glutamate NMDA receptor is knocked out—that
is, deleted from its genome. Specifically, they knocked out this
gene but only in one particular region of the mouse's hippocampus. They showed that in this animal it was not possible to induce LTP in this region, even though LTP induction was normal
in another region of its hippocampus. The NMDA receptor is necessary for the induction of LTP in this region. Furthermore, these
animals were markedly impaired in a spatial maze-learning task.
Accordingly, there were abnormalities in the place field organiza-

tion of this region. The place fields in normal mice are localized to particular places in the environments. The knockout mice showed much larger place fields with less discrete organization.

Conclusion

This research on the possible mechanism of memory suggests a working hypothesis about how memories are formed and stored in the brain: A learning experience induces rapid functional changes in neurons such as LTP. Over a period of minutes to hours and days, a complex series of events involving CREB and other biochemical processes acting via the DNA results in changes in the structures of synapses, the growth of new synapses, and other changes in the neurons resulting in the establishment of long-term memories. But we hasten to add that for most forms of memory we do not actually know where in the brain these memories are formed and stored or the actual molecular/synaptic mechanisms involved.

Processes like LTP, synaptic growth, and other changes in neuron excitability may indeed occur when memories are formed. Will our knowledge of these processes enable us to understand memory storage in the brain? The answer is clearly *no*. All these changes do is alter the transmission of information at neurons where they occur. The nature of the actual memories so coded is determined by the particular neural circuits in the brain that form the memories. The memory for the meaning of the word "tomato" is not in molecules or at particular synapses; it is embodied in a complex neural network embedded in larger complex networks that can code and store the meanings of words.

Molecular genetic analysis may someday tell us the nature of the mechanisms of memory storage in the brain, but it can never tell us *what* the memories are. Only a detailed characterization of the neural circuits that code, store, and retrieve memories can do this. We are still a long way from this level of understanding of memory.

10

The Future of Memory

It is always entertaining to look into the crystal ball and predict the future—entertaining but very speculative. The study of the brain in all its aspects, from genes to neurons to consciousness, is expanding at an almost exponential rate. Much of this new knowledge will impact our understanding of memory and the ways that memory processes might be altered or even enhanced in the future.

Genetic Engineering

Some people are disturbed by the notion that we can alter genes. There is even opposition in some parts of the world to the use of food products genetically engineered to be more resistant to disease or to have a longer shelf life. Actually, people have been doing genetic engineering for thousands of years: selective breeding. The huge variety of dogs, from the Chihuahua to the Great Dane, have all been selectively bred from ancestral wolves. The only difference between this kind of genetic manipulation and genetic engineering is that we can now alter the genes directly.

Memory abilities, like other human abilities and characteristics, have a significant genetic basis, called *heritability*. But genetic influences are by no means complete. As with other human attributes, memory abilities are influenced by genes and by development and experience, that is, by the environment.

In a classic study done many years ago at the University of California at Berkeley, Robert Tyron selectively bred rats to be maze-bright or maze-dull. After many generations the two groups diverged completely in their ability to learn mazes: The worst-performing maze-bright rat did better than the best-performing maze-dull rat. Maze learning in rats does indeed have a genetic basis.

In another experiment, discussed in Chapter 9, many mutated flies were much impaired in olfactory learning, but a genetically engineered fly with the enhanced biochemical CREB function learned much faster than normal flies. Similar results hold for mice. Impairing the function of the NMDA receptor molecule on neurons in the hippocampus impairs maze-learning ability. Joe Tsien, of Princeton University, engineered mice with enhanced NMDA function in hippocampal neurons, and these mice were super maze learners.

But what about people? Thanks to our knowledge of genetics and metabolism, some serious forms of mental retardation can now be prevented. A marvelous success story concerns a condition called *phenylketonuria*. The labeling on diet drinks warns that a sweetener called aspartame is used. This is actually the amino acid phenylalanine, which is present in certain foods. Some infants are born with a genetic defect in their ability to normally metabolize phenylalanine. Instead, they convert it to a toxic substance that can kill nerve cells. If untreated, these infants will develop brain damage and mental retardation.

As it happens, this disorder can be diagnosed in newborn babies by a simple urine test; many newborns are now routinely tested. If the disorder is present, the treatment is simply to avoid all foods containing phenylalanine, and this prevents the disorder.

With modern genetic engineering techniques it may be possible to alter this genetic defect in phenylketonuria directly and thus not only prevent the disorder but also cure it. A number of attempts have been made to treat human genetic disorders directly using genetic engineering methods—methods developed in animal studies—but the results have been mixed.

There are reports that a single gene may be involved in determining high intelligence. Should we genetically engineer all infants to be smart? This raises serious ethical and moral questions. Aldous Huxley's novel *Brave New World* is a frightening prediction of what might happen when genetic engineering is applied to people in a totalitarian society. Even the notion of selective breeding of humans, as the Nazis attempted in World War II, is abhorrent to most of us.

Individual people, of course, engage in a form of selective breeding when they marry. It sometimes happens that older wealthy or famous women marry much younger, attractive men, and vice versa. The beautiful dancer, Isadora Duncan, once propositioned the famous writer George Bernard Shaw to have a child with her. "Think of the incredible outcome," she said, "a child with my body and your brain." "But madam," he replied, "what if it had my body and your brain?"

These are questions that extend beyond science. Part of the problem is that far too little is known about the genetic basis of complex human characteristics. Perhaps someday it will be possible to genetically alter humans so that they will all be healthy, intelligent super-learners. But should we? The ethical questions remain.

Brain, Mind, and Machine

The activity of neurons in the brain generates electrical signals that can easily be recorded from the surface of the scalp, using the electroencephalogram (EEG). Considerable information is contained within the EEG record, which averages the activity of many neurons. We can tell if someone is aroused or resting, if they are directing their attention, or whether they are awake or in either of the two sleep states. Patrick Suppes of Stanford University and Zhong-lin Lu of the University of Southern California and their colleagues appear to have succeeded in decoding "thoughts" from EEG records. They presented subjects with 48 different sentences about European geography, and in each case recorded brain EEG activity for many different electrodes on the surface of the scalp. Using complex mathematical analysis of the EEG records, they were able to correctly recognize 90 percent of the brain waves generated by the 48 different sentences! Although this is just a beginning, it is conceivable that it will someday be possible to decode thoughts from records of brain activity.

If this could be done, a person could communicate directly—electrically—with a computer. In fact, monkeys have been made to do just that. Electrodes are implanted directly into areas of their cerebral cortex, which gives much better resolution of the electrical activity than records from the scalp. Miguel Nicolelis of Duke University has recorded the activity of many individual neurons from electrodes in a region of the motor cortex when a monkey subject is making an arm movement. He then uses the recording via a computer to generate the same movement of an artificial arm. In this way he is able to have the monkey control the movement of the artificial arm just by thinking about the movement.

Richard Andersen and his colleagues at the California Institute of Technology have gone even further. There is a posterior region of the cerebral cortex in monkeys and humans in front of the visual cortex that is critical for sensory-motor integration. It functions as the place in the cortex where intentions to act are formed—that is, high-level cognitive plans for movements, including eye movements, reaching movements, and grasping movements. In monkeys, Andersen recorded the activity (action potentials) from neurons in this region that responded prior to the animal making arm and eye movements and was able to computer decode the activity patterns of the neurons in terms of what movements the animal intended to make. He then used such recordings to correctly generate the movements the animal was planning to make before it made them (see Figure 10-1).

These studies by Nicolelis and Andersen raise the very real possibility of helping people who have lost limbs or been paralyzed. Paralysis is typically due to damage to the spinal cord or to the motor neurons that control muscles. The brain systems that control movements and intentions to move are still intact and functional. It may someday be possible to record the neuronal activity that codes skilled learned movements, perhaps in the cerebellum, for such patients so that they can yet again "play" the piano.

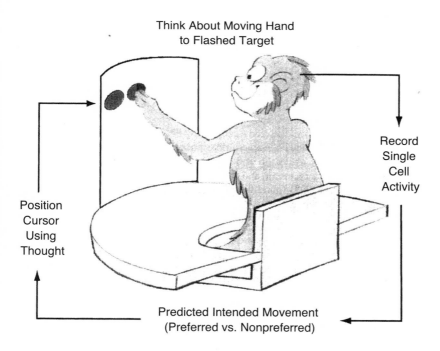

FIGURE 10-1 Neuronal activity in a region of the monkey brain code the animal's intention to make movements before it makes them. By recording from the neurons, that is by reading the thought, the movement can be made before the monkey makes it.

As more and more is learned about the detailed circuitries of the human brain and how they generate their extraordinary achievements, from consciousness to science, music, art, and literature, it will be increasingly possible to re-create these circuits in computers and even in hard-wired transistor circuits. The brain, after all, is like a computer, granted an extremely complex one with both hardware (neurons) and wetware (chemicals) and with feelings like pain and joy that computers have yet to achieve. Present-day computers cannot yet approach the complexity of the brain (each of the millions of Purkinje neurons in the cerebellum receives synaptic contacts from 200,000 or so different granule neurons, for example). But perhaps it is only a matter of time until sufficiently complex computers will become available.

Along these lines, Theodore Berger and his associates at the University of Southern California have analyzed the information-processing capabilities of the mammalian hippocampus. They simplified the problem by using an engineering approach, treating the hippocampus as a "black box." They sent a wide range of electrical signals into a hippocampal slice (from a rat) and recorded the output. Knowing the basic neural circuitry of the hippocampus, they were able to construct a computational model of the circuit in a computer, at least in terms of information processing.

Berger and his colleagues then built a physical model of the hippocampal computer circuit using electronic chips (see Figures 10-2 and 10-3). This device, like the computer circuit it simulated, processed information like the hippocampus. Amazingly, this electronic hippocampus turned out to be a language recognition system. In fact, it outperformed all commercially available English-language recognition devices. This sort of unexpected outcome is a particularly clear example of how basic research on the brain can lead to extremely useful applications in society.

The long-term goal of this project is to develop electronic chips that simulate brain circuits and that can actually serve as replacements for damaged circuits in the human brain, particularly circuits like the hippocampus that are critical for memory storage. The project involves marrying silicon chips to neurons so

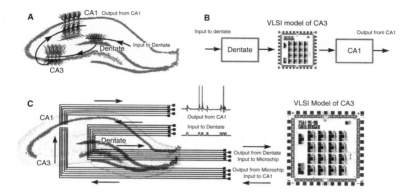

FIGURE 10-2 The way Berger characterized the activity of neurons in the hippocampus (CA1, CA3) as they analyze information. A silicon chip is then constructed to represent these regions of the hippocampus.

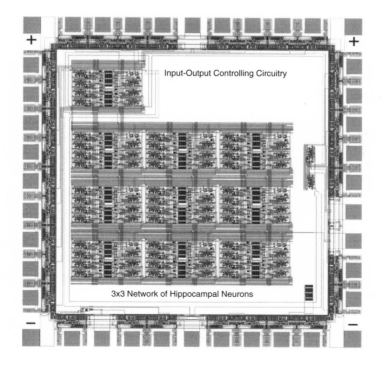

FIGURE 10-3 The electronic hippocampus.

they can communicate with one another, which has already been accomplished on a small scale. Roberta Brinton, at the University of Southern California, has succeeded in growing neurons in a cell culture on electronic chips that can intercommunicate.

The idea that nth-generation computer chips can serve as replacements for damaged brain regions sounds very much like science fiction—the creation of "cyborgs." But if this can be achieved, the human brain can be "plugged in" to nth-generation computers, vastly expanding the memory and information-processing capabilities of the human brain. This may well be in our future.

Suggested Readings

Ackerman, S. (1992). Discovering the Brain. Washington, DC: National Academy Press.

Allman, J.M. (1999). Evolving Brains. New York: Scientific American Library.

Andreasen, N.C. (1984). The Broken Brain: The Biological Revolution in Psychiatry. New York: Harper & Row.

Bruck, M., and Ceci, S.J. (1999). The suggestibility of children's memory. *Annual Review of Psychology, 50*, 419-430.

Campbell, R., and M. Conway. (1995). Broken Memories: Case Studies in Memory Impairment. Cambridge, MA: Blackwell.

Dawes, R.M. (1994). House of Cards: Psychology and Psychotherapy Built on Myth. New York: The Free Press.

Donahue, A. (2000). Electroconvulsive therapy and memory loss: A personal journey. *Journal of ECT, 16*, 133-143.

Dowling, J.E. (1998). Creating Mind: How the Brain Works. New York: W.W. Norton.

Dowling, J.E. (2004). The Great Brain Debate: Nature or Nurture? (Science Essentials). Washington, DC: Joseph Henry Press.

Dudai, Y. (2002). Memory From A to Z: Keywords, Concepts, and Beyond. New York: Oxford University Press.

Ebbinghaus, H. (1964). Memory. New York: Dover.

Endler, N. (1990). Holiday of Darkness. New York: Wall and Thompson.

Fink, M. (1999). Electroshock: Restoring the Mind. New York: Oxford Press.

Gluck, M.A., and C.E. Myers. (2001). Gateway to Memory: An Introduction to Neural Network Modeling of the Hippocampus and Learning. Cambridge, MA: MIT Press.

Gopnik, A., A.N. Meltzoff, and P.K. Kuhl. (1999). The Scientist in the Crib: What Early Learning Tells Us About the Mind. New York: Harper Collins.

Gottesman, I.I. (1991). Schizophrenia Genesis: The Origins of Madness. New York: W.H. Freeman.

Hermelin, B. (2001). Bright Splinters of the Mind: A Personal Story of Research With Autistic Savants. London: Jessica Kingsley.

Heston, L.L., and J.A. White. (1983). The Vanishing Mind: A Practical Guide to Alzheimer's Disease and Other Dementias. New York: W.H. Freeman.

Hobson, J.A. (2002). Dreaming: An Introduction to the Science of Sleep. New York: Oxford University Press.

Kotre, J. (1995). White Gloves: How We Create Ourselves Through Memory. New York: The Free Press.

LeDoux, J. (2002). Synaptic Self: How Our Brains Become Who We Are. New York: Viking Press.

Loftus, E.F., and K. Ketcham. (1994). The Myth of Repressed Memory: False Memories and Allegations of Sexual Abuse. New York: St. Martin's Press.

McGaugh, J.L. (2003). Memory and Emotion: The Making of Lasting Memories. New York: Columbia University Press.

McNally, R.J. (2002). Remembering Trauma. Cambridge, MA: The Belknap Press of Harvard University Press.

Rabinowitz, D. (2003). No Crueler Tyrannies: Accusation, False Witness, and Other Terrors of Our Time. New York: The Free Press.

Schacter, D.L. (1996). Searching for Memory: The Brain, the Mind, and the Past. New York: Harper Collins.

Shenk, D. (2001). The Forgetting: Alzheimer's: Portrait of an Epidemic. New York: Doubleday.

Thompson, R.F. (2000). The Brain: A Neuroscience Primer. New York: Worth.

Tulving, E., and F. Craik. (2000). The Oxford Handbook of Memory. New York: Oxford University Press.

Weiskrantz, L. (1997). Consciousness Lost and Found: A Neuropsychological Exploration. Oxford: Oxford University Press.

Wilding, J., and E. Valentine. (1997). Superior Memory. East Sussex, UK: Hove.

Notes

Chapter 1

p. 3. *Quote.* Milner, B. (1966). Amnesia Following Operation of the Temporal Lobes. Pp. 112-115 in C.W.M. Whitty and O.L. Zangwill (eds.). Amnesia. London: Butterworths. P. 115.

pp. 4-5. *Quote.* Luria, A.R. (1968). The Mind of a Mnemonist. Translated from the Russian by Lynn Solotaroff. New York: Basic Books.

p. 6. *Quote.* Neisser, U. (1981). John Dean's memory: A case study. *Cognition, 9,* 1-22.

p. 14. *Quote.* Sharpless, S., and H.H. Jasper. (1956). Habituation of the arousal reaction. *Brain, 79,* 655-680. P. 655.

Chapter 2

p. 26. *Figure 2-1.* Atkinson, R.C., and R.M. Shiffrin. (1971). The control of short-term memory. *Scientific American, 225,* 82-90. *P. 84.*

p. 30. *Figure 2-2.* After Glanzer, M. (1972), Storage Mechanisms in Recall. In G.H. Bower (ed.). The Psychology of Learning and Motivation. Vol. 5. New York: Academic Press. P. 144.

p. 38. *Figure 2-3.* Rees, G., C. Russell, C.D. Firth, and D. Driver.

(1999). Inattentional blindness versus inattentional amnesia for fixated but ignored words. *Science, 286,* 2504-2507. P. 2505.

p. 40. *Figure 2-4.* Simons, D.J., and C. Chabris. (1999). Gorillas in our midst: Sustained inattentional blindness for dynamic events. *Perception, 28,* 1059-1074. P. 1070.

p. 43. *Figure 2-5.* Woolsey, C.N., and H.F. Harlow. (1958). Biological and Biochemical Bases of Behavior. Madison, WI: University of Wisconsin Press. P. 5.

Chapter 3

p. 51. *Figure 3-1.* Rovee-Collier, C., H. Hayne, and M. Colombo. (2001). The Development of Implicit and Explicit Memory. Philadelphia: John Benjamins Publishing Co. P. 148.

p. 53. *Figure in Box 3-1.* Shatz, C.J. (1992). The developing brain. *Scientific American, 267,* 60-67.

p. 58. *Figure 3-2.* Kaye, K.L., and T.G.R. Bower. (1994). Learning and intermodal transfer of information in newborns. *Psychological Science, 5,* 287-288. P. 287.

p. 59. *Figure 3-3.* Pascalis, O., M. de Haan, and C.A. Nelson. (2002). Is face processing species-specific during the first year of life? *Science, 296,* 1321-1323. P. 1322.

p. 61. *Figure 3-4.* Rovee-Collier, C., H. Hayne, and M. Colombo. (2001). The Development of Implicit and Explicit Memory. Philadelphia: John Benjamins Publishing Co. P. 99.

p. 62. *Figure 3-5.* Meltzoff, A.N. and M.K. Moore. (1977). Imitation of facial and manual gestures by human neonates. *Science, 198,* 75-78. P. 75.

p. 70. *Figure 3-6.* Dehaene, S. (2002). Single-neuron arithmetic. *Science, 297,* 1652-1653. P. 1652.

pp. 70-71. *Quote.*   Flavell, J.H., P.H. Miller, and S.A. Miller. (2002). Cognitive Development. New Jersey: Prentice Hall. Pp. 187-188.

pp. 74-75. *Quote.*   *Time* Magazine. (May 6, 2002). Pp. 50-51.

pp. 84-85. *Quote.*   National Research Council. (2001). Knowing What Students Know: The Science and Design of Educational Assessment. J. Pelligrino, N. Chudowsky, and R. Glaser (eds.). Washington, DC: National Academy Press. Pp. 106-107.

Chapter 4

p. 87. *Quote.*   Ebbinghaus, H. (1964). Memory. New York: Dover Publications. P. 1.

p. 87. *Quote.*   Ebbinghaus, H. (1964). Memory. New York: Dover Publications. P. 4.

p. 88. *Figure 4-1*. Slameck, N.J., and B. McElree. (1983). Normal forgetting of verbal lists as a function of their degree of learning. *Journal of Experimental Psychology: Learning, Memory, and Cognition, 9*, 384-397. P. 387.

Chapter 5

p. 119. *Figure 5-1*. Bear, M., B. Connors, and M. Paradiso. (1996). Neuroscience: Exploring the Brain. Philadelphia: Williams & Wilkins.

p. 123. *Figure 5-2*. Thompson, R.F. (2000). The Brain: A Neuroscience Primer. New York: Worth.

p. 125. *Figure 5-3*. Squire, L.R., and E.R. Kandel. (2000). Memory: From Mind to Molecules. New York: Scientific American Library. P. 11.

p. 130. *Quote*. Endler, N. (1990). Holiday of Darkness. New York: Wall and Thompson.

p. 131. *Quote*. Fink, M. (1999). Electroshock: Restoring the Mind. New York: Oxford University Press. P. 16.

p. 133. *Quote*. Donahue, A. (2000). Electroconvulsive therapy and memory loss: A personal journey. *Journal of ECT, 16*, 133-143.

p. 134. *Figure 5-4*. Helmuth, L. (2001). Boosting brain power from the outside in. *Science. 292*, 1284-1286.

pp. 136-137. *Quote*. Heston, L.L., and J.A. White. (1991). The Vanishing Mind: A Practical Guide to Alzheimer's Disease and Other Dementias. New York: Freeman and Company. Pp. 1-5.

p. 138. *Figure 5-5*. Woodruff-Pak, D.S., R.G. Finkbinder, and D.K. Sasse. (1990). Eyeblink conditioning discriminates Alzheimer's patients from non-demented aged. *NeuroReport, 1*, 45-48.

Chapter 6

p. 143. *Quote*. Bruck, M., and S.J. Ceci. (1999). The suggestibility of children's memory. *Annual Review of Psychology, 50*, 419-430. P. 420.

p. 144. *Quote*. Rabinowitz, D. (2003). No Crueler Tyrannies: Accusation, False Witness, and Other Terrors of Our Time. New York: Free Press.

p. 147. *Quote*. McNally, R.J. (2002). Remembering Trauma. Cambridge, MA: The Belnap Press of Harvard University.

p. 147. *Quote*. Bruck, M., and S.J. Ceci. (1999). The suggestibility of children's memory. *Annual Review of Psychology, 50*, 419-430. P. 420.

p. 159. *Figure 6-1*. Gonsalves, B., and K.A. Paller. (2000). Neural events that underlie remembering something that never happened. *Nature Neuroscience, 3*, 1316-1321. P. 1317.

p. 160. *Quote*. Dawes, R.M. (1994). House of Cards: Psychology and Psychotherapy Built on Myth. New York: Free Press. P. 180.

Chapter 7

p. 163. *Figure 7-1* Munch, E. (1893). The Scream. BONO (Norwegian Visual Artists Copyright Society).

p. 164. *Figure 7-2*. Watson, J.B., and R. Rayner. (1920). Conditioned emotional reactions. *Journal of Experimental Psychology, 3*, 1-14.

p. 168. *Quote.* Neisser, U., and N. Harsch. (1992). Phantom Flashbulbs: False Recollections of Hearing the News About Challenger. Pp. 9-31 in E. Winograd and U. Neisser (eds.). *Affect and Accuracy in Recall: Studies of "Flashbulb Memories."* Cambridge, MA: Cambridge University Press.

p. 172. *Figure 7-3*. Helmuth, L. (2003). Fear and trembling in the amygdala. *Science, 300*, 568-569. P. 569.

p. 172. *Table 7-1*. Davis, M. (1992). The role of the amygdala in fear and anxiety. *Annual Review of Neuroscience, 15*, 353-375. P. 354.

p. 174. *Figure 7-4*. Adolphs, R., D. Tranel, H. Damasio, and A.R. Damasio. (1995). Fear and the human amygdala. *Journal of Neuroscience, 15*, 5879-5891. P. 5888.

p. 176. *Figure 7-5*. Vuilleumier, P., J.L. Armony, J. Drive, and R.J. Dolan. (2003). Distinct spatial frequency sensitivities for processing faces and emotional expressions. *Nature Neuroscience, 6*, 624-631. P. 625.

pp. 183-184. *Quote.* Bagby, E. (1928). The Psychology of Personality. New York: Holt.

pp. 184-185. *Box 7-1*. Cahill, L., B. Prins, M. Weber, and J.L. McGaugh. (1994). b-Adrenergic activation and memory for emotional events. *Nature, 371*, 702-704. P. 702.

pp. 186-187. *Quote.* Bandura, A. (1975). Perceived Effectiveness: An Explanatory Mechanism of Behavioral Change. Pp. 562-563 in G. Lindzey, C.S. Hall, and R.F. Thompson (eds.). *Psychology.* New York: Worth.

pp. 187-188. *Quote.* Leshner, A.I. (1997). Addiction is a brain disease, and it matters. *Science, 278*, 45-47.

p. 193. *Figure 7-6*. NIDA Notes. (1996). *National Institute on Drug Abuse, 11*, 1-20.

p. 195. *Quote.* Helmuth, L. (2001). Moral reasoning relies on emotion. *Science, 293*, 1971-1972.

Chapter 8

p. 198. *Quote.* Saffran, J.R., A. Senghas, and J.C. Trueswell. (2001). The acquisition of language by children. *Proceedings of the National Academy of Sciences, 98*, 12874-12875. P. 12874.

p. 200. *Figure 8-1*. Holowka, S., and L.A. Petitto. (2002). Left hemisphere cerebral specialization for babies while babbling. *Science, 297*, 1515.

p. 205. *Figure 8-2.* Max Planck Research (2002). How language hits a nerve. *4/2002*, 53-57. P. 53.

p. 206. *Figure 8-3.* Geschwind, N. (1972). Language and the brain. *Scientific American, 226*, 76-83.

p. 209. *Figure 8-4.* Helmuth, L. (2001). Where the brain tells a face from a place. *Science, 292*, 196-198. P. 196.

p. 210. *Figure 8-5.* Jacobs, B., M. Schall, and A.B. Scheibel. (1993). A Quantitative dendritic analysis of Wernicke's area in humans. II. Gender, hemispheric, and environmental factors. *Journal of Comparative Neurology, 327*, 97-111.

p. 211. *Quote.* Dowling, J.E. (1998). Creating Mind: How the Brain Works. New York: W.W. Norton & Company. P. 141.

p. 216. *Figure 8-6* Allman, J.M. (1999). Evolving Brains. New York: Scientific American Library. P. 152.

p. 217. *Figure 8-7.* Massaro, D. Personal Communication.

Chapter 9

p. 249. *Figure 9-2.* Wilson, M.A., and S. Tonegawa. (1997). Synaptic plasticity, place cells, and spatial memory. *Trends in Neuroscience, 20*, 102-106.

Chapter 10

p. 255. *Figure 10-1.* Andersen, R.A., and C.A. Buneo. (2002). Intentional maps in posterior parietal cortex. *Annual Review of Neuroscience, 25*, 189-220.

p. 257. *Figure 10-2.* Berger, T.W. Personal Communication.

p. 257. *Figure 10-3.* Berger, T.W. Personal Communication.

Index